Inflow of foreign aid, mainly in the form of consumer goods, was somewhat helpful in alleviating inflationary pressures, but it could not serve as a basic remedy for inflation. Therefore severe inflation continued, coupled with inappropriate management of money supply. The inflation caused instability of national life, misallocation of resources, rash speculation, and low domestic savings vitally needed for growth, which in turn acted as deterrents to economic development.

During the eight years following the Armistice between 1954 and 1961 wholesale prices rose 4.3 times, at an average annual rate of 22.2 per cent. In particular, prices skyrocketed during the three years from 1954 to 1957. Inflation was temporarily suppressed in 1958, attributable to the large-scale influx of aid as well as the sudden drop in grain prices, but it became serious again in 1960.

Chronic inflationary pressures and economic instability were main factors impeding efficient mobilization of domestic savings for development. Since gross national product grew only at an average annual rate of 4.4 per cent over the period 1953-61, per capita gross national product stood at a low level of 83 dollars in 1961. Such low per capita income inevitably resulted in a low national savings ratio of 4.3 per cent, and caused the economy's heavy dependence upon foreign aid for capital finance.

As interest rates on bank deposits at that time were far below the rising rate of prices, private individuals had no motive to save. Under the circumstances, the national economy as well as households had no alternative but to incur deficits.

Spiralling Inflation

Refugees during the Korean War

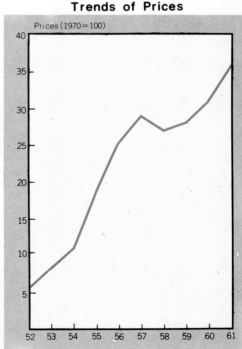

Trends of Prices

Prices (1970=100)

Development Aspirations

A development plan entails three basic decisions: who implements the plan, what are its main objectives, and what ways and means should be adopted to carry it out. Of these, who formulates and implements the plan is the most important factor.

There was a proposal as to the formulation of an economic development plan in Korea by the Liberal Party regime in the latter 1950's but it did not materialize. In the following Democratic Party regime of the Second Republic, 1960-61, a three-year plan and a five-year plan were prepared, but also proved abortive because of the collapse of the regime.

It was the Third Republic that made the 1960's the decade of development, inspired the will to develop, and marked a turning point in the history of modernization in Korea. The revolutionary regime that pledged "to solve the problem of starvation and raise the standard of living of the people" promptly started to formulate a five-year economic development plan, and the successive government of the Third Republic implemented the plan with firm determination and will for development.

Economic development and industrialization are the only ways to cast off long stagnation and dependence, and furthermore indispensable to prove the superiority of our own system to that of north Korea. This will provide a sound basis for the eventual unification of the country.

In order to obtain overwhelming support of the general public for the plan, it was imperative for the government to show the people the blueprint of development, the First Five-Year Economic Development Plan put into force in 1962.

The eventual goal of this plan was to break out of the vicious circle of poverty, and to consolidate the foundation for a self-supporting economy. To achieve the goal, the gross national product during the plan period was to be increased at an annual rate of 7.1 per cent, or by 40.7 per cent as of the target year, 1966. At that time, the growth target seemed so high that the plan was criticized as being over-ambitious in view of the previous performance of the economy. This is but one proof of the strong volition of the government for economic development.

The government ultimately succeeded in obtaining full cooperation of private individuals and enterprises in carrying out the plan. As a result, the allegedly over-ambitious initial targets of the First Five-Year Plan were exceeded.

Plant under construction and river embankment in rural area

Creation of the Preconditions for Development

To achieve development goals it is necessary to adopt proper means and to exert reasonable efforts. The government not only had to formulate the plan, but also to make great efforts to stimulate voluntary participation of the people to take the path to development.

Basic direction of the Five-Year Plan was as follows:

First, the basic economic system was to be free enterprise, respecting as much as possible the freedom and creativity of private individuals. However, with regard to key industries, the government took either a direct or indirect part in rendering guidance. In other words, the system of 'guided capitalism' was adopted as a basic principle.

Second, as the ultimate course of the Korean economy lies in industrialization, capital formation to meet investment requirements was an important problem to solve. The government, therefore, exerted utmost efforts to increase domestic savings and to induce the inflow of foreign capital.

Refinery at Ulsan

The facade of Bank of Korea

Controlling Inflation

Economic stabilization is the most urgent task to be performed in the process of economic development. In order to execute a long-range development plan that lasts five to ten years, a national economy should be kept on a sound basis, like the physical condition of a marathon runner.

Development inflation is a serious risk in the course of development, endangering success of a plan. Vicious inflation must therefore be suppressed above all to carry out a developmemt plan smoothly. In 1962, the year in which the First Five-Year Plan was launched, the government undertook an emergency currency reform in an effort to curb inflation and to mobilize domestic savings.

Although the currency reform was not fully successful in obtaining expected results, with this reform as precedent the goal of stabilization of the national economy has been steadily pursued. In 1963 the government initiated the Financial Stabilization Program to curb inflation and in 1965 adjusted interest rates to realistic levels.

19

Creation of
an Attractive
Investment Climate

The slogan of the First Five-Year Plan was ''increase production, exports and construction.'' The most urgent task in launching the plan was to expand such social overhead capital as electric power, transportation and communications, which form the foundations of industrialization. An environment in which private enterprises erect factories and enhance production activities could be created only through the expansion of the infrastructure.

Therefore, during the First Five-Year Plan period (1962-66) the government allocated 32 per cent of total fixed capital investment to the expansion of social overhead capital. It is difficult, in general, for a private enterprise to invest in the social overhead sector because the gestation period of capital in that sector is too long. Consequently, it was inevitable that the the government itself had to make the requisite investments. Even in the case of government investment, the long gestation period of capital is likely to give rise to inflation, so the government employed flexible fiscal policies in encouraging expansion of electric power and transportation capacity.

During the period of the First Five-Year Plan, social overhead capital was expanded as follows:

First, the generating capacity of electric power doubled, rising from 367,000 kilowatts in 1960 to 769,000 kilowatts in 1966, thereby making an unrestricted supply possible from April 1964.

Second, the length of railway lines for industrial use was extended by 240 kilometers to 1,699 kilometers. The government built or imported 2,740 coaches and freight cars and 215 locomotives to cope with transportation demand, increasing 20 per cent annually. At the same time, the government expanded the network of roads for industrial use, constructed or restored 400 bridges, improved 122 kilometers of old roads, and newly paved 500 kilometers. The capacity of marine transportation also increased through better use of ports.

Investment and Savings

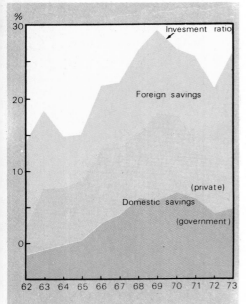

Composition Ratio of Domestic and Foreign Savings

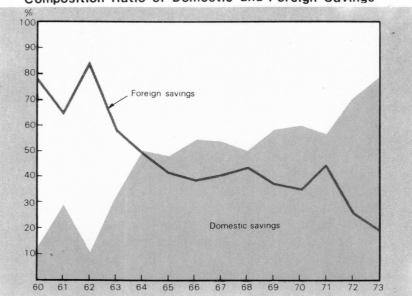

20

Strengthening International Cooperation

The government established a system for inducement of foreign capital in order to raise investment funds smoothly, because financing of domestic capital formation was the key to success of the development plan. The Foreign Capital Inducement Law contains such essential incentives as reductions or exemptions of taxes, guarantee of remittance of dividends, and a payment guarantee system that permits foreigners to lend funds without risk. At the same time, the government strengthened cooperation with the friendly developed nations.

At the beginning of the plan, official loans to Korea from the United States and Germany constituted a major part of foreign capital induced, on account of premature conditions for development and poor creditworthiness of private enterprises. But commercial loans based on private credit and direct investments were also introduced gradually.

From 1965, inducement of commercial loans on a private basis increased sharply, thanks to the creditworthiness of the Korean economy which began to be recognized internationally, following the approval of Stand-by Arrangements with the International Monetary Fund, and the normalization of diplomatic relations with Japan. Lenders were diversified, from the United States and Germany to Japan, France, the United Kingdom, Italy, and such international financial institutions as the International Monetary Fund and International Bank for Reconstruction and Development.

Foreign capital thus formed 52 per cent of total investment during the First Five-Year Plan. Along with promoting international cooperation, the government devoted itself to the expansion of exports, converting the economic system into an open one. As a result, exports rose remarkably, at an annual average growth rate of 43 per cent.

Characteristics of the First Five-Year Plan

The Third Five-Year Plan is now under implementation and further such plans will continue to be pursued. The common objectives of these economic plans are, of course, to develop the economy and improve the standard of living. However, the major content and emphasis in development may differ from plan to plan, since progress must be pursued step by step because of the limitation of available capital and capacity.

Taking this into account, the government established as its ultimate aims the modernization of industry and achievement of a self-supporting economy. Within this framework, the objective of the First Five-Year Plan was set as the providing of a basic foundation.

Until the national economy reached a certain level, it was inevitable for the government to take the lead in mobilizing the need-

A night view of Chungju Fertilizer Co.

ed capital and developing such key industries as energy for the sake of laying the foundations of a self-supporting economy. During the First Five-Year Plan, the government established the basis for mobilizing investment funds for developing such energy industries as coal, electric power and oil refining. At the same time the government prepared groundwork for self-sufficiency in fertilizer, which was a key point for agricultural improvement.

The goals of the Second Five-Year Plan were ① to propel industrialization full speed, ② to expand the foundations of agricultural production through farmland consolidation and expansion of irrigation facilities, ③ to maintain a high rice price policy and to carry out special projects for the increase of farm and fishery incomes in order to equalize living standards with the industrial sector.

On the foundations of industrialization achieved during the First Five-Year Plan, the government pushed forward during the Second Plan, with mobilization of investment funds as a prime mover. Development of such heavy and chemical industries as steel, machinery and petrochemicals began, and export industries were fostered further. Epoch-making progress was made in the development of electric power with the construction of 15 hydroelectric or thermal power plants and six diesel power plants.

Following the Ulsan Oil Refinery that had been built in 1964 the Honam Refinery and Kyungin Energy Co. began to operate in 1969 and 1971 respectively, thereby tremendously expanding the energy supply.

Besides, such export industries as textiles and plywood grew conspicuously, contributing to export increases. In consequence, Korea became a world-famous exporting country for textiles and plywood. The value of commodity exports already exceeded 700 million dollars in 1969, the original goal for the target year, and recorded 1,352 million dollars in 1971.

Characteristics of the Second Five-Year Plan

Textile industry led economic growth during the Second Plan

Characteristics of the Third Five-Year Plan

With the successful implementation of the First and Second Five-Year Plans, Korea achieved rapid economic growth, greatly increased exports, and laid a firm foundation for a self-supporting economy. In the Third Plan period, heavy and chemical industries for industrial modernization were emphasized. Policies for development of farming and fishing villages to a new level grew in accordance with the New Community Movement.

Development of heavy and chemical industries was the last step in industrial modernization and achievement of a self-supporting economy. Light industries that had led export expansion had already reached certain limitations, and it became inevitable to increase imports according to export increases, due to the high dependency on foreign raw materials. Therefore, it was required to construct heavy and chemical industries in order to fundamentally improve the trade structure by reducing dependency on imported raw materials and increasing exports still further.

New policies to develop farming and fishing villages were carried out for self-supply of food and balanced progress of the national economy.

Major Objectives of Each Development Plan

First Plan (1962–66)	Second Plan (1967–71)	Third Plan (1972–76)
1. Development of energy industries such as electricity and coal. 2. Expansion of social overhead capital. 3. Export increase and development of import substitution industries. 4. Increase of agricultural productivity.	1. Improvement of industrial structure through construction of heavy industries such as steel, machinery, etc. 2. Expansion of exports and promotion of import substitutes. 3. Increase of farm household incomes. 4. Advancement of scientific technology.	1. Development of heavy and chemical industries. 2. Self-supply of food, increase of incomes of farmers and fishermen and improvement of living conditions. 3. Expansion of exports and improvement of trade structure. 4. Coordinated development of national land. 5. Evolution and teaching of scientific technology.

Heavy and chemical industry being constructed during the Third Five-Year Plan
Petrochemical Complex (left)
Atomic Power Plant (below)

Major Policy Measures under the Development Plans

In order to implement an economic development plan successfully, there must be among other things adequate financing of investment funds. Moreover, the increase in domestic savings is a driving force for the constant growth of an economy. To mobilize maximum financial resources for use as industrial funds, since 1962 the government has not only encouraged the induction of foreign capital but has also taken various measures to mobilize domestic capital efficiently, some of which are summarized as follows:

First, the government executed a currency reform on June 10, 1962. The aim of the reform was to mobilize hoarded capital and utilize it as industrial funds, and to curb the galloping inflation owing to the increased money supply since 1960.

Second, the interest rates were raised to realistic levels on September 30, 1965. The increase in interest rates on deposits and loans of banking institutions, which had remained at unrealistic levels lower than the rates of price increases, played a decisive role in accelerating the mobilization of financial savings by boosting time and savings deposits, and suppressing disguised demand for bank loans. According to the adjusted interest rates, time and savings deposits in banking institutions increased by about 50 per cent, from 19.9 billion won at the end of 1964 to 30.6 billion won at the end of 1965. This increment was made within three months after the raising of the interest rates. Thereafter, time and savings deposits continued to expand rapidly, reaching 1,214.2 billion won in 1973, 83.7 times the level at the time of the reform. Subsequently, along with price stabilization, interest rates were reduced step by step to moderate burdens of enterprises. In 1972 the interest rates were reduced to levels even below those prior to the reform; nevertheless, time and savings deposits continued to grow.

Third, the government enforced the "August Economic Emergency Measures" in 1972 in order to rationalize the supply of funds for enterprises, which were suffering from oppressive interest burdens and low efficiency of capital, because they depended upon curb markets for raising funds. With the Emergency Measures, interest rates of banking institutions were adjusted downward and extant curb market loans were frozen, so as to break the bottleneck confronting enterprises.

Main contents of the Emergency Measures were: ① establishment of new terms and conditions for curb market loans, under which loaned money should be paid back in installments over a period of five years after a three-year grace period, and interest rates limited to 16.2 per cent per annum, ② loans up to 200 billion won aiming at shifting short-term loans to long-term loans with lower interest rates, ③ enlargement of credit guarantee system, ④ raising of Industrial Rationalization Funds, ⑤ efficient operation of public finance, ⑥ downward adjustment of interest rates of banking institutions.

The Emergency Measures contributed to price stabilization by reducing interest burdens and moderating the tight financial situation of enterprises, and together with the increase in exports brought about an economic boom never experienced before.

Interest Rates of Banking Institutions
—September 30, 1965—

(per cent per annum)

		Before revision	After revision
Deposits	Time Deposits		
	3 months	9.0	18.0
	6 months	12.0	24.0
	1 year or more	15.0	26.4~30.0
	Installment Savings Deposits	10.0	30.0
Loans and Discounts	Discounts on Commercial Bills	14.0	24.0
	Discounts on Other Bills	16.0	26.0
	Overdrafts	18.5	26.0
	Call Loans	12.0	22.0

Diversification of Means of Saving

Provision of various means for saving plays an important role in increasing savings. There are many categories of potential savers. Some may have a sizable sum of money in hand, while others save penny by penny. Some attach greater importance to returns rather than safety, while others feel the opposite. Therefore, various kinds of institutions and means for saving should be provided to meet the needs of savers.

Before 1962 there was no institutional way to save except by bank deposits, which were handled by only four commercial banks. Accordingly, people frequently formed loan clubs or utilized curb markets that were inefficient and caused many abuses.

In implementing its economic development plans, the government diversified the banking business by establishing various specialized banks, enlarged insurance companies so that they could take

Banking institutions endeavor to increase savings

over a part of long-term savings, and encouraged capital markets to make it possible for enterprises to raise industrial funds directly. In addition, short-term finance companies and mutual credit companies were established.

At the beginning of 1961 the only banks existing in Korea were the Bank of Korea, Korea Development Bank and four commercial banks. Since that time the government has established many specialized banks in order to diversify banking business, and to meet the needs of the expanding economy. Most importantly, in July 1961 the Agricultural Cooperatives were reorganized and the Medium Industry Bank was established. Financing for small and medium enterprises was urgently required because it was very difficult for such enterprises to gain access to commercial banks, which dealt mainly with large corporations. The Fisheries Co-

operatives, too, were reorganized in January 1962, and in December of the same year the mutual savings and loan banks were merged into the Citizens National Bank taking charge of petty loans for the populace.

In January 1967, the government established the Korea Exchange Bank for foreign exchange business in order to assist international trade. Also the Korea Housing Bank and the Korea Trust Bank were established in July 1967 and December 1968 respectively. In addition, ten local banks have been established since March 1967, and nine branches of foreign banks—three American, four Japanese, one British, and one French—have been approved to operate in Korea.

Policies for the insurance business were improved and strengthened remarkably. Until 1960, insurance companies in Korea remained small in scale, depending mainly upon revenues from fire insurance accompanying bank loans in the case of non-life insurance, and upon group insurance in the case of life insurance.

But the system of direct insurance and reinsurance were rationalized by the consolidation of smaller companies, enlargement of scale through capital increases after special supervision of the insurance business in 1962, and establishment of a government-managed reinsurance corporation. Thereafter, the insurance business expanded by no less than 45 times during ten years, and Korea became one of the 30 major countries in which insurance businesses are being operated successfully.

Reviewing the assets of all insurance companies as of 1973, the total amount of investments in securities and loans that could be considered to have been mobilized as industrial funds came to 32.1 times that of 1963, increasing from 1.6 billion won to 51.2 billion won. These figures show the increased mobilization of domestic capital through insurance companies.

Concurrently, the capital market was promoted by a series of thoroughgoing measures to foster a sound securities market as a source of industrial investment funds.

However, the securities market remained in a stunted condition until 1968, for there was no issuance market to supply superior securities, and the trading market played only a minor role, in which a few listed bonds and securities were traded. The Korea Stock Brokerage Association was established in 1953 and the Korea Stock Exchange as the trading market in 1956. An issuance market was not formed until 1968, and then out of order with the normal development sequence of a securities market, since in developed countries an issuance market comes into being initially.

Accordingly, while making efforts to foster the securities market, the government has hastened to promote an issuance market since 1968. In November of that year, the Law on Fostering the Capital Market was promulgated, and the Korea Investment Development Corporation, established in December, started to take charge of promoting the issuance market.

Rapidly growing insurance companies

In 1969 the Corporate Income Tax Law was revised for the purpose of providing tax concessions to publicly-owned corporations. The Public Corporation Inducement Law was enacted in 1972, and in May 1974 the President especially ordered the cabinet to devise necessary measures to induce corporations to open to the public.

As a result of such policy assistance for the securities market, the value of public offerings of new shares in the issuance market mushroomed from 8.1 billion won in 1969 to 57.8 billion won in 1973, while the value of securities traded grew from 42.3 billion won to 167.5 billion won during the same period.

Development of the short-term finance market and petty loans were aimed at diversifing financial channels to mobilize domestic savings and institutionalizing private loans through the supplementary economic emergency measures of August 1972. In the past, the major reason the curb market was given much more weight than the public money market was that public loans could not supply sufficient funds quickly and flexibly enough to meet needs.

On this score, the Short-Term Financing Business Act of August 1972 helped eight short-term finance companies to come into being. The Mutual Credit Company Act of the same month paved the way for former pseudo-financial companies, which had been deeply ingrained in the financial structure until 1972, to be organized as open mutual credit companies.

Modernized securities market

Foreign Capital Inducement Policy

In the early stage of foreign capital inducement, the government enacted the Law for the Encouragement of Foreign Capital Inducement in 1961, and took necessary steps to bring about conditions suitable for introducing foreign capital and coping with the sharply swelling demand for foreign loans, in conformity with the economic development plan and the decreasing trend of U. S. aid. To achieve successfully the targets of the First Five-Year Plan launched in 1962, the "Basic Guidelines for the Operation of Foreign Capital Inducement" were enacted to permit legitimate foreign loans without examining their types, conditions or amounts concerned, and to provide government guarantees of repayment, if needed.

In view of the increase in the amount of government repayment guarantees, and the high rate of downpayments according to mounting inflow of foreign loans, the government changed its policy from quantitative preference to qualitative screening in order to curtail private foreign capital inflow which required government guarantees or downpayments, by stipulating "Guidelines for Handling Applications of Nonprojects" in 1963 and the "Basic Guidelines for the Promotion of Private Commercial Loans" in 1964.

After the normalization of Korea-Japan diplomatic relations in 1965 and a favorable foreign exchange situation, more emphasis was laid on efficient administration of foreign loans already pro-

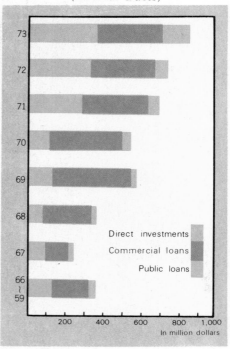

Foreign Capital Inflow
(Arrival Basis)

Direct investments
Commercial loans
Public loans

In million dollars

cured rather than on foreign capital inducement. As a result, various laws and regulations concerned were consolidated into the Foreign Capital Inducement Law.

In the light of the exchange risk on the part of enterprises borrowing foreign funds resulting from drastic changes in foreign exchange rates in the 1970's, the government began encouraging direct investment rather than foreign loans. Consequently, a series of measures was taken, such as applying a ceiling system on commerical loans by maturities, establishing the new Foreign Capital Deliberation Committee for effective administration of foreign capital, and inducing foreign direct investments by providing industrial facilities through a law providing for the establishment of free export zones.

Subsequently, approval procedures for foreigners' investments were simplified as much as possible in October 1972. The Foreign Capital Inducement Law and its enforcement decree were again revised to utilize more effectively such long-term development funds as those needed for New Community projects and heavy and chemical industries.

The "Principles of Foreign Investment Ownership" was enacted in 1973, stipulating as a general rule joint investment with foreigners' share of fifty per cent or less.

The free export zone in Masan

Exports as Leading Sector

Industrialization and export promotion have been the major policy goals in the course of economic development efforts. Therefore, redirecting the Korean economy into an open system has been a prerequisite since the beginning of the First Five-Year Plan. In spite of the lack of natural resources needed for industry, Korea is endowed with an abundant supply of labor of a high level of education. This suggests the need for labor-intensive export products. In addition, exports are expected to augment national wealth by earning foreign exchange, and to enhance production and employment through increased demand.

Therefore the government has pushed strenuous promotion policies for exports since the First Five-Year Plan. Export promotion conferences, inaugurated in December 1962 and chaired by the President, have been held monthly ever since. Export promotion has been advocated as of first importance among all economic policies, and the primary concern in making policies for trade administration, taxes, financing and fiscal matters has been positive export promotion.

To cope with various unfavorable domestic economic factors, the exchange rate was readjusted to a realistic level in 1964. The measure resulted in drastic improvement in export profitability. Also, tax concessions and adequate financing were adopted as two main props supporting effective and preferential export promotion. In addition, the government took various appropriate measures for improving trade administration and developing export industries.

First, export financing is the most important part of export support. Export industries have been provided operation funds through low-interest loans and equipment funds through foreign capital inducements and foreign currency loans. Especially, export industries have benefited from a variety of assistances through selective financing of priority order over other kinds of financing.

Second, the government prepared in the tax system such supports as exemption from customs and commodity taxes on imported raw materials for exports and exemption from business and commodity taxes on export producers' shipments. Besides, some discounts on such public utility charges as power and railway freight have been allowed for export products which were in need of much help.

Third, administrative support was provided. The Monthly Export Promotion Conference under the direct supervision of the President has handled all sorts of administrative measures concerning exports. The Trade Transaction Law of 1967 formulated legislative administration of exports and imports, and systematically provided the simplification of trade services and modernization of trade administration.

Fourth, the government has given maximum support to the enlargement of production capacities of export industries and to environmental protection. Domestic loans in foreign currency and foreign

Increase of Commodity Exports

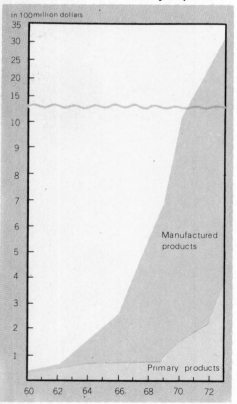

In 100 million dollars

35
30
25
20
15
10
9
8
7
6
5
4
3
2
1

Manufactured products

Primary products

60 62 64 66 68 70 72

loans were accorded highest priority, and export industrial estates have been established. In addition to major export industrial estates in Guro Dong, Incheon and Gumi, as well as the Masan Free Export Zone, industrial estates for small and medium enterprises have been established in every province. The Office of Industrial Estates Management was set up for efficient assistance to them.

Lastly, the government has continuously strengthened economic diplomacy and exploitation of foreign markets for export promotion. Private traders' efforts to develop foreign markets have been supported vigorously, and also the Korea Trade Promotion Corporation (KOTRA) was instituted in June 1962. KOTRA's activities, including participation in international exhibitions and the holding of commodity expositions, have obtained excellent results, and sharply increased performance in facilitating transactions has been brought about through dispatching trade missions.

Korea has participated in 133 international exhibitions since 1963

Export commodities on show

International Exhibitions and Transaction Facilitation

	International Exhibitions (number)	Commodity Exhibitions (number)	Transaction Facilitating Performance (in thousand dollars)
1963	2		4
1964	3	1	12,319
1965	2		148
1966	4	1	798
1967	2	9	13,936
1968	1		130
1969	10	2	17,843
1970	28		34,732
1971	16	21	86,562
1972	19	25	116,145
1973	22	35	146,437
1974	24	26	245,109
Total	133	120	674,162

and commodity expositions have been held on 120 occasions since 1964. Besides, 'Korea Weeks' at leading department stores overseas have been held to advertise commodities. Commodity exhibitions held in Eastern Europe since 1972 have made a great contribution to increasing exports and enhancing the nation's prestige. Reflecting these efforts, export markets have diversified so that the number of countries buying Korean goods increased from 25 in 1961 to 116 in 1973.

With the aid of the measures mentioned above, commodity exports rose from no more than 32 million dollars in 1960 to 3,257 million dollars in 1973.

Owing to the reorganization of the industrial structure led by export growth, the emphasis of the export structure changed from primary commodities such as farm and marine products to manufactured products. Especially, exports of heavy and chemical products such as electronic goods and ships have outpaced products of light industries including textiles. Marine and mineral goods accounted for 82 per cent of total export commodities in 1960, whereas by 1973 manufactured products occupied a full 88 per cent of the total.

Updating Science and Technology

Progress in science and technology is the most important factor for industrial modernization in the course of economic development. A nation's welfare depends on the increase of per capita income, and the most important element in raising productivity is technical progress.

The government made promotion of technology one of the goals of the First Five-Year Plan along with science education and business management. Improving the levels of technology and productivity were also targets in the Second Five-Year Plan.

Aspects emphasized include introduction of advanced foreign technology, systematic research and development, diffusion of technical education, improvement of industrial technology, cooperation between industry and education, and strengthening of the administrative system.

First, introduction of foreign technology occurred in only four instances in 1965, but increased to 82 cases in 1973. There was also a shift in emphasis from consumer goods sector, such as textiles and food, during the First Plan period to the heavy and chemical industry sector, such as machinery and fabricated metal products, during the Second Plan period. Utilization of advanced technology has considerably assisted development of new products, productivity enhancement and export growth.

Second, a firm foundation for technical progress and think-tank activity was formulated with the strengthening of systematic

An overall view of the Korea Institute of Science and Technology

research and development in the nation. The Korea Institute of Science and Technology (KIST) was established as a research center in 1966. A year later the government revised the laws and ordinances concerned and promulgated the Science and Technology Promotion Law in 1967. In addition the government created the independent Ministry of Science and Technology and established the Korea Advanced Institute of Science, the Korea Development Institute, and the Korea Atomic Energy Research Center. A research and development area was constructed in Seoul. At present, the building of an innovative research town in Daedeog is under way.

At the same time, yearly research and development expenditure rose from 1.3 billion won in 1963 to 15.6 billion won in 1973, a 12 times increase. This has stimulated vigorous research and development activities in all kinds of research institutes, colleges and enterprises. The number of private research institutes grew from 62 in 1963 to 120 in 1972, almost a twofold increase; college research institutes rose from 9 in 1963 to 66 in 1972, a 7.3 times increase; and enterprises carrying out research and development swelled from 12 to 133.

Third, substantial efforts have been made to meet increasing demands for technicians through technical education and training. Education in Korea was developed with a view toward quantity after 1945, but it has also been readjusted qualitatively, in line with need for the improvement of technical skills in the course of the economic development of the 1960's. Since 1963, efforts have been made to strengthen vocational training, and students in technical high schools rose from 34,000 that year to 82,000 students in 1972, a 2.4 times increase, and engineering school enrollment from 15,000 to 38,000, a 2.5 times increase. Also junior technical colleges, which were not known in 1963, were established from 1967 and had 19,000 students in 1972.

Fourth, the government has also worked for the improvement of industrial technology through direct policy supports. In line with industrialization policies, the proportion of heavy and chemical industries in the whole industrial structure rose, and labor force needs changed from simple manual workers to skilled technicians. This created problems of technical training.

In 1967 scientific and technical manpower 3.9 per cent of total industrial employment of 8,717,000, but by 1972 had in these sectors expanded to 551,000 or 5.5 per cent of total industrial employment of 10,559,000.

Especially in the mining and manufacturing sectors, which have absorbed most of the technical employment, scientific and technical manpower increased from 244,000 in 1967, accounting for 21.4 per cent of the total employment of 1,115,000, to 390,000 in 1972, or 26 per cent of the total employment of 1,499,000.

Enlargement of the technical labor force will be further accelerated in the future with the development of heavy and chemical industries, and the proportion of scientific and technical manpower

Experimenting with gamma rays

Technical education

in mining and manufacturing is expected to be 52.1 per cent, or more than half of total employment, by 1981.

To meet the increasing demand for skilled manpower, the government has implemented short and long-term manpower development plans, stressing on-the-job training programs. Thanks to these plans, the number of trained workers increased to 48,640 in 1973 from 10,738 in 1967, and 88 per cent of them are employed. Posts available for on-the-job training also have been enlarged from 50 to 124.

The spread of on-the-job training and the improvement of industrial skills have not only laid a foundation for the development of the nation's heavy and chemical industries, but also enabled Korean technology to operate abroad. Technical assistance for foreign countries increased rapidly, from 46 cases in 1965 to 197 in 1973, of which 177 involved Asian countries, six African nations, three Latin American states and five elsewhere.

Highways in Korea were constructed entirely by Korean technology, and the Seoul subway, which opened on August 15, 1974,

Triumphal parade of craftsmen from the International Vocational Training Competition

was built on schedule in only three years and four months without any dependence on foreign technology. Further a super oil tanker of 260,000 dead-weight tons was built by the Hyundai Shipbuilding and Heavy Industries Co., Ltd., incorporated in 1971, in only two years, without any foreign technical assistance.

The superiority of Korean technology has been displayed throughout the world by Korean craftsmen who, with six gold medals, ranked second at the 21st International Vocational Training Competition held in August, 1973 in Munich. The fact that the gold medals were obtained in such skilled fields as fitting, press tool making, and turning augurs well for the future development of the heavy and chemical industries of the nation. To utilize vocational education in the field more effectively, the government is hastening to establish a system called "cooperation between education and industry," which aims to train vocational students in collaboration with enterprises to meet increasing requirements for technical manpower. The government has established a basis for cooperative relations between education and industry by revising pertinent laws.

First, the Regulations governing the Education-Industry Cooperation Council were promulgated in 1972 in order to encourage students of agricultural schools to participate in agricultural development plans.

Second, the government revised the Enforcement Ordinance of the Industrial Education Promotion Act in 1973 to offer vocational students opportunities for practical training. Along with these measures, business associations such as the Korean Traders Association raised an education-industry cooperation fund in order to provide scholarships for students in vocational schools.

In 1973, a crafts education system was introduced to institutionalize vocational training of young people in basic crafts needed for improving vocational know-how. The basic idea of this system is to expand the skilled labor force by training people in basic skills from youth, and to promote recognition of the importance of crafts and skills.

Seoul subway train (above)
Subway station (lower right)
Subway under construction
(lower left)

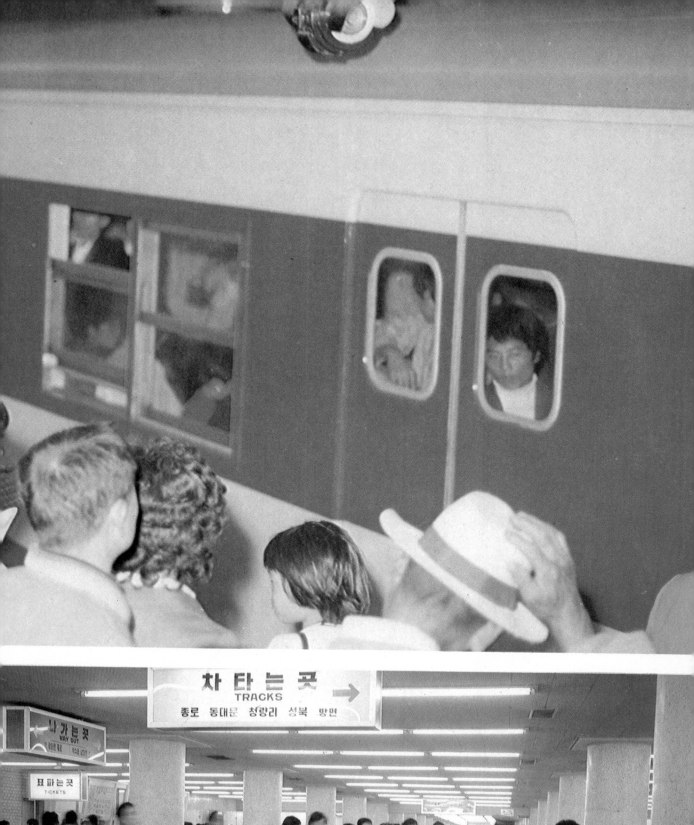

Achievements of the Development

During the past 12 years, the Korean economy has showed an unprecedented high rate of growth. The First and Second Five-Year Economic Development Plans, spanning 1962-71, were successful and the Third Plan is in its fourth year in 1975. From 1962 to 1973, the average annual growth rate of the Korean economy recorded a high level of 9.6 per cent.

During the First Five-Year Plan (1962-66) the average annual growth rate reached 7.8 per cent, exceeding the planned target of 7.1 per cent which had been alleged to be too ambitious at the beginning, and surpassing the average 5.1 per cent of the developed countries and 5.5 per cent of the Southeast Asian countries.

During the Second Plan (1967-71), the economy gathered further momentum, recording an average annual growth rate of 10.5 per cent. This exceeded not only the planned target, but also the 5.3 per cent of the developed countries and the 6.7 per cent of the Southeast Asian countries during the same period.

During the first two years of the Third Plan (1972-73), the Korean economy further accelerated its growth rate: average gross national product growth rate in this period reached 11.8 per cent, far above the planned rate of 8.6 per cent and a level double the 5.1 per cent of the developed nations and the 5.9 per cent of Southeast Asian countries during the same period. The average rate of growth of 9.6 per cent during the past 12 years from 1962 to 1973 presents a striking contrast to that of the preceding eight years (1954-61), when the average annual growth rate was only 4.4 per cent.

As a result of such rapid economic growth, gross national product rose to 12.4 billion dollars (4,928.7 billion won) in 1973, 5.9 times the 2.1 billion dollars in 1961, before economic de-

Gross National Product

	Gross National Product		Per Capita Gross National Product	
	in billion won	in million dollars	in won	in dollars
1961	297.0	2,124	13,301	83
1966	1,032.4	3,655	35,648	126
1971	3,151.5	8,747	99,020	275
1973	4,928.7	12,374	148,414	376

velopment plans existed in Korea. The per capita gross national product increased to 376 dollars in 1973, 4.5 times the 83 dollars of 1961.

By industry, during the past 12 years the average annual growth rate of mining and manufacturing reached 18.2 per cent, social overhead capital and other services 10.3 per cent, while agriculture, forestry and fisheries recorded a somewhat lower level of 3.8 per cent, mainly due to several obstacles such as bad weather and slow realization of development results. But it was low only compared with the conspicuous growth of the other sectors, and was still high compared with other developing countries.

In short, the impressive performance of the Korean economy has been led mainly by the rapid growth of the manufacturing and social overhead capital and other services sectors. The manufacturing sector in particular has shown a remarkable 22.2 per cent annual average growth rate since the Second Plan.

The industrial structure has undergone gradual change. The share of the mining and manufacturing sector in the overall industry of the country has increased steadily, and that of social overhead capital and other services has shown a somewhat slower increase trend. As a result, the share of primary industry decreased sharply. This phenomenon should be regarded as inevitable in the course of economic development.

According to statistics, it is clear that by 1973 the industrial structure of the Korean economy had become similar to that of a developed economy while in the 1960's Korea had the typical structure of an underdeveloped economy. Between 1961 and 1973, the share of primary industry fell from 40.2 per cent to 26.0 per cent while the share of mining and manufacturing rose from 15.2

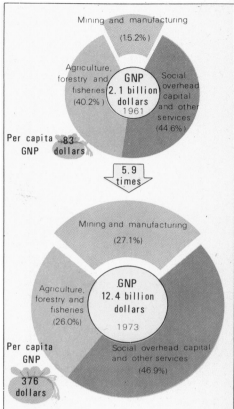

Growth by Industry and Industrial Structure

Mining and manufacturing (15.2%)

Agriculture, forestry and fisheries (40.2%)

GNP 2.1 billion dollars 1961

Social overhead capital and other services (44.6%)

Per capita GNP 83 dollars

5.9 times

Mining and manufacturing (27.1%)

Agriculture, forestry and fisheries (26.0%)

GNP 12.4 billion dollars 1973

Social overhead capital and other services (46.9%)

Per capita GNP 376 dollars

Industries leading economic growth

per cent to 27.1 per cent, and of social overhead capital and other services from 44.6 per cent to 46.9 per cent.

The manufacturing sector has led the growth of the national economy by attaining an average annual growth rate of 19 per cent during 1962-1973. During the First Plan period, energy industries including coal mining, electric power and oil refining, basic industries like fertilizer and cement, and light industries such as textiles developed markedly. With the beginning of the Second Plan, development priorities were put mainly on such heavy and chemical industries as iron and steel, machinery and petrochemicals.

Regarding shortage of energy supply as a severe bottleneck, the government has urged development of the energy industry from the beginning of the First Plan.

The capacity of electric power doubled to 769 thousand kilowatt-hours with the construction of five new power plants during the First Plan period. Five additional hydropower plants, ten thermal power plants and six diesel plants were built during the Second Plan period. As a result, the power generated totaled 14,826 million kilowatt-hours in 1973, 8.4 times the 1,773 million kilowatt-hours in 1961.

The output of anthracite, which is an important primary energy source in Korea, increased to 13.6 million tons in 1973, 2.3 times the output of 1962.

Oil refining capacity reached 395,000 barrels (BPSD) at the end

of 1973. The Ulsan Oil Refinery went into operation in 1964, the Honam Oil Refinery in 1969 and the Kyungin Energy Co. in 1971. Thus, refining capacity increased by about eleven times compared with 35,000 barrels (BPSD) in 1964 when oil refining began in this country. In 1974, the total refining capacity of the nation rose to 435,000 barrels (BPSD) with the completion of expansion of the Korea Oil Corporation to meet increasing demand for petroleum products. The government, in collaboration with foreign oil companies, is also expediting exploration for submarine oil resources by continuing boring in potential seabed oil fields.

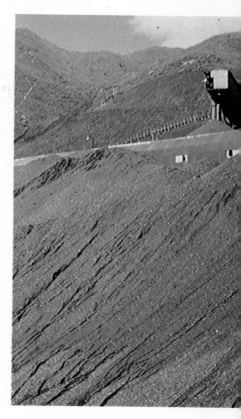

The iron and steel sector, which plays a vital role in modern industry, has shown remarkable expansion in production capacity. Total annual production capacity increased to 931,000 tons in 1972 from 148,000 tons in 1960 owing to the continuous enlargement of production facilities during the First and Second Plans to meet the increasing demand for iron and steel products. The completion of the integrated iron and steel mill of the Pohang Iron and Steel Co. in 1973 raised the production capacity to 2,367,000 tons per year. As a result, the output of iron and steel products increased to 2,868,000 tons in 1973, about 33 times the 87,000 tons of 1961, making it possible to export surplus products. To meet the rapidly increasing domestic demands the first facility expansion, at Pohang, is now underway, aimed at expanding the annual production capacity to 2.6 million tons. The government also

plans to build a second integrated iron and steel mill with an annual production capacity of 7 million tons.

The machinery industry, which plays a pivotal role in industrialization, has shown vigorous growth in every field including general, electrical and transport machinery through establishing of a mass-production system, specialization, and vertical integration of the machinery industry, and by expanding production scale. The output of the industry thus increased sharply during the period 1961–1972 : 2.3 times in general machinery, 14.6 times in electrical machinery, and 9.8 times in transport machinery.

The shipbuilding industry, which is both an integrated machinery sector and a labor intensive industry, has been developed by the government with strong emphasis as a strategic export industry. As a result, total ships built expanded from 4,600 gross tons in 1962, to 163,500 gross tons in 1973, a tremendous increase of more than 35 times during this period. Moreover, by launching two super-tankers of 260,000 dead-weight tons in 1974, the Hyundai Shipbuilding and Heavy Industries Co., Ltd., with an 750,000 gross tons capacity, has made Korea one of the foremost shipbuilding countries. Korea will no doubt emerge as one of the ten largest shipbuilding countries in the world when three more shipyards go into operation.

Production capacity of the chemical fertilizer industry increased from zero before 1960 to 170,000 tons per year in 1963 with the construction of the Chungju Fertilizer Plant in 1960 and the Honam Fertilizer Plant in 1963, both with 85,000 tons capacity. Also, 498,000 tons of urea and 361,000 tons of compound fertilizer were added to the total capacity by the construction of three more plants. Accordingly, the nation's total annual production capacity increased to 1,521,000 tons in 1973, more than 17 times that of 1961, and will see greater expansion in the near future with the construction of a seventh plant.

With abundant local reserves of limestone, cement manufacturing has also shown rapid growth. In 1961, the country had only two plants with combined production capacity of 720,000 tons. However, during the period of the First and Second Five-Year Plans, six new plants were built and total production capacity increased to 8,290,000 tons, 11.5 times that of 1961. Such a rapid expansion of production capacity increased output to 8,175,000 tons in 1973, 15 times the 523,000 tons of 1961, enabling export of surplus production.

Finally, the petrochemical industry, as one of the strategic industries, has developed markedly since 1968, parallel with the development of oil refining. The government built a naphtha cracking center with an annual production capacity of 100,000 tons on ethylene basis in the Ulsan Petrochemical Complex, and 13 satellite plants, all of which went into operation in 1974. Another large-scale petrochemical complex is now under construction in the Yeocheon district, due for completion in 1975.

Per capita gross national product increased to 376 dollars in 1973 from the low level of 83 dollars in 1961, thanks to the rapid growth of gross national product and continuous decline in the rate of population growth. It is very important to keep population growth under control because per capita gross national product will never increase if the rate of population growth exceeds the growth rate of gross national product.

The popultion growth rate remained at a high level of 3.0 per cent and 2.9 per cent in 1961 and 1962 respectively. However, it declined to 2.2 per cent in 1966, the final year of the First Five-Year Plan, and showed a further decline to 1.7 per cent in 1971, the final year of the Second Plan. It is expected that the rate will be reduced to 1.5 per cent in 1976. the last year of the Third Five-Year Plan.

On the other hand, the rapid growth of such labor-intensive industries as mining and manufacturing, social overhead capital and other services has offered increased employment opportunities.

Consequently, unemployment has been sharply reduced. Until 1963 the unemployment ratio remained at the high level of 8.1 per cent, but declined almost every year thereafter: to 7.1 per cent in 1966, 4.5 per cent in 1971 and further to 4.0 per cent in 1973.

Population and Employment

National Income and Capital Formation

Along with the growth of per capita gross national product, per capita income has also increased, which, in turn, has brought about a sharp rise in the national savings ratio. The amount of gross national product in 1960 was 1,129.7 billion won at 1970 constant prices, of which the share of private consumption expenditure was 942.6 billion won, 83.4 per cent of the total amount, and that of fixed capital formation 97.0 billion won, only 8.6 per cent. In 1973, however, gross national product had grown to 3,522.7 billion won, equivalent to more than three times that of 1960, and gross domestic capital formation increased to 851.9 billion won, or 24.7 per cent of the whole amount, eightfold that of 1960, so that the ratio of capital formation to gross national product has continued rising for the past 12 years. The ratio of gross investment to gross national product rose from 13 per cent in 1962, the beginning year of the First Five-Year Plan, to 26.4 per cent in 1973. Moreover, the domestic saving ratio has risen sharply to 22 per cent from the low level of a mere 2.2 per cent in 1962.

If capital formation is broken down into saving and investment, dependency of capital formation on domestic savings in the initial year of the First Five-Year Plan (1962) was 12.0 per cent compared with dependency on foreign savings of 83.5 per cent (discrepancy due to errors and omissions). The former, however, rose to 54.6 per cent while the latter declined to 39 per cent in 1966. In 1971, they changed further to 56.9 per cent and 44 per cent respectively. During the Third Five-Year Plan, dependence on foreign savings continued to fall to 15.4 per cent in 1973, while dependence on domestic savings rose to 84.3 per cent. There will be almost no need to depend on foreign savings by 1976, the final year of the Third Five-Year Economic Development Plan.

Before implementation of the economic development plans, Korea suffered from vicious inflationary spirals due mainly to shortages in supply of goods. From the middle of the 1960's, however, price levels began to stabilize, thanks to the successful implementation of the First Five-Year Economic Development Plan. In the course of the plan, factors responsible for price increases were gradually uprooted by virtue of favorable domestic production, improvement of the foreign exchange situation in external transactions with the liberalization of trade, and enforcement of the overall price stabilization policy. As a result, price increases witnessed annual rates of 10.0 per cent in 1965, 8.9 per cent in 1966 and 6.4 per cent in 1967.

Toward the latter part of the 1960's, pressures on prices which has accumulated due to excess demand during the past decade were considerably reduced by the favorable supply of goods. However, entering the 1970's, prices reacted to unusual cost-push pressures due mainly to the world-wide inflation.

In order to alleviate the serious cost-push pressures, the government promulgated the President's Emergency Decree for Economic Stability and Growth in August, 1972. The measures contributed remarkably to improving the business financial structure, and also provided a momentum for price stability and business recovery. As a result, price levels stabilized at an increase of around 3 per cent from August 1972 to August 1973. However, the world economy was drawn into the whirlpool of heavy inflationary pressures and a business recession due to the unexpected oil upheaval in the wake of the Mideast War in October, 1973. The Korean economy, which is heavily dependent on imports, could not be an exception in the prevailing worldwide inflation.

In order to overcome this serious situation, the government promulgated the Presidential Emergency Decree of January 14, 1974, which included the alleviation of tax burdens on low income groups, stabilization of the nation's livelihood, and upward adjustment in prices of major items to realistic levels. Along with the decree, a series of new price stabilization policies was introduced.

Price Stabilization

Annual Increase Rate of Prices

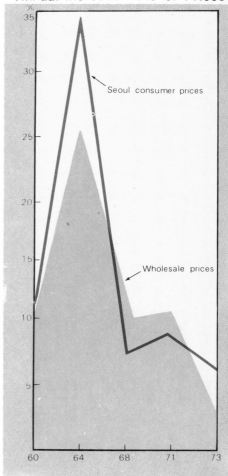

Seoul consumer prices

Wholesale prices

PROFILE OF
INDUSTRIALIZATION

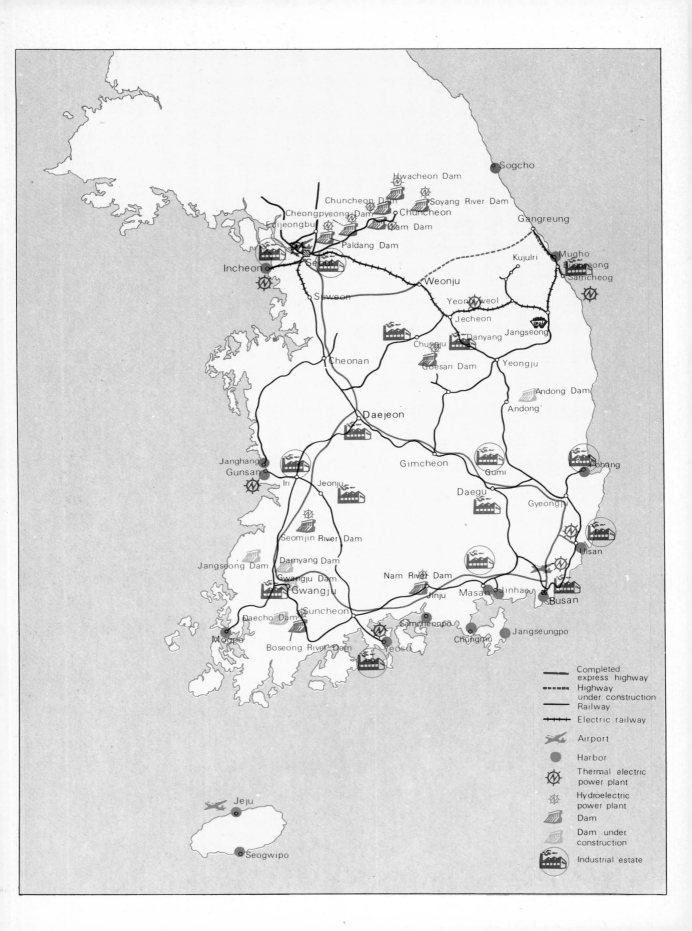

Iron and Steel Industry

The level of production and consumption of iron and steel is regarded sometimes as a barometer of a nation's prosperity and industrial development. Therefore, this industry plays a significant role in the development of a modern economy.

Before the liberation from Japan, Korea had an annual production capacity of 600,000 tons of iron and 160,000 tons of steel but most of the plants were located in north Korea. In south Korea there was only the small-scale Samhwa Iron Works Co. The Korean War dealt a near-fatal blow to this plant. After the Korean War, Daehan Heavy Industry (the predecessor of the Incheon Iron Works Co.) was established as the nation's first steelmaking and rolling industry, aimed at processing scrap iron. Existing worn-out equipment was partly replaced and blooming and slabbing mills, and scalp facilities were newly installed. Thus, in 1960 the nation's total production capacity of iron, steel and rolling plants amounted to 48,000 tons, 148,000 tons, and 318,000 tons respectively. In addition, a foundry pig iron plant with an annual production capacity of about 100,000 tons was established. However, most of the plants were so small and obsolete that their products were limited to only a few items. As a result, large amounts of iron and steel products indispensable for the development of modern industry were inevitably imported.

Tapping

Construction of Pohang Integrated Iron and Steel Mill

With the successful implementation of the First and Second Five-Year Economic Development Plans in the 1960's, the iron and steel industry began to develop rapidly. Reviewing the expansion of production facilities, in the ironmaking sector the small-scale blast furnace (60 cubic meters) of the Dongkuk Steel Mill Co. and electric preheater of the Incheon Iron Works Co. were newly installed in 1965 and 1969. In steelmaking the Pusan Iron, Dongkuk Steel and Kuckdong Steel Companies newly installed or enlarged existing converters and electric furnaces. Finally, in the rolling sector, production capacity was vigorously expanded, and the products diversified with cold rolled sheets, plate mills, etc.

Thus, by 1971, the final year of the Second Five-Year Economic Development Plan, the total production capacity of iron, steel, and rolling plants reached 203,000 tons, 911,000 tons, and 2,025,000 tons respectively.

It was a milestone in the iron and steel industry when the Pohang Iron and Steel Company Ltd., with an annual production capacity of 950,000 tons of iron, 1,032,000 tons of steel and 950,000 tons of rolling, was completed in July, 1973 as the nation's first integrated iron and steel mill. The construction of this mill with a modern and large-scale production system has contributed to rational and stabilized development in this sector.

Even up to 1972, when the mill had not yet been completed, there was really no integrated iron and steel mill with interrelated ironmaking, steelmaking and rolling facilities in Korea. Furthermore, existing plants could hardly compete with large-scale plants in efficiency. Only a few plants had a unit production capacity exceeding more than 100,000 tons a year. To make matters worse, iron making facilities were specialized only in the final rolling facilities. Consequently, large quantities of semi-processed iron and steel products had to be imported for industrial construction.

With the construction of the Pohang Mill, the imbalance among ironmaking, steelmaking and rolling facilities was greatly dimin-

Casting

Converter

The Pohang Iron and Steel Mill Co.

Billet Rolling Mill

Trend of Production Capacity in Iron and Steel Industry

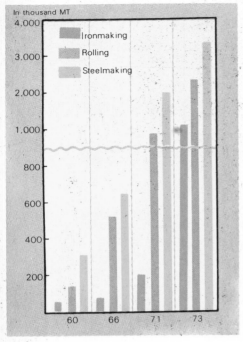

In thousand MT

- Ironmaking
- Rolling
- Steelmaking

(Bar chart with vertical axis values: 4,000 / 3,000 / 2,000 / 1,000 / 800 / 600 / 400 / 200; horizontal axis years: 60, 66, 71, 73)

Production Capacity of the Pohang Integrated Iron and Steel Mill

Plant	Products	Production Capacity (thousand MT)
Blast Furnace	Pig Iron	950
Steelmaking Plant	Molten Steel	1,032
Blooming and Slabbing Mill	Slab and Bloom	890
Billet Mill	Billets	141
Hot Strip Mill	Hot Coils	606
Plate Mill	Plates	336
Foundry Pig Iron Plant	Foundry Pig Iron	150

ished. Thus the nation's production capacity expanded to 1,153,000 tons of iron, 2,367,000 tons of steel, and 3,422,000 tons of rolling products. Before the construction of the Pohang Mill, we had exported most of our iron ore and on the other hand imported iron scrap. But with the Pohang Mill construction, the nation's iron-making facilities were greately reinforced. Now we import the once exported iron ore and have reduced remarkably our imports of iron scrap with the addition of rolling facilities, a blooming and slabbing mill with production capacity of 890,000 tons a year, billet mills, hot strip mills, etc., all kinds of rolled products including slabs, billets, and hot coils can now be produced domestically. As a consequence small and medium-sized producers, who specialized in processing imported semi-finished products in the past, have achieved linkage relations with the Pohang Iron and Steel Mill.

The construction of the Pohang Mill was planned in the early 1960's but did not materialize then because of various difficulties. However the construction work commenced finally in April, 1970, thanks to commerical loans from Japan and to the partial utilization of the Property and Claims Fund.

The construction period was only 39 months, half the period of normal construction. Also, normal operation of the mill was achieved in only four months, a period unprecedented in the history of construction of steel mills. In the past year, the mill earned enormous profits of 24.2 billion won, close to 20 per cent of total funds invested. This was accomplished not only by producing good-quality products, by no means inferior to foreign items, but also by selling at more moderate prices than imported counterparts.

Finishing mill pulpit

Shift from Import to Export

Since the 1960's, production of iron and steel products has rapidly increased and diversified. At the same time the quality of goods has reached international levels. As a result, most iron and steel products, which were entirely imported previously, ranging from a small needle to structural steel, motor vehicles, and ocean-going vessels, now are completely domestic in origin. Many iron and steel products are exported.

In 1960, the total demand for steel products in Korea amounted to only 168,000 tons, of which 31 per cent was imported because of poor production facilities. In particular, such major items as plate and scalp were entirely imported. With the progress of industrialization the nation's total demand for these products during the period 1962–71 increased at an average annual rate of 25.9 per cent, equivalent to about five times the world level. As a consequence, net imports of iron and steel products continued to increase year after year.

However, thanks to the steel industry development plan, the annual production of iron and steel products increased to one million tons around the end of the 1960's, and the self-sufficiency ratio of the products was greatly enhanced. Net imports were thus much reduced. As the First and Second Five-Year Economic Development Plans were successfully accomplished, all iron and steel products could be supplied domestically. With completion of the Pohang Mill in 1973 demand for such major products as plate and section rolling, which had to be partly imported during the past decade, could also be met fully by domestic supply.

Actual Demand and Supply of Steel Products

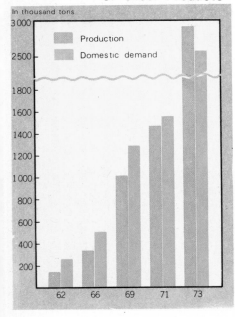

In thousand tons

Production

Domestic demand

3 000
2500
1800
1600
1400
1200
1000
800
600
400
200

62   66   69   71   73

Meanwhile, exports of iron and steel products increased very rapidly after 1970, with a record of 100 million dollars in 1972 and 208 million dollars in 1973, accounting for 6.4 per cent of total exports. Export items have been diversified, ranging from plates to steel pipes, reinforcing bars, wire rope and cast iron products. The market for exports has also expanded, with scalp being exported to 31 countries.

Since the completion of the Pohang Mill with its annual production capacity of 950,000 tons the supply-demand situation of raw materials in this industry has been improved by importing more iron ore and by reducing imports of pig iron and iron scrap.

Plates

It is natural for the demand of iron and steel products to increase, parallel with the development of such related industries as shipbuilding, machinery, vehicles, and electrical machinery, as well as the enlargement of social overhead capital, including railways, harbor facilities and other construction. In this connection, exports of iron and steel products are expected to continue to grow, judging from the fact that the output of industrialized countries including the United States and Japan is anticipated to slow down gradually, reflecting various factors such as wage increases, labor shortages, pollution control, and plant site problems.

To meet rapidly increasing demand, the government is actively pushing plans to expand the Pohang Mill, and to construct another integrated iron and steel mill with an initial capacity of 7,000,000 tons by the beginning of the 1980's. The plant site is planned to be on Asan Bay. The government also plans to systematize the linkage between related industries.

Hot coils

The Pohang Mill, with a capacity of 1,030,000 tons of crude steel a year, plans to expand capacity to 2,600,000 tons by 1976, and again to 7,000,000 tons by 1980. The first expansion project was started in December, 1973.

Besides these plans, private enterprises are also actively pushing plans to enlarge and modernize their production facilities. When the plants and the equipment installation planned by both the government and private enterprises are completed, the nation's steel production capacity will increase greatly.

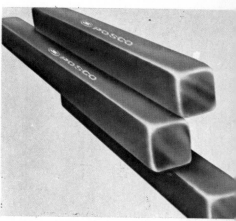

Billets

Exports of Steel Products			
			(In thousand MT)
	1971	1972	1973
Plates	8.1	39.7	111.0
Scalps	155.3	424.3	542.2
Steel Pipe	8.3	51.2	93.9
Reinforcing Bars	19.0	110.0	41.9
Foundry Pig Iron	1.8	3.0	20.7
Others	8.8	38.0	51.6
Total	201.3	666.2	861.3

Nonferrous Metals

Production of nonferrous metals cannot match the total output of iron and steel but, nevertheless, they are recognized as basic materials indispensable for the development of modern industry. They cover about 70 different items and have a wide variety of uses. Thus, the consumption level of nonferrous metals, as in the case of iron and steel, is regarded as a barometer of a nation's prosperity and industrial development.

The nonferrous metals industry in Korea was in a primitive stage until the end of the 1950's. The Janghang smelting works, the earliest facility for smelting and refining, built in 1936, produced only a small quantity of copper and lead. To make matters worse, the smelter was unable to maintain normal operations because of worn-out equipment and sluggish supply of required ores. In order to overcome the difficulties, intensive efforts were made toward the partial replacement of worn-out equipment and expansion of attached facilities by the United Nations Korean Reconstruction Agency (UNKRA) funds, but the operation was still stagnant because many difficulties remained unsolved.

However, beginning in the 1960's, with the rapidly increasing demand for various nonferrous metals along with vigorous industrialization, the Janghang smelting works producing copper and lead, was expanded several times; at the same time zinc and aluminum refinery plants were newly built.

The Janghang smelting works, playing a leading role in this sector, was merged into the Korea Mining and Smelting Corporation run by the government during the First Five-Year Economic Development Plan. Thereafter, copper smelters with an annual production capacity of 3,000 tons expanded to a level of 7,000 tons and lead smelters with an annual production of 3,600 tons were newly established. To meet the continuously increasing demand, a production facility expansion plan was accelerated during the Second Economic Development Plan. The annual production capacity of the Janghang smelting works amounts to 18,000 tons of copper and 6,500 tons of lead. Thus the self-sufficiency ratio of nonferrous metals was enhanced. In 1971 when the full operation started, the Janghang smelting works again came under private management.

The Janghang smelting works

Overall view of the Janghang smelting works

In the field of smelting zinc ores, the Tongshin Chemical Products Co. Ltd. with an annual capacity of 2,500 tons and the Seogpo factory of the Youngpoong Trading Co. Ltd. with an annual capacity of 9,000 tons were inaugurated in 1965 and 1970 respectively. Moreover, in the case of Seogpo factory, its capacity was expanded to 21,000 tons in October, 1974. In the absence of domestic facilities Korea formerly had to export zinc ores and import zinc ingots to smelt them. In this context, the establishment of these new facilities contributed considerably to elimination of the balance-of-payments bottleneck resulting from this kind of unfavorable trade.

In 1969, the Ulsan plant of the Aluminum of Korea, Ltd, was established with an annual capacity of 17,000 tons, thereby laying down the basis for domestic production of one of the most important nonferrous metals for modern industrial development. The plant overcame its initial difficulties by inducing Aluminum Pechiney of France to participate in its investment program and now plans to double its capacity in the near future to meet the ever-growing demand for its products on the part of domestic industries.

With regard to melting facilities for nonferrous scrap metals, there are ten copper melting companies, including the Taehan Electric Wire Co. and the Kunsul Co. Ltd., with total annual capacity of 18,000 tons, and three zinc smelting companies with annual capacity of 1,500 tons. These facilities make a great contribution to the saving of metal resources by rejuvenating waste metallic scraps.

Smelting Facilities Expanded

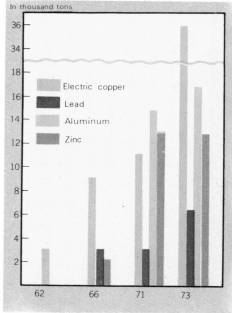

Smelting Capacity

In thousand tons

Electric copper
Lead
Aluminum
Zinc

62   66   71   73

Ulsan plant of the Aluminum of Korea Ltd.

Along with intensive efforts directed toward rapid industrialization, demand for various nonferrous metals showed a sharp increase during the period from 1960 to 1973: demand for copper increased on average by 30.2 per cent per annum for zinc by 30 per cent, for lead 22.5 per cent and aluminum 36.2 per cent. All these growth rates are above that of steel products except in the case of lead.

In the meantime, the output of nonferrous metals expanded to a great extent as a result of enlargement of smelting facilities. Output of electroyltic copper in 1973 amounted to 18,000 tons as compared with 1,000 tons at the beginning of the 1960's. During the same period output of lead and zinc ingots increased to 5,500 tons and 13,000 tons from less than 500 tons and 100 tons, respectively. Production of aluminum ingots, which was initiated toward the end of the 1960's, is estimated to exceed 16,000 tons per year presently.

Zinc smelter (Bonghwa)

The expansion of these production facilities has resulted in steady increases in self-support ratios in various nonferrous metals. The ratios in 1973 were 75 per cent for electrolytic copper, 50 per cent for lead ingots, 57 per cent for zinc ingots and 79 per cent for aluminum ingots. Domestic demand for nonferrous metals is expected to be fully met by domestic production in the near future.

In an effort to meet growing demand for nonferrous metals in tandem with the development of heavy and chemical industries, the government is planning to construct four large-scale smelters at a coastal area near Onsan, Gyeongnam Province, which is earmarked as a site for the development of a complex for the smelting industry. Combined with the various expansion programs for exsisting facilities initiated by private enterprises, the projects are expected to be an epoch-making event in the history of the smelting industry in Korea.

Regarding the construction timetable, copper and zinc smelters, with annual capacities of 100,000 tons and 80,000 tons, are scheduled to be completed in 1976, followed by an aluminum smelter with annual capacity of 100,000 tons in 1978 and a lead smelter with annual capacity of 50,000 tons in 1980.

Construction of New Large-Scale Smelters

Construction Plans of Large-Scale Smelters

	Major Products and Annual Capacity		Construction Period
	(thousand tons)		
Copper Smelter	Electrolytic copper	100	Jul. 1974~Dec. 1976
Zinc Smelter	Zinc	80	Jul. 1974~Dec. 1976
Aluminum Smelter	Aluminum	100	Mar. 1976~Sept.1978
Lead Smelter	Lead	50	Jan. 1979~Jun. 1980

Interior of the Aluminum of Korea, Co., Ltd.

Output of Nonferrous Metals

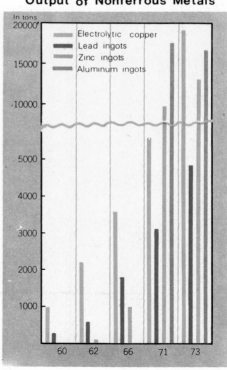

In tons

Electrolytic copper
Lead ingots
Zinc ingots
Aluminum ingots

20000
15000
10000
5000
4000
3000
2000
1000

60   62   66   71   73

Promotion of Machinery Industry

The machinery industry in Korea has seen remarkable growth in recent years. Formerly most machinery products needed in the process of industrialization had to be imported from abroad, as there was hardly any local machinery industry worth mentioning, except for plants producing small-size motors, farming implements and electrical products such as light bulbs and transformers, all of which were equipped with primitive technology and obsolete facilities.

Under these circumstances, the government initiated a series of measures to boost local industries, and to improve the balance of payments by substituting home-made products for imported ones. The Act for Promotion of Machinery Industries was put into force in 1967 and loans designed to promote the development of the industries began to be released in accordance with the basic promotion programs adopted by the government in 1968.

Machinery industry promotion loans are extended not only to manufacturers producing designated machinery products but also to

Tractors made by G.M. Korea Co.

those who use home-made equipment. A total of 69 billion won of loans was supplied during the period from 1968 to July 1974 on a long-term basis and at preferentially low interest rates. The magnitude and terms of the loans are expected to improve substantially as the National Investment Fund is added to the existing sources from 1974.

Moreover, to encourage the use of home-made products, in 1968 the government began to restrict the importation of machinery competitive with domestic products after plants have been introduced by the government or government-owned enterprises.
In addition, those who use home-made machinery were given the privilege of a 10 per cent tax deduction on their investments.

Owing to these favorable measures, the output of machinery industries in recent years has increased by ten times since 1960 and the share of machinery industry in the total manufacturing sector rose from 5 per cent to 10 per cent.

Trend of Machinery Promotion Loans (In million won)

Year	Amount Authorized	Amount Released	Loans Outstanding
1968	2,400	2,400	2,400
1969	17,427	8,631	9,895
1970	9,411	16,501	20,521
1971	10,300	9,401	21,453
1972	15,000	11,928	24,471
1973	10,217	13,963	31,552
1974 (end of July)	6,683	6,211	34,928
Total	71,438	69,035	

Note: Includes funds from National Investment Fund in 1974.

Assembly line in Korea Machinery Co.

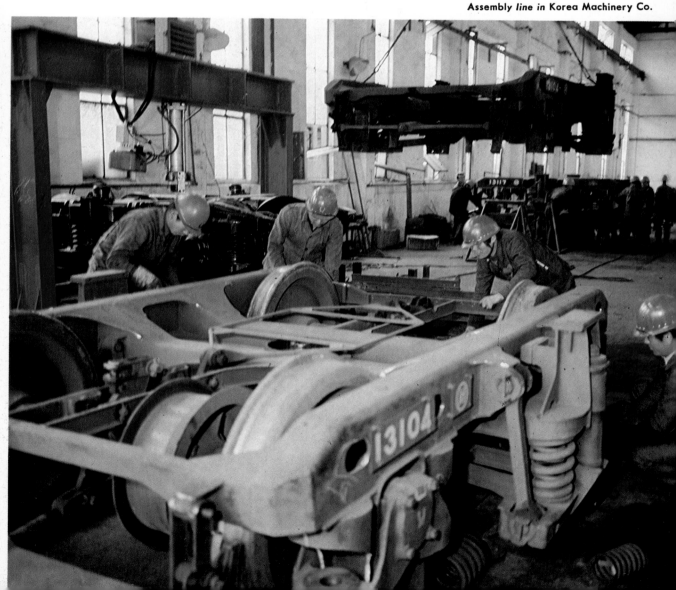

Increased Production of Farming Machinery

Until the beginning of the 1960's, manufacturers of agricultural equipment in Korea generally concentrated on the production of small farming implements such as weeding hoes, shovels, and ploughs. However, since the mid-1960's, the production pattern has shifted to the manufacturing of such modern farming machinery as power tillers, power sprayers, power thrashers, and water pumps, thanks mainly to various government policies designed to modernize agriculture. In particular, the number of power tillers produced in 1973 reached 18,495 sets. The production of tractors, made possible since the early 1970's, constitutes an epoch-making event in reforming generation's-old primitive farming practices in Korea.

Most of the parts used in these machines are produced by domestic firms and, even in assembling tractors, 34 per cent of the components are made domestically.

In addition, long-term loans for procurement of agricultural machines are extended to farmers at preferentially low rates of interest to the extent of 50 to 100 per cent of required funds in order to facilitate the use of home-made products.

As of the end of 1973, some 38,000 power tillers, 11,000 power thrashers, 62,000 water pumps, and 280 tractors are under actual utilization in farming.

Output of Major Farming Machinery

| | | 1962 |
| | | 1973 |

In thousand

Manufacturing power tillers at
Daedong Industrial Co. Ltd.

Increased Output of Electrical Equipment and Appliances

Output of Electric Machinery and Appliances

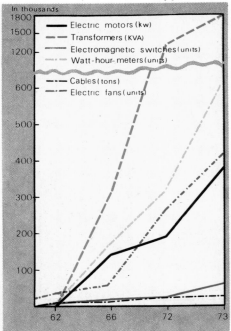

In thousands

- Electric motors (kw)
- Transformers (KVA)
- Electromagnetic switches (units)
- Watt-hour-meters (units)
- Cables (tons)
- Electric fans (units)

1800 1500 1200 600 500 400 300 200 100

62 66 72 73

It was not until the early 1960's when electric power began to be supplied without restrictions that the electrical machinery industry achieved momentum for modernizing its facilities and introducing foreign loans and advanced technology.

In the field of electrical equipment for industrial use, the output of electric motors and transformers increased sharply during the latter half of the 1960's and in 1969 even extra-high-voltage transformers of 154 kilovolts were turned out.

On the other hand, the production of electrical appliances for household use has also been expanded to a great extent, in accordance with the growth of national income and brisk demand for quality goods on the part of consumers.

The output of electric fans and refrigerators, both of which had been in the trial stage in the early 1960's, reached 410,000 and 50,000 units respectively in 1973. In the meantime, enlargement of the production scale and technical advances have been instrumental in increasing exports of electrical products, which soared in value to 17 million dollars in 1973, with substantial diversification of export items, ranging from light electrical appliances such as light bulbs and electric fans to heavy equipment such as cables, transformers, motors, watt-hour-meters, etc..

Automotive Industry

The automobile industry in Korea came into existence with the introduction of a modern assembly plant in 1962. It was a small plant with an annual production capacity of 6,000 Saenara (New Country) passenger cars assembled by the semi-knockdown method.

In 1966, a private enterprise, the Shinjin Motor Co., Ltd., took over the plant and operated it with technical cooperation from the Toyota Motor Company of Japan to assemble passenger cars, buses, and trucks through the complete knockdown method.

Later the Company broke relations with Toyota and established G.M. Korea Co., Ltd., with General Motors of America as partners, in a joint venture.

In the meantime, the Hyundai Motor Company was established

Assembling passenger cars in Kia Industrial Co.

Output of Automobiles

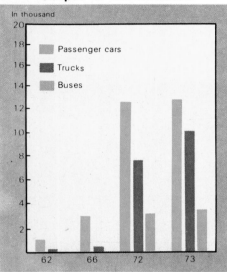

In thousand

Passenger cars
Trucks
Buses

62   66   72   73

in 1968 under a technical cooperation agreement with the British Ford Motor Company, and the Asia Motor Co. began to assemble its passenger cars in cooperation with the Fiat Motor Company of Italy in 1970. The Kia Industrial Co., Ltd., which had been assembling motorcycles and three-wheel halftrucks, finished its assembly plant for four-wheel trucks with technical assistance from the Toei Industrial Co., Ltd. of Japan. With these four companies competing with one another, the automotive industry in Korea seems to be on the threshold of rapid development.

As of the end of 1974, the annual capacity of automobile assembling firms totaled 63,100 units : 31,000 passenger cars, 7,200 buses and 24,900 trucks. The G.M. Korea Co., Ltd. leads the other three companies in market share.

The production of automobiles expanded remarkably in the latter half of the 1960's in parallel with the growth of national income and increase in demand for transportation services.

The number of automobiles assembled in 1973 reached 26,314 (12,751 passenger cars, 3,494 buses and 10,069 trucks). These compare with no more than 17,000 home-made passenger cars and 67 trucks produced in 1962.

Furthermore, in consideration of the strategic importance of the automobile industry in the growth of the national economy, the government prepared a long-term plan to promote the automotive industry in January 1974, which envisions establishment of a mass-

production system and substitution of domestic products for imported auto parts.

The production of motor vehicles in Korea has been dependent upon imports of knockdown parts from abroad rather than on domestic products.

Recently, however, a series of government measures to foster industries manufacturing automobile parts and components has caused a substantial rise in the ratio of domestic components to the total. The ratios now stand at 62 per cent in the case of passenger cars, 83 per cent for buses, and 53 to 80 per cent for trucks. Moreover, prospects for further import substitution in the automotive industry are bright as G. M. Korea and the Kia Industrial Co. launched construction of plants in 1974 to manufacture their own automobile engines, with combined annual capacity totaling 50,000 units.

In order to achieve complete domestic production of automobiles by 1975, the government plans to realign diversified auto part industries according to their specialties, while the Kia Industrial Co. and Hyundai Motor Co. are to complete their press plants in 1975.

In addition, existing companies are subject to a government program to realign the industry on the basis of one company for one type of automobile. Small low-cost passenger cars for the general public are scheduled to be produced in 1975.

Automobile Output Capacity by Company
(In thousand units)

	Passenger Cars	Buses	Trucks	Total
G.M.Korea (Bupyeong)	16.0	3.0	6.0	25.0
Hyundai (Ulsan)	7.8	1.8	6.9	16.5
Asia (Gwangju)	7.2	2.4	3.6	13.2
Kia (Seoul)	—	—	8.4	8.4
Total	31.0	7.2	24.9	63.1

Manufacturing automobile engines in Kia Industrial Co.

Construction of the Changweon Machinery Industrial Estate

Korea's machinery industry has made great strides in recent years. Production facilities, however, are still limited with each firm producing a variety of items with relatively small-scale facilities.

For this reason the competitiveness of the products is behind that of developed countries in both price and quality.

Facing these problems, the government has established a long-term development plan to promote the industry as a strategic sector for development of heavy and chemical industries. According to this plan, by the 1980's 43 types of business and 128 major items will be promoted intensively, and the Changweon Machinery Industrial Estate will be constructed to secure effective

Plan for Plant Constructions

	Industries (Number of Items	Number of Plants	Invest-ment
			million dollars
Total	43 (128)	322	2,186
Chang-weon Estate	37 (117)	104	968
New construction other than the Estate	5 (7)	13	206
Extension of designated plants	40 (122)	205	819
Others	—	—	193

alignment of the related plants. Also, a total of 322 plants will be newly set up or will expand their facilities in the course of implementation of the plan.

The construction of the Changweon Estate was started in 1973 and the first construction area was completed in 1974. With the completion of the first area, 20 of the 104 invited to use the Estate confirmed their entry, and 12 already began their factory construction.

The completion of the Estate will make a great contribution to self-supply of machinery by realizing domestic production and supply of components or parts required for the machinery industry, including the automobile and shipbuilding industries.

A bird's-eye view of the Changweon Machinery Industrial Estate

Development of Korea's Shipbuilding Industry

Trend of Shipbuilding Capacity

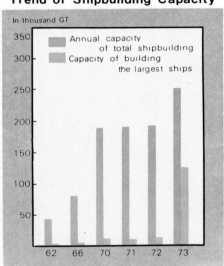

In thousand GT

Annual capacity of total shipbuilding

Capacity of building the largest ships

The shipbuilding industry purchases various required materials from no less than 50 other industries, including steel, machinery, electronics, chemicals, etc.. The industry, therefore, has far-reaching linkage effects, and requires a large labor force while using little energy. Accordingly, it is a very promising field for Korea, foreshadowing a leading role in developing heavy and chemical industries under the twin circumstances of poor resources endowment and the great advantage of abundant labor.

Nonetheless, development had stalled owing to the lack of recognition of its importance. At the time of the Liberation in 1945 the total shipbuilding capacity of 13 yards located in South Korea stood at no more than 19,000 gross tons. Thereafter, efforts were made to replace or extend the existing facilities, without any noteworthy results. Until the 1950's the industry's main business was nothing but repairing small wooden vessels. The total shipbuilding tonnage during 1954–61 was no more than 24,000 gross tons and 95 per cent of the total was occupied by wooden ships.

From the 1960's, however, the industry entered a new stage. The government established the Five-Year Shipbuilding Plan

parallel with the First Five-Year Economic Development Plan and promulgated the Shipbuilding Industry Encouragement Law in 1962 to subsidize the industry considering the unfavorable margin between the prices of home-made and foreign ships. Also, through the subsequent enactment of the Shipbuilding Promotion Law in 1967 and Machinery Promotion Law in 1969, the government has secured fiscal and financial support for the manufacturers and actual users of domestic ships.

Owing to these favorable measures, the total production capacity of the industry in 1966, the last year of the First Five-Year Economic Development Plan, recorded a twofold expansion. Compared with no more than 41,700 gross tons in 1962, capacity jumped to 190,000 gross tons in 1971, or 4.5 times the figure of 1962.

In addition, tonnage of the largest ship ever built in Korea, which was no more than 200 gross tons in 1962, grew to 6,000 gross tons in 1967 and 12,000 gross tons in 1971. Eventually, Korea's shipbuilding industry advanced to a new stage in the early 1970's when such large ships as deep-sea fishing vessels, cargo ships, passenger ships, etc., can be built.

Shipbuilding Reaches Level of Developed Countries

In the 1970's, thanks to the vigorous promotion of the heavy and chemical industries, shipbuilding has achieved remarkable progress as a strategic industry.

According to the measures taken on August 3, 1972, small and medium shipyards have been merged into large-sized ones, and the production facilities of major existing enterprises such as the Korea Shipbuilding Corporation have been extended. In addition, the establishment of the Hyundai Shipbuilding and Heavy Industries Co., Ltd. opened a new era in the development of the Korean shipbuilding industry. The annual production capacity has reached 750,000 gross tons and the largest ship that can be built is 350,000 gross tons.

As of June 1974, the annual production capacity of all shipyards in Korea reached 1.1 million gross tons. As many as 144 enterprises are involved in the industry, including the Hyundai Shipbuilding and Heavy Industries Co., Ltd. described above, the Korea Shipbuilding and Engineering Corporation with a capacity of 200,000 gross tons, the Daesun Shipbuilding and Engineering Co., Ltd. with 31,000 gross tons, etc., and 54 enterprises have the capability of building steel ships.

Reviewing the actual results of shipbuilding in Korea, the gross tonnage of total ships built in 1962 did not exceed 5,000 gross tons, but it rose about four times to 17,700 gross tons by 1966, and exceeded 40,000 gross tons in 1971. Further, it grew to an astounding 163,000 gross tons in 1973, almost the same level as the 171,000 gross tons, of all ships built during the entire period of the Second Five-Year Economic Development Plan. Moreover, since 1974 when construction of the Hyundai Shipbuilding and Heavy Industries Co. facility was completed, shipbuilding tonnage has accelerated. Also, the ratio of steel ships to total shipbuilding has risen sharply. The number of steel ships increased to 161 in 1973, accounting for about half the total, from only two small ships in 1962. In particular, the ratio of tonnage of the steel ships to total tonnage exceeded 90 per cent in 1971, grown from 8.2 per cent in 1962.

In the process of such rapid growth of the shipbuilding industry, 20 modern pelagic-fishing vessels were built in 1969 for export to Taiwan, a multipurpose cargo ship of 18,000 dead-weight tons was completed in 1972, an oil transport ship of 20,000 dead-weight tons was completed in June 1974, and two oil tankers of 260,000

Increased Shipbuilding and Export

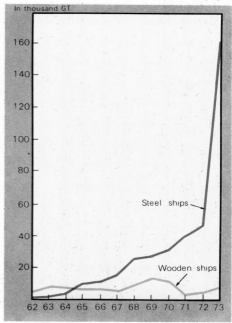

Actual Results of Shipbuilding
In thousand GT

Steel ships

Wooden ships

62 63 64 65 66 67 68 69 70 71 72 73

The Atlantic Baron, the oil tanker of 260,000 dead-weight ton class, built by the Hyundai Shipbuilding and Heavy Industries Co.

Exports and Imports of Ships

(In thousand dollars)

Year	Exports	Imports
1967	899	48,430
1968	1,228	40,606
1969	6,000	68,668
1970	3,000	33,810
1971	5,000	32,929
1972	9,000	48,648
1973	87,000	121,600

dead-weight tons were launched in February and June 1974 by the Hyundai Shipbuilding and Heavy Industries Co.. All these accomplishments enabled Korea to become one of the most promising shipbuilding countries in the world.

Korean ships were passed by examination of the International Ship Association in 1967, and the nation's shipbuilding technology was acknowledged worldwide.

From that time on, exports of ships increased continuously to mark 87 million dollars in 1973, and is expected to reach 260 million dollars in 1974, including the export of two supertankers built by the Hyundai Shipbuilding and Heavy Industries Co.. Buying orders from the rest of the world as of June 1974 totaled 59 ships or 668 million dollars, including pelagic-fishing vessels, cargo ships and oil tankers of supertanker scale.

Plan for Promotion of Shipbuilding Industry

Year	Building Capacity	Production Plan	Export Plan
	thousand GT	thousand GT	million dollars
1974	1,100	590	260
1975	1,440	1,014	300
1976	2,600	1,395	400
1980	5,950	3,730	1,000

Construction of Large-Scale Shipyards

Prospects for exports by the Korean shipbuilding industry are favorable because shipbuilding capacity of major developed countries falls short of the increasing demand for ships in the world market. In view of these favorable conditions, the government plans to promote the shipbuilding industry as a strategic export industry in the process of pursuing heavy and chemical industrialization. According to this policy, the facilities of the Ulsan shipyard of the Hyundai Shipbuilding and Heavy Industries Co. are scheduled to be extended to the capacity of two million gross tons by September 1975, and the Ogpo shipyard of the Korea Shipbuilding Corporation, equipped with a capacity of 1.2 million gross tons, and the Anjeong shipyard of the Samsung Heavy Industry Co., with a capacity of 750,000 gross tons are to be completed by 1976.

With these shipyards completed, the largest ship capable of being constructed is expected to reach 500,000 gross tons, and the total production capacity of Korea's shipbuilding industry will be extended to the level of no less than 6 million gross tons by the 1980's. Annual gross tonnage of shipbuilding also is expected to increase year by year to 4 million gross tons by the 1980's, exporting as much as one billion dollars of ships to the world market.

It was not until the early 1960's that Korea's electronics industry experienced notable development. Since that time the industry has marked conspicuous growth to become one of the most important export industries in Korea. In recent years the industry has earned as much as 400 million dollars in exports.

Such rapid development of this industry, achieved during a relatively short period of time, owes much to aggressive support by the government. Korea has favorable conditions for developing an electronics industry because the country has abundant skilled labor.

In consideration of these favorable prospects, in 1966 the government designated the electronics industry as a strategic export industry and provided it with various financial aids and preferential tax treatments. Also the Electronics Industry Promotion Law promulgated in 1969 has provided an institutional foundation to support the industry.

In addition, the continuous increase in domestic demand for electronic products such as radios, television receivers, etc., in response to the nation's rising living standards and an annual favorable increment of 10 per cent in overseas demand has contributed greatly to the conspicuous development.

Electronics as an Export Industry

Korea's electronics industry began with the production of vacuum-tube radio receivers in 1958, but until the early 1960's little headway was made because of the lack of technical know-how. At that time the main products were confined to radio sets, telephones and other relatively simple items.

In the course of implementing the First Five-Year Development Plan, the nation's electronics industry began to assume a new aspect as a modern industry. In 1965 the domestic production of record players was first attained and in 1966 the domestic assembling of television sets, one of the most important durable consumer goods, was realized. This was followed by production of various semiconductors such as transistors, integrated circuits and components for computers which spearheaded the development of electronic technology. From the 1970's such delicate appliances as tape recorders, desk-top calculators, color television receivers, etc., were added to the nation's electronic products.

By the end of 1973, a total of 351 enterprises were engaged in manufacturing electronic articles and their total output that year, covering 150 products, was valued at 185.2 billion won. Principal outputs included a total of 3,000,000 radio sets, 830,000 television receivers and 1,500,000 tape recorders. Among parts and components, transistors and integrated circuits produced in 1973 were valued at as much as 69 billion won.

The ratio of home-manufactured parts and components to finished products changed from 33 per cent in 1965 to 61 per cent in 1973, reflecting the rapid growth in the share occupied by domestic parts and components.

Output of Electronic Products

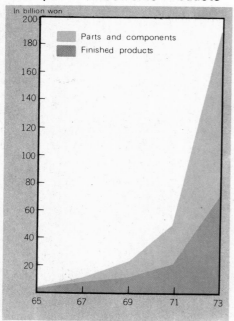

In billion won

Parts and components
Finished products

200
180
160
140
120
100
80
60
40
20

65   67   69   71   73

Assembling electronic appliances and equipment at the Dongyang Precision Co.

TV 설계의 새로운 도전! TCM2500-敎育用 COLOR TV

** DR TV**

Strategic Export Industry

Exports of electronic goods began with the sale of radio receivers in 1963, and increased year by year, accelerating in the latter half of the 1960's when the industry began experiencing remarkable growth. Exports rose from only 50 thousand dollars in 1963 to 4 million dollars in 1966, when the government designated the industry as a strategic export industry, and jumped to 369 million dollars in 1973, an increase of more than 92 times the level of 1966 and equivalent to 11.3 per cent of total Korean exports that year.

Export items also were diversified from a few simple products such as radio receivers in the early stage, to such delicate electronic machines as television receivers, record players, speakers, telephone exchanges, and varied components such as transistors, integrated circuits, etc..

In the 1970's tape recorders and desk-top calculators were added to export items and in early 1974 domestic production and export of color television sets and electronic clocks began.

As a result, the number of electronic items being exported swelled to 70 presently and some 80 per cent of present output goes to the world markets in more than 50 countries.

Exports of Electronic Products

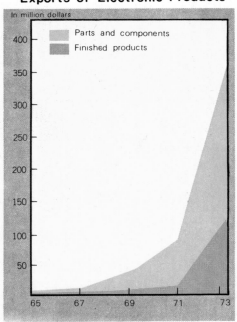

In million dollars

Parts and components
Finished products

400
350
300
250
200
150
100
50

65   67   69   71   73

To further stimulate development of the electronics industry and to strengthen the competitiveness of Korean electronic products in world markets the government has established a long-term promotion plan and is directing its efforts toward construction and extension of electronics industrial bases.

In October 1973, a large electronics industrial base of 583,000 square meters, was established in Gumi, Gyeongbug Province. By June, 1974, 50 enterprises had already settled in the base with 22 of them in operation. The base is expected to be completed by 1977 with accomodation of 300 enterprises. Thereafter, imports of elementary materials will be substituted by domestic products and exports produced in the base alone are expected to exceed 400 million dollars on annual average. Accordingly, from 1976 the base will play the role of an advanced post for exports of electronic products as well as the supply of essential parts and components.

Construction of the Gumi Electronics Industrial Estate

Promising Petrochemical Industry

The petrochemical industry had its beginning during the 1920's but it was only after World War II that it experienced rapid growth, especially in the developed countries.

Formerly the organic chemical industry depended for its raw materials on coal, carbide and animal and vegetable oils. However, it was not possible to supply these raw materials in the quantities required and cheaper hydrocarbons did not provide a sufficient degree of purity. Consequently, the chemical industry gradually shifted to petroleum as a raw material source.

Now modern chemical industries depend for their raw materials upon petroleum or natural gas, which are more suitable in availability, practicality and cost.

With successive technological innovations, the petrochemical industry has produced a wide variety of products of wide uses, ranging from raw materials for other industries to plentiful and inexpensive daily necessities. Because of these advantages, most

countries have put high priority on development of their own petrochemical industry.

In Korea, completion of the Ulsan Oil Refinery was followed by rapid development of related petrochemical industries, such as synthetic resins, synthetic fibers, synthetic rubber and detergents, which use petrochemicals as raw material. At the time, demand for petrochemical intermediate products increased markedly. As a result, the need arose for development of a petrochemical industry to improve balance of payments through import substitutions and to foster domestic industries through domestic supply of raw materials.

Thus, the development of a petrochemical industry became one of the most important projects during the Second Five-Year Economic Development Plan, and the government has provided concentrated support to help this field develop as a strategic industry in the pursuit of a fully industrialized society in the 1980's.

Naphtha cracking center of the Korea Oil Corporation

Petrochemical Processing Diagram

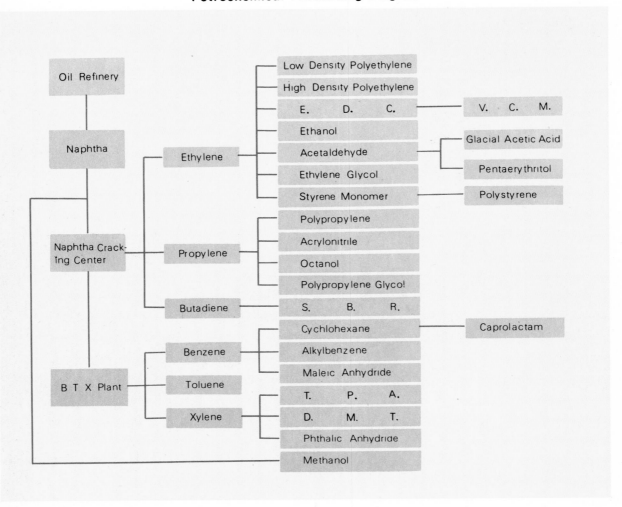

Oil Refinery

Naphtha

Naphtha Cracking Center

B T X Plant

Ethylene
- Low Density Polyethylene
- High Density Polyethylene
- E. D. C. → V. C. M.
- Ethanol
- Acetaldehyde → Glacial Acetic Acid / Pentaerythritol
- Ethylene Glycol
- Styrene Monomer → Polystyrene

Propylene
- Polypropylene
- Acrylonitrile
- Octanol
- Polypropylene Glycol

Butadiene
- S. B. R.

Benzene
- Cyclohexane → Caprolactam
- Alkylbenzene
- Maleic Anhydride

Toluene

Xylene
- T. P. A.
- D. M. T.
- Phthalic Anhydride

Methanol

Production Capacities of Ulsan Petrochemical Complex

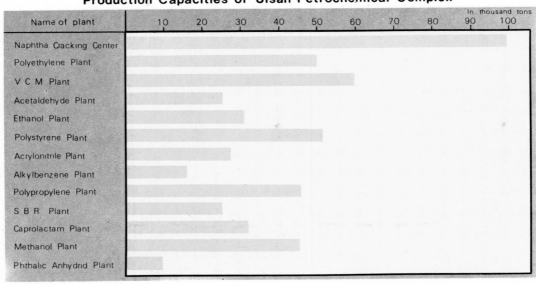

In thousand tons

Name of plant	10	20	30	40	50	60	70	80	90	100
Naphtha Cracking Center										100
Polyethylene Plant		20								
V C M Plant						60				
Acetaldehyde Plant		25								
Ethanol Plant			32							
Polystyrene Plant					50					
Acrylonitrile Plant			28							
Alkylbenzene Plant		17								
Polypropylene Plant				45						
S B R Plant			27							
Caprolactam Plant			33							
Methanol Plant				45						
Phthalic Anhydrid Plant	11									

Implementation of the petrochemical industry development plan began with the establishment of the Integrated Development Plan for the Petrochemical Industry in November, 1966. Physical development began in March, 1968 when the construction of the Ulsan Petrochemical Complex commenced.

A petrochemical industry includes a naphtha cracking center which supplies various basic raw materials to other petrochemical downstream plants producing many industrial raw materials. The group is called a petrochemical complex.

The first development plan of the Ulsan Petrochemical Complex provided for the construction of thirteen petrochemical plants, including a naphtha cracking center, all of which were already completed and in normal operation in 1974.

The construction of a large-scale naphtha cracking center, the pivot of the petrochemical complex, was undertaken by the Korea Oil Corporation in October, 1972. The annual production capacity is 100,000 tons of ethylene, beside which such basic raw materials as propylene, butadiene, etc., are extracted in the process of naphtha cracking.

In the complex there are five satellite plants consuming ethylene as raw material: a polyethylene plant with an annual capacity of 50,000 tons; a VCM (vinyl chloride monomer) plant with an annual capacity of 60,000 tons, finished in October, 1972; a polystyrenes plant with an annual capacity of 50,000 tons, finished in December 1973; and ethanol and acetaldehyde plants completed in November 1974.

There are three downstream plants using propylene as raw material. The acrylonitrile plant, providing raw material for the production of chemical fibers, and the polypropylene plant supplying raw materials for the production of chemical fibers and synthetic resins, were finished in October, 1972. The alkylbenzene plant which supplies raw materials for the producion of synthetic detergents was completed in February, 1973.

Meanwhile the SBR (styrene butadiene rubber) plant, producing synthetic rubber from butadiene, was completed in May 1973. The methanol plant supplying raw material for the production of paint, solvents and plywood, was finished in July, 1971 by the Daesung Timber Company. Finally, a caprolactam plant, supplier of the material for manufacturing nylon fiber, was completed in June, 1974.

In addition, a utilities and service center was constructed in March 1972 by the Petrochemical Service Center to supply water, electric power, steam and various services at low cost to the thirteen downstream plants mentioned above.

Construction of Ulsan Pertrochemical Complex

Production of polypropylene by Korea Petrochemical Industry Co.

Hankook Caprolactam Co.

Demand for various oils used as industrial raw materials has increased rapidly since construction of the Ulsan Petrochemical Complex. Accordingly, interrelated industries which use intermediate petrochemical products as raw materials have recorded rapid growth.

The synthetic resins industry, representative of petrochemical interrelated industries, has made remarkable progress since the first PVC plant was constructed in 1966 by the Daehan Plastics Co. with an annual production capacity of 6,600 tons. By the end of 1973 the annual aggregate production capacity had expanded to 231,000 tons.

The chemical fiber industry, another important petrochemical industry, marked a production capacity of 314 tons per day as of the end of 1973, due mainly to the expansion of production facilities of synthetic fibers such as nylon, polyester, polypropylene, etc., since 1967.

The synthetic detergents industry, a prime user of alkylbenzene, was initiated in 1966 and recorded an output of 39,000 tons in 1973. Meanwhile, various organic chemicals derived from petrochemicals began to be produced in 1968.

Formerly, petrochemical interrelated industries relied heavily on imported raw materials. At present, however, the petrochemical industry in Korea is making great progress in its import substitution as various petrochemicals have begun to be produced since 1973 with completion of the Ulsan Petrochemical Complex.

Development of Related Industries and Import Substitutes

A part of Korean Synthetic Rubber Co.

Imports of Major Petrochemical Products

(In tons)

	1969	1972	1973	Percentage Changes between 1972 and 1973
Polyethylene	33,535	63,947	38,470	−40.0%
Polypropylene	3,586	18,209	7,173	−60.6
Acrylonitrile	14,560	24,700	5,766	−76.6
VCM	20,365	41,438	4,768	−88.5
Methanol	35,815	19	10,781	−69.9[1]
Benzene	2,493	3,165	10	−99.7
Phthalic Anhdride	1,841	3,573	963	−73.0
Acetaldehyde	273	4,199	2,962	−29.5
Caprolactam	16,416	30,841	37,193	20.6
Orthoxylene	15	5,387	10,463	94.2
D.M.T	13	32,747	45,908	40.2
Ethylene Glycol	1,418	13,214	18,214	37.8
Toluene	5,407	1,334	6,456	19.4[1]

Note: 1) Compared between 1969 and 1973.

Expansion of Petrochemical Complex

In spite of the achievement of considerable import substitution of major petrochemicals since the construction of the Ulsan Petrochemical Complex, the petrochemical industry in Korea still relies heavily upon imports. Many kinds of petrochemicals have to be imported to meet domestic demand, which seems to increase in tandem with the development of interrelated industries.

Accordingly, the government has a plan to foster the petrochemical industry as part of overall strategy for heavy and chemical industry. This plan consists of the expansion of existing facilities of the Ulsan Petrochemical Complex and construction of a second petrochemical complex in the Yeocheon area.

The expansion plan for the Ulsan Petrochemical Complex includes the following enlargements: the naphtha cracking center to 150,000 tons on an ethylene basis; the low-density polyethylene plant from 50,000 tons to 100,000 tons; the vinyl chloride monomer plant from 60,000 tons to 120,000 tons; the acrylonitrile plant from 27,000 tons to 113,000 tons; the polypropylene plant from 45,000 tons to 90,000 tons; the styrene butadiene rubber plant from 25,000 tons to 75,000 tons; the caprolactam

Tongsuh Petrochemical Co.

Second-Stage Construction Plan of Ulsan Petrochemical Complex

(In thousand tons)

	Sponsor	Present Capacity	Total Capacity after Expansion	Completion Year
Expansion of Existing Facilities				
Naphtha Cracking Center	Korea Oil Corp.	100	150	1977
L.D. Polyethylene	Korea Pacific Chemical Corp.	50	100	1978
VCM	Korea Pacific Chemical Corp.	60	120	//
Polypropylene	Korea Petrochemical Industry Co.	45	90	//
Acrylonitrile	Tongsuh Petrochemical Co.	27	113	//
Caprolactam	Hankook Caprolactam Co.	33	133	//
SBR	Korea Synthetic Rubber Industry Co.	25	75	//
Phthalic Anhydride	Samkyung Chemical Industry Co.	8.4	20	//
New Construction				
Naphtha Cracking Center	Not yet determined		200	1978
H.D. Polyethylene	Korea Petrochemical Industry Co.		35	1975
Styrene Monomer	Ulsan Petrochemical Co.		60	1978
Polypropylene Glycol	Korea Polyol Co.		5	//
EDC	Oriental Diamond Co.		110	//
Octanoic Butanol	Lucky Chemical Co.		50	//
DMT	Sunkyung Petrochemical Co.		120	//
TPA	Samsung Petroleum Co.		100	//
Maleic Anhydride	Daenong Petrochemical Industry Co.		10	//

plant from 33,000 tons to 133,000 tons; and the phthalic anhydride plant from 8,400 tons to 20,000 tons. Further, it is planned to construct another naphtha cracking center with an annual production capacity of 150,000–200,000 tons, and nine other plants for high-density polyethylene, polypropylene glycol, DMT, TPA, etc.. Most of the plants under expansion or construction are to be completed by 1978.

Meanwhile, the industrial site of 4.26 square kilometers for the Yeocheon Complex is now under construction, with the Yeosu Petrochemical Corporation undertaking all the construction projects.

By 1977, eleven downstream plants will be finished. It is estimated that a total of 1 billion dollars will be required for the construction.

The government is making utmost efforts to induce participation of domestic and foreign capital in this project. It is expected that the construction of the petrochemical complex in Yeocheon will bring about self-sufficiency in petrochemical products and enable Korea to export surpluses.

Fertilizer Contributes Increasing Food Production

The chemical fertilizer industry supplies not only various kinds of fertilizers essential to agricultural production but also such basic chemicals as ammonia, phosphorus and nitrogen necessary to the petrochemical industry.

In Korea, modern chemical fertilizer production originated with the construction of the Heungnam Fertilizer Plant in 1930, with an annual capacity of 480,000 tons. After liberation from Japan, there were several small-scale fertilizer plants in South Korea, including Samcheog Industrial Development Co., the Incheon Plant of the Chosun Chemical Co., the Mogpo Potassium Alumite Plant, etc., but all of these plants were destroyed during the Korean War.

Consequently the government gave special priority to the development of the industry. The Chungju Fertilizer Plant was constructed in 1960 and the Naju Fertilizer Plant in 1963. Thereafter, the chemical fertilizer industry has recorded rapid growth, due to steady construction of large-scale fertilizer plants of the Yongnam Chemical Co., Chinhae Chemical Co., the Korea Fertilizer Co., etc..

In June 1973 the Chungju Fertilizer Co. and Honam Fertilizer Co. merged into the Korea General Chemical Corporation which, as a holding company, controls such affiliated companies as the Yongnam Chemical Co. and Chinhae Chemical Co., and to undertake completion of the Sixth Fertilizer Complex (ammonia

Bagging at Chungju Fertilizer plant

Urea tower of the Korea Fertilizer Company

plant) and construction of the Seventh Fertilizer Complex. Thereby, a sound foundation will be laid for smooth development of the chemical fertilizer industry as an integrated chemical industry.

As regards production capacity of chemical fertilizers, urea expanded more than 10 times: from 85,000 tons annually in the early 1960's to 968,000 tons in 1974. There are presently six urea plants, including the Chungju Plant, Naju Plant, and the newly built ammonia center all belonging to the Korea General Chemical Corp., plus plants operated by the Yongnam Chemical Co, Chinhae Chemical Co. and Hankook Fertilizer Co.

Compound fertilizer containing the three major elements of nitrogen, phosphorus and potash is produced by the Yongnam Chemical Co. and Chinhae Chemical Co., with a total annual production capacity of 361,000 tons.

The production capacity of fused phosphate by the Kyungki Chemical Co. and Pungnong Chemical Co. has reached 158,000 tons per year, and that of calcium cyanamide stands at 25,000 tons per year.

The Pohang Iron and Steel Co. has also been producing ammonium sulphate as a by-product since 1973, and the Hankook Caprolactam Co. has been in operation since 1974. As of the end of 1974, the total production capacity of ammonium sulphate amounted to 148,600 tons, of which the Pohang Iron and Steel Co. Ltd. provided 8,600 tons and the Hankook Caprolactam Co. 140,000 tons.

Fertilizer Production Capacity

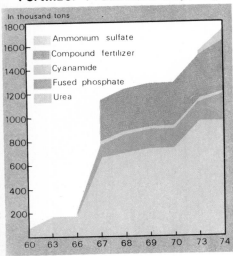

In thousand tons

- Ammonium sulfate
- Compound fertilizer
- Cyanamide
- Fused phosphate
- Urea

Fertilizer Production

In thousand tons

Increased Production of Fertilizer

The domestic production of chemical fertilizer has increased year by year with consecutive construction of new fertilizer plants and expansion of existing production facilities. As a result, production of chemical fertilizer grew from 13,000 tons in 1960 to 190,000 tons in 1966, the last year of the First Five-Year Economic Development Plan. At the same time, diversified types of fertilizers, such as nitrogen, phosphate and potash, began to be produced. In 1968, with full operation of the Korea Fertilizer Co., Yongnam Chemical Co. and Chinhae Chemical Co., production of fertilizer topped the 1,000,000 ton level for the first time. By 1973 it had increased further to 1,428,000 tons.

In 1973 output consisted of 698,000 tons of urea, 566,000 tons of compound fertilizer, 159,000 tons of fused phosphate, and 4,500 tons of ammonium sulfate. In terms of fertilizer elements, production in 1973 consisted of 442,000 element tons of nitrogen, 160,000 element tons of phosphorus, and 65,000 element tons of potash, making a total of 667,000 element tons. Up to the first half of the 1960's annual imports of fertilizer hovered around 800,000 tons, equivalent to 60 million dollars. Since then, fertilizer imports have showed a rapid downward trend, hitting a low of 2,280,000 dollars in 1973. On the other hand, exports of fertilizers have increased gradually since 1968, when urea fertilizer was first exported. Fertilizer exports surpassed imports by 1970. In 1973 total exports of urea and compound fertilizer reached 6.4 million dollars, three times imports in the same year.

Completion of Large-Scale Compound Fertilizer Plant

Since the beginning of the 1970's, domestic consumption of fertilizer has increased rapidly. During the period from 1962 to 1972, the average annual rate of increase in domestic consumption of fertilizer was 8 per cent. Especially in 1973, the consumption showed a drastic increase of 22 per cent over the previous year. Such a striking increase in fertilizer consumption is attributed to extensive use of fertilizer for enhancing agricultural productivity, cultivation of profitable crops, and expansion of arable land.

In order to meet the increased demand for fertilizer, the government plans to construct the Seventh Plant in Yeocheon, Jeonnam

Exports and Imports of Fertilizer

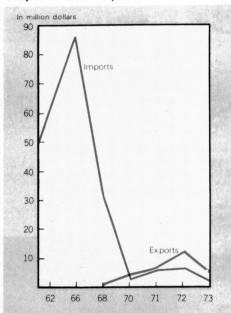

In million dollars

Imports

Exports

A general view of the Chinhae Chemical Co.

Province. This will be undertaken by the Namhae Chemical Co., one of the subsidiaries of the Korea General Chemical Corporation, and will have a production capacity of 700,000 tons of urea and 330,000 tons of compound fertilizer, comparable in capacity to that of all existing plants. In addition, the plant will also produce sulphuric acid, phosphoric acid, nitric acid and ammonium nitrate. Upon completion of the plant in 1977, the nation will attain self-sufficiency in fertilizers of nitrogen, phosphate and potash constituents. Furthermore, it will be possible to export fertilizers in the amount of 50 million dollars annually.

Annual Production of Cement Reaches 10 Million Tons

Unlike most other manufacturing industries which are forced to rely on imported raw materials, the cement industry has no difficulty in procuring limestone, the main raw material, since it is found abundantly throughout the country. Together with the local limestone, the cement industry enjoys the great advantage of using domestic production technology which has been developed since the early 1950's.

Until the latter 1950's, there were only two companies, Tongyang and Korea Cement Manufacturing Co.'s, engaged in cement manufacturing in Korea. In 1961 upon completion of the new Samcheog and Mun-gyeong Plants, they were able to double their annual production capacities to 720,000 tons.

Since the 1960's, the domestic demand for cement has increased substantially, due mainly to augmentation of infrastructure and construction projects in conjunction with implementation of the ambitious economic development plans. In order to cope with the accelerated increase in demand the Ssangyong Plant, with an annual capacity of 400,000 tons, Hanil Plant, with an annual capacity of 400,000 tons, and Hyundai Plant, with an annual capacity of 200,000 tons, were established in 1964, and the Asia Cement Plant, with an annual capacity of 400,000 tons, in 1966. As a result, by 1966 when the First Five-Year Economic Development Plan had ended, total installed capacity of the cement industry reached 2,120,000 tons, a threefold increase over the early 1960's.

During the Second Five-Year Economic Development Plan, production capacity continued to expand considerably. In 1968 the 2nd Ssangyong Cement Plant, with an annual capacity of 1,700,000 tons and the largest in Korea, was completed and followed in 1969 by the Sungsin Cement Plant, with an annual capacity of 1,000,000 tons. More recently, the Korea Cement Plant, with a production capacity of 660,000 tons per year, was completed in 1973. The Hyundai Cement Plant doubled its capacity and the Ssangyong Cement Plant upped its capacity to 4.6 million tons.

By 1974 the total domestic production capacity of eight cement manufacturers with nine cement plants amounted to 9,490,000 tons per annum. Besides, the Union Cement Plant, which was completed in 1964, began producing 30,000 tons of white cement per year. As can be seen from the above, the domestic cement industry has witnessed a remarkable expansion since the early 1960's.

Supply and Demand of Cement

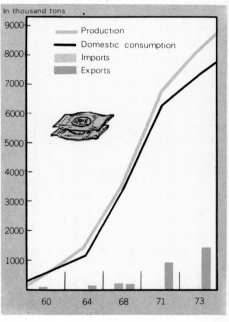

In thousand tons

- Production
- Domestic consumption
- Imports
- Exports

Cement Production Capacity

(In thousand tons)

	1962	1966	1971	1973	1974
Tongyang, Samcheog Plant	360	360	950	950	950
Korea, Mun-gyeong Plant	360	360	480	480	480
Ssangyong, Yeongweol Plant	—	400	700	1,700	1,700
Ssangyong, Donghai Plant	—	—	1,700	1,700	2,900
Hanil, Danyang Plant	—	400	1,000	1,000	1,000
Hyundai, Danyang Plant	—	200	400	400	400
Asia, Jecheon Plant	—	400	500	400	400
Sungsin, Danyang Plant	—	—	1,000	1,000	1,000
Korea, Jangseong Plant	—	—	—	660	660
Total	720	2,120	6,630	8,290	9,490

Cement Production Increases Rapidly

With new cement plants coming into being one after the other, domestic production of cement increased in tandem.

From 464,000 tons in 1960, production rose to 1,000,000 tons in 1964, to 3,570,000 tons in 1968 and 8,170,000 tons in 1973.

As a result Korea, which had depended heavily upon imported cement in the 1950's, was able to meet most of the domestic demand from its own production in the 1960's.

By 1970 the country achieved self-sufficiency and was able to begin exporting. In 1972 cement exports reached 1,000,000 tons.

Considering Korea's share in world cement trade volume, the country has become one of the large cement exporters not only in Northeast Asia but in the world as well.

Smooth transportation is very important for the cement industry. Most cement factories are located in the mountainous eastern parts of Gang-weon and Chungbuk Provinces and cement has a heavy seasonal demand from spring to autumn. Therefore, with a view to solving the bottleneck in transportation, many sub-factories were established near major cities, where the clinker, an intermediate product for cement, is moved, stored, crushed and packaged for shipment.

At present, nine clinker grinding factories are located in such large consumption cities as Seoul, Daegu, Daejeon etc.. In 1973 their annual grinding capacity reached 1,350,000 tons, which represents more than 10 per cent of total domestic cement production. In addition, four cement packaging factories were establised in Mugho, Yeosu, Ulsan and Busan.

Establishment of Clinker Plants

103

Cement Exports

Developed countries have begun restricting the expansion of cement production facilities because of the pollution problem but foreign demand for cement has been increasing rapidly due mainly to the vigorous economic development of the oil-producing countries in the Middle East.

Accordingly, prospects for the cement industry are highly promising in view of favorable production conditions and world demand.

To keep pace with rapidly growing domestic and overseas demand, efforts are being made to expand the production capacity of the cement industry. Five cement manufacturers plan to raise their capacities an additional 10,600,000 tons. Upon completion of these plans in 1977, total cement production capacity will hit 21,000,000 tons and exports are expected to reach 7,000,000 tons.

Cement stevedoring at Mugho Port

Textile Industry Reaches International Standards

Interior of the Dongyang Nylon Co.

The textile industry is one of the oldest and foremost manufacturing industries in Korea, with cotton and wool yarns and fabrics in the forefront.

In the course of economic reconstruction after the Korean War, emphasis was first placed on the textile industry, especially cotton and woolen textiles, to meet the clothing requirements of the time. Consequently the textile industry was the leading industry during the 1950's.

In the 1960's textile manufacturers expanded production facilities for cotton and woolen textiles and exports of textile products increased year by year. Thus, the textile industry developed rapidly as the most important export-oriented industry. In the latter half of the 1960's, the textile industry faced a new stage of growth with the coming into vogue of chemical fibers.

Production facilities of major manufacturers expanded remarkably; in the case of cotton textiles, fine spinning machines and weaving machines increased from 462,000 spindles and 10,000 looms in the early 1960's to 1,308,000 spindles and 44,000 looms in 1973, reflecting a sharp increase in demand for cotton products from the developed countries. The average number of fine spinning machines per factory increased from about 30,000 spindles in the early 1960's to 70,000 spindles in 1973, exceeding international competitive level of 50,000 spindles.

On the other hand, woolen textile makers also expanded their production facilities to meet the increasing demand for woolen

Production Facilities of Major Textile Industries

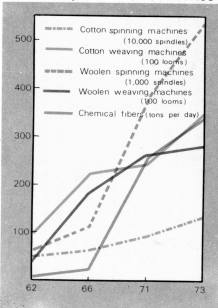

Cotton spinning machines (10,000 spindles)
Cotton weaving machines (100 looms)
Woolen spinning machines (1,000 spindles)
Woolen weaving machines (100 looms)
Chemical fibers (tons per day)

products, in line with the rise in income. Therefore, fine spinning machines and woolen weaving machines increased from 50,000 spindles and 500 looms in the early 1960's to 520,000 spindles and 38,000 looms in 1973.

The average number of fine spinning machines per factory increased from 8,000 spindles to 18,000 in 1973.

With the expansion of production facilities up to international levels, the output of cotton and woolen textile products by 1973 had increased sharply compared with the beginning of the 1960's,

Production of Major Textile Products

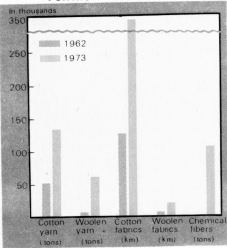

In thousands

1962
1973

Cotton yarn (tons) · Woolen yarn (tons) · Cotton fabrics (km) · Woolen fabrics (km) · Chemical fibers (tons)

Exports of Textile Products

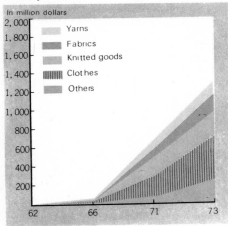

In million dollars

Yarns
Fabrics
Knitted goods
Clothes
Others

showing a threefold increase in cotton yarn and twentyfold increase in woolen yarn.

Furthermore, from the mid-1960's, when the domestic chemical fiber industry began to develop, cotton and woolen textile manufacturers not only produced chemical yarns and fabrics but also developed various mixed-spun products. In other words, the textile industry has made remarkable progress both in quantity and quality, and Korea has become one of the more important textile producing countries in the world.

Interior of the Jeil Woolen Textile Co.

Textiles: Leading Export Industry in Korea

At the beginning of the 1960's, the textile industry was only able to meet domestic demand.

Thereafter however, the textile industry grew so fast that exports already amounted to 24 million dollars by 1964, 100 million dollars in 1967 and a phenomenal 1,200 million dollars in 1973.

The share of textile exports in total exports increased from a negligible amount at the beginning of the 1960's to 38 per cent in 1973. Originally, exports of textile products consisted mainly of fabrics, including cotton cloth. However, exports of final goods processed with yarns or fabrics showed a rapid increase after the mid-1960's.

By 1968 exports of knitted goods exceeded those of fabrics and accounted for 40 per cent of total textile exports. However, fabrics again assumed dominance in the early 1970's.

Interior of the Bangrim Spinning Co.

This has been conducive to improving balance of payments and coping with import restrictions in foreign markets. Highly processed textile products have come to occupy a major share of total exports. Reviewing exports of textiles by fiber, cotton products accounted for most textile exports until the middle 1960's. However, exports of chemical fiber products began increasing from about that time so that by 1973 their share of 35 per cent exceeded that of cotton products, 29 per cent. This implies that the foundation for export of textile products has been greatly strengthened.

Interior of the Hanil Synthetic Fiber Co.

Rapidly Growing Chemical Fiber Industry

Supply and Demand for Chemical Fibers

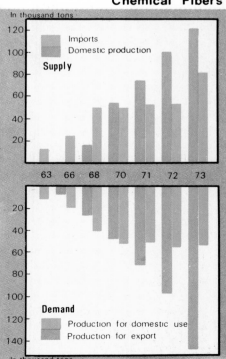

In thousand tons

Imports
Domestic production

Supply

120
100
80
60
40
20

63 66 68 70 71 72 73

20
40
60
80
100
120
140

Demand

Production for domestic use
Production for export

In thousand tons

The chemical fiber industry has made rapid progress parallel with the development of the petrochemical industry. This is because continuous production of chemical fibers is possible regardless of weather conditions, whereas the production of natural fibers depends heavily on geography and the forces of nature.

It was in 1959 that the first chemical fiber plant in Korea, the Mijin Chemical Fiber Co., began production of vinylon.

As the demand for chemical fibers increased rapidly in the early

1960's, production facilities for nylon were established in 1963, and thereafter viscose rayon, acrylic fiber, polypropylene fiber, polyester fiber, acetate rayon etc., were successively produced from 1966 to 1969.

The increasing demand for chemical fiber products gave rise to strong competition and enlargement of chemical fiber producing equipment.

As a result, production capacity per day expanded from 21.5 tons in 1966 to 344.3 tons in 1973, an increase of 16 times. The production of chemical fibers also increased dramatically to 122,000 tons in 1973.

Production Capacity of Chemical Fibers

(Tons per day)

	Beginning year of production	1962	1966	1971	1973	1974
Nylon (4)	1963	–	3.8	68.2	91.9	121.4
Acryl (2)	1967	–	–	73.5	88.5	193.5
Polyester (7)	1968	–	–	65.0	78.0	291.0
Polypropylene (3)	1966	–	0.7	22.0	49.2	49.1
Vinylon (PVA) (1)	1959	2.0	2.0	7.0	7.0	7.0
Viscose (1)	1966	–	15.0	15.0	22.2	32.2
Acetate (1)	1969	–	–	7.5	7.5	7.5
Total		2.0	21.5	258.2	344.3	701.7

Note : Figures in parentheses are numbers of enterprises. In case of polypropylene, the figure in parentheses indicates only the number of large-scale firms.

Chemical fibers have provided intermediate materials for other textile manufactures of cotton yarns, woolen yarns and rayon fibers. By 1970 the production of chemical fibers was sufficient to meet domestic requirements and by 1973 was 69,000 tons in excess. The chemical fiber industry in Korea has solidly established its position as an export-oriented industry and has contributed markedly to the improvement of balance of payments.

Most of the raw materials, including caprolactam, AN monomer, PP resins, etc., were previously imported from abroad, since Korea did not possess the advanced petrochemical plants needed to supply these raw materials. However, the construction of the Ulsan Petrochemical Complex enabled domestic production of intermediate petrochemicals used as raw materials for synthetic fibers. As a result, imported raw materials have been gradually eliminated since 1973. Domestic production of AN monomer, one of the major raw materials, supplied more than 80 per cent of domestic demand in 1973 and imported caprolactam has also been replaced to a great extent by domestic products since 1974.

Until the end of the 1950's the rubber industry in Korea was represented only by the manufacturing of rubber footwear. Owing to the fast growth of such industries as automobiles, etc., the production of rubber goods for industrial use, including tires and rubber belts, has increased remarkably since the early 1960's.

The production capacity of tires increased from 200,000 in the early 1960's to 3,300,000 in 1973, of rubber belts for industrial use 500 million plies in 1973, an increase of 10 times compared with the early 1960's, and of rubber footwear 133 million pairs, thanks to an explosive increase in overseas demand.

In step with these increases, production has markedly risen since the latter half of the 1960's. During 1973, exports of rubber footwear reached more than 100 million dollars, while those of tires and rubber belts for industrial use amounted to 11 million dollars and 8 million dollars respectively. Korean tires are very popular in Southeast Asia and the Middle East due to their low prices and high quality. Thus, the rubber industry has come to occupy a strong position as an export-oriented industry in Korea.

A SBR synthetic rubber manufacturing plant with an annual production capacity of 25,000 tons was completed in the Ulsan Petrochemical Complex in May 1973, the first in Korea. As a result, a considerable amount of SBR synthetic rubber, which formerly had been imported, could be supplied domestically. Imports of natural rubber reached 51,000 tons and of synthetic rubber 28,000 tons in 1973. The domestic production of synthetic rubber was enough to meet more than 80 per cent of domestic needs, and the production capacities are to be increased twofold by 1978.

Other Steadily Growing Industries

Production of Rubber Goods

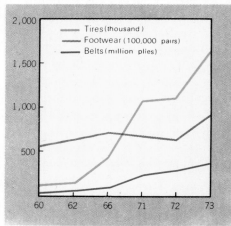

Paper Industry Reaches Self-Sufficiency

Supply and Demand for Paper

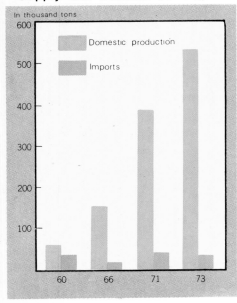

In thousand tons

Domestic production

Imports

600
500
400
300
200
100

60   66   71   73

Though the paper industry was well established relatively earlier than other industries, its production facilities could not meet the increasing domestic demand. Therefore, about 40 per cent of total domestic consumption had to be imported until the end of the 1950's.

Since the early 1960's, the demand for paper has increased at a fast pace, parallel with the recent outstanding improvement of national living standards and vigorous cultural and industrial activities.

With such a growth in consumption, the industry has seen considerable expansion, both in production facilities and output. The annual production capacity of the paper industry, which was a mere 100,000 tons in the early 1960's, grew twofold during the period 1962–1966 and accelerated during the Second Five Year Economic Development Plan, reaching 626,000 tons. Reviewing the annual production capacity for major kinds of paper in 1973, newsprint reached 121,000 tons, printing paper 144,000 tons, kraft paper 111,000 tons, paper board 203,000 tons, and others 47,000 tons.

With such an expansion of production facilities, paper output amounted to 537,000 tons in 1973, ten times production in the early 1960's. Accordingly, approximately 94 per cent of total domestic demand, 572,000 tons, was supplied by domestic paper production in 1973. Moreover, 29,000 tons of printing

Interior of the Sedae Paper Co.

paper and kraft paper, equivalent to 18 million dollars, were exported. In view of present condition of supply and demand, paper production in Korea seems sufficient to meet domestic demand from 1974 onward.

However, much of the pulp providing the raw material for paper has been imported year after year, owing to the shortage of domestic timber resources. To minimize the heavy dependence on imports of raw materials, chemical pulp plants were established in 1964, and three pilot plants using raw materials such as straw and corn stalks were constructed in the early 1970's.

In 1973, the annual production capacity of the paper industry amounted to 107,000 tons, of which ground pulp and chemical pulp accounted for 82,000 tons and 25,000 tons respectively, and pulp production reached 81,500 tons. Nevertheless, the domestic supply of pulp amounted to only a little over 20 per cent of total pulp consumption, owing to the rapidly growing demand for paper, especially for high-class paper.

Four straw pulp plants with 21,000 tons of annual production capacity are under construction, and 3 large-scale chemical pulp plants with an annual production capacity of 264,000 tons will be completed by 1977.

Accordingly, at the time when the Third Economic Development Plan ends, the paper industry will no longer depend for its raw materials on imports.

Supply and Demand for Pulp 1973
(In thousand tons)

	Domestic Production	Imports	Domestic Consumption	Self-Sufficiency Rate (%)
Ground Pulp	76.8	6.3	83.1	92.4
Chemical Pulp	4.7	295.2	299.9	1.6
Total	81.5	301.5	383.0	21.3

Interior of the Taeryong Pulp Co. (straw pulp)

Export-Oriented Plywood Industry

The plywood industry met domestic demands in the mid-1950's, and has since grown into one of the nation's major export-oriented industries, because it is relatively labor-intensive and needs few highly-skilled techniques.

The Dongmyung Timber Company, with an annual production capacity of 80 million square feet of plywood, was constructed in 1954. Most of the plywood produced went to meet the domestic demand until 1956. It was almost the end of the 1950's before plywood began to be exported.

The plywood industry has expanded rapidly since 1964, when the industry was designated as an export-oriented industry to be supported with preferential financing.

Accordingly, the annual production capacity increased from 300 million square feet in 1969 to 5 million square feet in 1973. Korea today ranks fourth among the world's plywood-producing coun-

Production and Export of Plywood

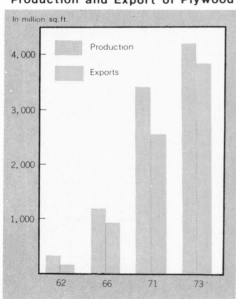

tries.

Furthermore, the plywood industry, which established a mass-production system through expansion of modern facilities, has reached international standards of production.

Parallel with the remarkable expansion in production facilities and new plant construction, output of plywood has shown a rapid increase since the latter half of the 1960's. As a result, plywood production by 1973 had increased about 18 times over 1962.

Most plywood products have been exported to advanced countries, among which the United States has been the major customer. Exports of plywood amounted to 100 million dollars in 1970 and 286 million dollars in 1973, an increase of 140 times over the early 1960's. With such a rapid increase in exports, Korea has secured a strong position as one of the most important plywood-exporting countries in the world.

The Dongmyung Timber Co.

MODERNIZATION OF AGRICULTURE AND FISHERIES

New Community Movement and Rural Development

The Saemaul Undong (New Community Movement) launched in the early 1970's has brought about major renovations in long-stagnated rural areas. It has spread from villages to cities, from island to inland and from home to working places over the past three years.

Villages have replaced straw-thatched roofs, rebuilt walls and improved sanitation. They have built wells, water supply facilities, meeting halls, storehouses, public baths and other utilities. Roads in villages and farm fields have been levelled and broadened, so that networks of rural roads connected to national and local highways have been formed to promote the transport of agricultural products and mechanization of farming. At the same time, irrigation facilities and dikes between paddy fields have been improved and arable lands have been consolidated to prepare a sound basis for increase of food production.

In addition to these improvements in living surroundings and farming environment, villagers have carried out projects for increasing income such as planting fruit trees, raising livestock and managing village farms with united efforts. Gambling and superstitions have disappeared and wasteful wedding and funeral ceremonies have been simplified. The general way of living in rural areas has become more sound.

The most important result of the Movement is the renovation in the way of thinking of village residents. Villagers, once lost in resignation and idleness, have united around leaders and have worked hard, learning the spirit of cooperation and diligence and thus confidence in a better life has taken root.

These are the most valuable lessons and assets for the nation's development.

In the past, there were rural rehabilitation movements but none of these attained comparable results. The New Community Movement is a nationwide campaign for modernization initiated by the faith and determination of President Park, differing from previous movements in its goals and scope.

Although they were proud of a long history and glorious cultural traditions, the Korean people never experienced modernization by their own initiative, passively relying on other nations for help. They did not foster the spirit of independence which would have enabled them to attempt development by themselves and to take responsibility for what they did. They used to blame poverty and other difficulties on their predecessors, or to accept conditions as predestined, falling into resignation and apathy.

Working by Torchlight

Philosophy of the New Community Movement

The 1960's witnessed a historic turning point which broke the vicious circle of poverty and paved the way to development. Having made every effort to lay a foundation for industrialization through the First and the Second Five-Year Economic Development Plan which began in 1962 and 1967 respectively, the government has launched special projects to increase income of farmers and fishermen since 1968. During the Third Five-Year Plan, emphasis is being placed on rural areas for the purpose of exploring intensively the economic capacity accumulated during the 1960's. The people's will and confidence in a better life began to increase when they saw the nation's economy improving to the level of semi-advanced countries.

This, in turn, created an atmosphere for modernization of the country. Especially farmers and fishermen realized that the will for a better life, perseverance, and a spirit of self-help and cooperation were necessary conditions for modernization of their fatherland. The accomplishment of economic development, confidence in a better life, and a new attitude form the firm basis for the New Community Movement.

But better life for an individual presupposes better life for all, through concerted effort and cooperation. It ultimately aims to hand over a better country to posterity. The united efforts of two people obviously bring forth results on a geometric rather than arithmetic progression. This is the background of the philosophy of the New Community Movement. This is why the spirit of diligence, self-help and cooperation has become the principle of conduct for the Movement. Looking back upon past days, great achievements of a nation or a people were propelled by high morale. This is illustrated by the 'Spirit of the Mayflower' which built the world's strongest nation on virgin land. The reconstruction movement of Denmark is another example. In a word, the spirit of the New Community Movement is the driving force for the advance of the nation.

In addition, real democracy suitable to the needs of the nation can take root through the Movement. In the process of selecting village leaders, choosing projects by taking account of villagers' opinions, and pushing the projects forward with coordinated efforts, the methods and spirit of true democracy are developed.

At the same time, the Movement for better villages has encouraged the love for villages which in turn has led to love for the country. The fruits ripened with sweat and efforts through diligence, self-help and cooperation constitute the very core of real patriotism.

Also, the New Community Movement has rendered the living philosophy for the accomplishment of the October Revitalizing Reform of 1972. The October Revitalizing Reform aims to eliminate all inefficient and unproductive factors and promote the national strength and wealth by uniting all the people under the same objective and mind and this can be realized by the New Community Movement.

Selecting a New Community leader

Improving the Village Environment

The New Community Movement started in 1970 and was initiated to improve village environment by utilizing the idle farming season, which extends from November to February. With village development committees of provinces as pivots, projects for improving living environment were carried out by the villagers' own efforts, assisted by 335 bags of cement for each village subsidized by the government.

The New Community Movement started with projects for improving village environment in order to encourage inhabitants to participate in the Movement by recognizing good results accomplished by their own efforts.

With all the difficulties, the projects achieved results worth more than three times the 4.1 billion won cost of the free cement. Village leaders were trained and effective methods of government support were also learned in the process of implementing these projects.

With these lessons, in 1971 the government systematized the implementation of the Movement and broadened it still further in 1972.

Thus 1971 marked the experimental period, while in 1972 the Movement made real progress and spread throughout the nation.

Village renewed by New Community Movement

Perpetuation of the New Community Movement

In 1972, the government selected 16,600 villages which had attained excellent results in projects for improving village environment, and encouraged their self-help spirit by supplying 500 bags of cement and one ton of reinforcing steel to each village. At the same time a training center was established to educate leaders, concentrating on discipline methodology.

In 1973, the Movement was expanded and scope of participation enlarged, so it became virtually a national movement. Emphasis was also shifted from basic projects for improving environment to projects for increasing income, based on cooperation among the villagers to realize a better life.

In 1973 classification of all villages into three categories (according to stage of development, 18,415 underdeveloped villages, 13,943 developing villages and 2,307 developed villages), was completed to help them carry out the Movement according to their capabilities. The basic villages were given support of 500 bags of cement and one ton of reinforcing steel for improving facilities and infrastructure. The developing villages were directed to undertake improvement of land, towns, and rivers along with projects for improving environment. The developed villages were guided in such projects for increasing income as afforestation, livestock raising and other subsidiary tasks.

They were also encouraged to implement productive programs including collective cultivation of crops, along with cultural and welfare projects such as electrification of rural areas, construction of standard houses and establishment of water facilities, village

communication facilities and methane gas facilities in order to promote welfare and income of the village residents. During the last three years, the rural areas of the country have shown remarkable development. Construction of key roads contributed to smooth circulation of agricultural products and mechanization of farming. Comparing the performances with the targets, about 70 per cent of the target was accomplished in farm road maintenance, while improvement of village streets and construction of small bridges reached 91 per cent and 98 per cent respectively.

Residential conditions of rural areas were greatly bettered by improving roofs, walls and toilets. The improvement of roofs and construction of laundry facilities and drains were completed by 43 per cent and 70 per cent respectively.

Along with these improvements, cultural and welfare facilities have been greatly increased. As of the end of 1973, the ratio of households which were supplied electricity to total households in rural areas marked 52 per cent, and communication facilities of villages were greatly expanded. Sixty nine per cent of villages have built town halls for better discussion and cooperation, and more than half of all villages have established water supply facilities.

Meanwhile, the basis for increasing agricultural production has been laid and irrigation has been improved. Village warehouses, joint workshops, libraries and storehouses have been established. Intangible as well as material benefits have resulted. The Movement provided an opportunity for removal of traditional discord among clans or villages in rural areas, and promoted the spirit of cooperation. There are 12,569 villages managing more than one joint project for increasing income, and 2,200 villages carrying out

Cottage production of straw bags and mats

more than five joint projects. These projects cover a wide range, including raising livestock and planting cash-crop vegetables, crops for industrial use, and fruit trees. Cooperation among villagers is shown even in small villages with only a hundred households, which have constructed bridges worth five or six million won.

Antiquated conventions and useless formalities in rural life have disappeared and new morals and orders have begun to emerge. Every village has adopted a town code banning gambling and superstition, and simplifying wedding and funeral ceremonies. Gambling has faded away while 12,480 villages have got rid of

taverns. Since the beginning of the New Community Movement, savings in rural areas have increased more than four times.

Farmers have learned the true meaning of democracy in the process of discussing subjects of common interest, making decisions, and implementing them by themselves.

This contributes greatly to the formulation of a national consensus. Thus, farmers have become able to discover their infinite potentialities, and to gain the confidence and pride that they can accomplish whatever they want with their own will and efforts. This is the most valuable asset, once lost but newly discovered.

Self-Sufficiency in Food Grains

Korea suffered food grain shortages periodically until the 1950's. Annual rice production had not been more than three million tons, far below the needs. In spite of a rationing system, rising cereal prices triggered general price instability and threatened the people's livelihood. The government's efforts for boosting cereal production had been limited to importation of fertilizers and sporadic construction of irrigation facilities. Traditional antiquated techniques of farming, shortage of fertilizer and agricultural chemicals, and meager finances had resulted in poor harvests, and average yield per danbo (992 square meters) marked only 260 kilograms.

Grain aid from the United States began from 1957, alleviating shortages of food, but in the long run this aggravated the situation by depressing grain prices and dampening farmer's incentives for

more production.

However, from 1961 the government, realizing the pressing need for self-reliance in food grains, not only for stabilization of national life but also for national security, launched an ambitious plan to achieve renovation in agriculture.

For this purpose, the government set increases in food production and farm household income as one of the major objectives of the First and Second Five-Year Economic Development Plans.

Under the Plans the government renovated the agricultural administrative system and pushed such projects as construction of irrigation facilities, water resources development, implementation of intensive fertilization techniques, prevention and extermination of blights and insect damage, and popularization of new farming techniques.

Cooperative work in the paddy field

Improving Fertilizer Distribution and Production

In 1961, the government improved the fertilizer distribution system. Until the beginning of the 1960's, little fertilizer was directly distributed by the government to farmers at favorable prices, and a large portion of fertilizer had to be purchased at unstable prices in the free market. Prices were high and shortages in farming seasons occurred frequently. However, since 1961 the National Agricultural Cooperatives Federation (NACF), established in the same year, has administered distribution and sale of all fertilizers and farmers have been able to acquire enough in the right season at stable prices.

Moreover, the government lowered prices of fertilizers for farmers below international market prices and expanded sales on credit at low interest rates in order to lessen farmers' burdens and thereby increase their income. Owing to such policies, the average price of fertilizer only doubled while the average price of cereals increased

Shipment of fertilizer at a NACF storehouse

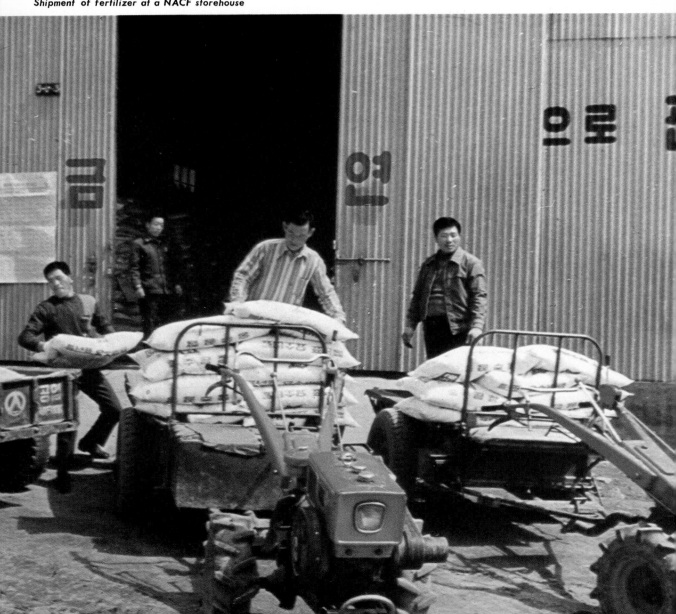

six times during the period 1962–1973.

In addition, the government took proper steps to attain self-reliance in fertilizers. Until 1961, annual production of fertilizers was not more than 30,000 tons, all of which was nitrogenous. Inevitably, most fertilizers, amounting to 140,000 tons annually, were imported from abroad.

The government stepped up building fertilizer plants during the First and Second Five-Year Economic Development Plans. Five were constructed during the period 1961–1967. Production facilities of the Chungju Fertilizer Plant and the Honam Fertilizer Plant were enlarged in 1968 and 1969 respectively, with the construction of the plants, and annual domestic production of chemical fertilizers increased to 667,000 tons (element ton) in 1973. Particularly, domestic production of nitrogenous fertilizers sufficed for domestic demand, and production of other fertilizers such as compound and phosphorous fertilizers also increased rapidly.

Farmers, encouraged by the increased supply and improved distribution of fertilizers, have paid great attention to the modernization of farming through intensive fertilizations and technical improvement. Annual input of fertilizers in farming increased to 793,000 tons (element ton) in 1973 from 137,000 tons (element ton) in 1960. The input ratio of fertilizers by elements, — nitrogen, phosphorus, and potassium— improved from the ratio of 64:31:5 in 1960 to the ratio of 52:29:19 in 1973.

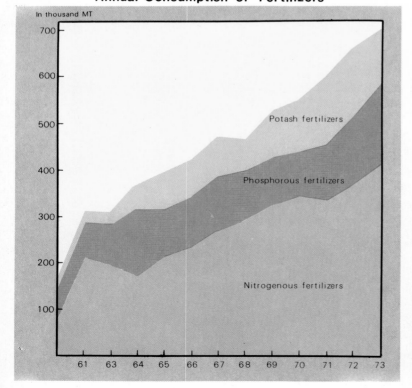

Annual Consumption of Fertilizers

In thousand MT

Potash fertilizers

Phosphorous fertilizers

Nitrogenous fertilizers

Compost production

Combating Blight and Insect Damage

One of the main improvements in agricultural techniques in the 1960's was blight control. Until the beginning of the 1960's agricultural chemicals had been used almost entirely for production of fruits and vegetables, not for cereals such as rice and barley. The annual losses in rice production due to blight damages had been estimated at 20 per cent of the total.

Therefore, the government enacted the Law on Prevention of Epidemics in Agriculture in December 1961, marking a turning point in prevention and combat of blights and insect damages. Under the Law, the government established an efficient system for preliminary investigation of such damages, and set up 48 investigation centers in rural areas, for early prevention and dissemination of techniques.

Blights-controlled areas were less than 460,000 hectares in 1962,

Insecticide spraying by a helicopter

but sharply expanded to 2,870,000 hectares in 1967, and extended to all cultivated areas in 1973, owing to the government's subsidies of more than one billion won per annum and cooperative effort rather than inefficient individual action. Especially from 1969, aerial prevention and extermination has been applied to large-scale paddy fields and contaminated areas.

Due to these measures, production of agricultural chemicals increased from 501 tons in 1962 to 17,000 tons in 1973. Agricultural chemicals were diversified to suit the various types of blights and insect damage.

Annual consumption of agricultural chemicals increased sharply, from 993 tons in 1962 to 13,692 tons in 1973. Paddy fields used 5,512 tons of agricultural chemicals in 1973, covering 6,041,000 hectares.

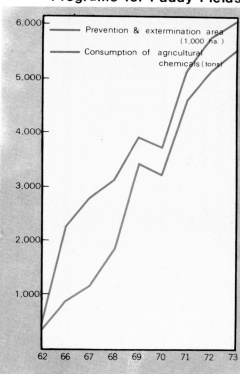

Prevention & Extermination Programs for Paddy Fields

Prevention & extermination area (1,000 ha.)

Consumption of agricultural chemicals (tons)

Agricultural Infrastructure Development

Since the beginning of the 1960's, the government has carried out projects for water resource development so that farming might be immune from drought and flood. Especially since 1969, the government has implemented projects ranging from developing small wells to construction of large dams and embankments, taking account of regional needs. As a result, the ratio of irrigated area to total paddy fields increased to 83 per cent in 1973 from 50 per cent in 1960. Projects for preservation and reclamation of farm fields have also been implemented under the Law on Preserving and Utilizing Farmland and the Law on Fostering Reclamation of Land.

By 1966, 110,000 hectares of land had been reclaimed and this was further expanded to 152,000 hectares by 1972. In 1973 laws were set up to strictly regulate the preservation of farmland and to prevent any diversion to other uses.

Yedang Reservoir

Since the beginning of the 1960's, the government had concentrated on developing high-yield varieties of cereals in order to accomplish a Green Revolution for self-sufficiency in food grains, and ultimately succeeded with 'Tong-il IR 667' in 1969, a rice strain which produces epochal yields, representing an increase of 30 per cent compared with common varieties.

After passing the productivity test in 1969 and adaptation test for cultivation in local areas in 1970, nationwide group cultivation of 'Tong-il' rice was tried on 2,750 hectares in 1971. The cultivation areas of 'Tong-il' rice were expanded to 139,000 hectares in 1973 and 307,000 hectares in 1974, corresponding to one-fourth of total paddy fields. Particularly in 1973, the average yield of 'Tong-il' rice per danbo (992 square meters) recorded 481 kilograms, 37 per cent more than with common varieties. Judging from the

The Green Revolution

Test cultivation of rice

increased eagerness for cultivation of 'Tong-il' rice by farmers, it is expected that it will become the main variety of rice grown in Korea.

Meanwhile, on high and cold mountainsides, a substantial increase in rice production was accomplished by moving the sprouting stage two weeks earlier than usual and by cultivating 'Suweon 242' which grows rapidly and yields the same amount as 'Tong-il' rice.

In the case of barley, the single-crop system was changed into a double-crop system in central and northern areas by cultivating new variety 'SB 6920', which has good resistance to lodging, grows in various kinds of soil, and yields 17–23 per cent more than common varieties. For soybeans, new 'Gangrim' and 'Dongbugtae' strains were developed and popularization of these varieties which bring increased yields of 13 per cent and 15 per cent respectively over common varieties, is being promoted.

In 1973 farmers were strongly persuaded to cultivate any of 21 improved varieties of rice and 20 varieties of barley, and it is planned to spur the seed improvement campaign with a World Bank loan in 1975.

The communal farming system for rice has been introduced and spread throughout the country since 1968 in order to improve farm yield by increasing efficiency and cooperation. The communal farming area increased to 206,000 hectares in 1973 from 2,000 hectares in 1968.

Since 1973, large-scale field consolidation has been fostered in order to improve farming techniques by facilitating common use of farming equipment and facilities, such as drainage and irrigation works. The large-scale farming areas range from 700 hectares to 5,000 hectares in size, while those of other communal areas are only 10 hectares or so.

Operational committees were organized within these areas, and responsible leaders encouraged farmers to employ basic skills to raise technical levels, in accordance with standard cultivation

Development of Cooperative Farming

methods presented by the government. In 1973 the number of large-scale areas reached 47 encompassing an acreage 111,000 hectares.

Meanwhile, in the case of barley, group farming has been under way since 1973 in order to popularize high-yield skills and to restrain spring ploughing, conducive to low harvests. In the case of beans, the government has induced farmers to use communal farming methods since 1974.

Rice Production Increases

The Third Five-Year Economic Development Plan specifies 'revolutionary development of rural areas' as a fundamental goal, and emphasis is being placed on food production, especially staple cereals, such as rice, barley and beans, in order to attain self-sufficiency in these cereals by 1976.

In 1973, the government conducted a 150-day campaign to elevate efficiency in transplanting of rice, damage control, mowing and reaping. Along with the establishment of new large-scale communal farms, inferior seed varieties were forbidden, and handling methods after reaping were improved.

Expansion of seedling hot beds was worthy of notice. In the past, low temperatures during the maturing period had been the substantial cause for decreased yields but this has been almost eliminated by planting and reaping rice earlier than usual. A campaign for earlier transplanting of rice and expansion of seedling hot beds was actively developed, so that areas of earlier

transplantation were expanded from about 8 per cent of total paddy in 1972 to 27 per cent in 1973, thereby bringing forth more abundant harvests.

The contract system for rice production was also introduced. Under the system, New Community villages were persuaded to plant rice in accordance with the standard cultivation methods given out by the government. Households achieving the target were awarded prizes and those failing were compensated. In a word, this system aimed to encourage farmers to increase rice production and to spread better farming techniques. In addition, the government set its rice production target for 1974 at 5,411,700 kiloliters of rice. For this purpose a 250-day campaign lasting from March 1 until November 10 made it possible to exceed the target with a production of 5,568,639 kiloliters.

Utilizing these methods the government plans to achieve self-sufficiency in staple cereals by 1976.

Seedling hot bed

Matured 'Tong-il' rice

Gradual Realization of Self-Sufficiency

Staple Food Production

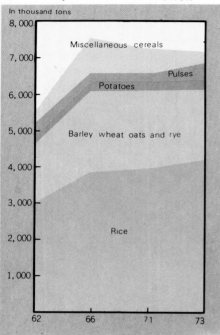

In thousand tons

Miscellaneous cereals
Pulses
Potatoes
Barley wheat oats and rye
Rice

Food Crops per Danbo

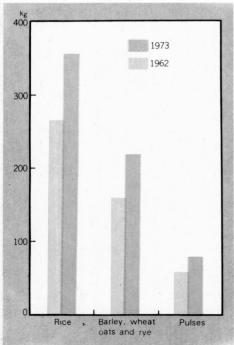

kg

1973
1962

Rice   Barley, wheat oats and rye   Pulses

Note: 1 danbo equals 992m²

Spurred by these energetic efforts, staple food production reached 7,160,000 tons in 1973, from 5,420,000 tons in 1962. The increase by 30.6 per cent during the period was the highest among Asian countries for the same period.

Particularly, rice production recorded 4,445,000 tons in 1974 representing an increase of 47.4 per cent over 1962 and the highest rice production so far in Korea. Also yields of wheat, barley, etc. increased by 15.7 per cent, pulses by 185.9 per cent, and potatoes by 235.7 per cent for the same period.

These increases are attributable to the enhanced productivity per unit of farmland rather than the expansion of cultivated areas. Yield of rice per danbo (992 square meters) increased to 356 kilograms in 1973 and 369 kilograms in 1974, from 265 kilograms in 1962.

The nation became third among the countries of the world in rice production per unit area, following Spain and Japan. With Korean unit productivity equal to 100 : Taiwan stood at 81 per cent, India and the Philippines, at 32 per cent, and Indonesia and Vietnam at 40 per cent. Although yields of barley and wheat have remained behind those of developed countries like Japan, they are already higher than those of most other countries.

On one hand, the government's continuous efforts have made it possible for Korea to keep a high level in production of food grains but, on the other hand, the increasing consumption caused by the growing population and the rising income level has made it difficult to realize self-sufficiency in food grains. Although rice production increased 47.4 per cent during the period from 1962 to 1974, rice consumption increased by 47.9 per cent during the same period.

As for total grains, production grew by 30.6 per cent, but consumption increased by 54 per cent during the same period. Taking account of the population growth rate of 24.5 per cent during the period, grain consumption per capita increased enormously.

Korea's ability to increase food grain production is seriously limited by the shortage of arable land.

Therefore the government, after studying productivity of various food grains, plans to import such grains as wheat which have low productivity and to encourage farmers to produce more rice, barley and beans, which have high productivity.

In view of the fact that in the past the rate of grain consumption increase was 1.7 times the rate of population growth, frugality in grain consumption is urgent in Korea.

All-Weather Agriculture and Farmland Expansion

Korea's agriculture heavily depended on the weather in the past. More than half of the paddy fields were not fully irrigated, but relied entirely on rainfall. Water utilization projects did not achieve successful results owing to shortage of capital, an ill-equipped administrative system, and shoddy construction.

In 1962 the government enacted the Law on Land Improvement Projects and transformed the Irrigation Association into the Land Improvement Association so as to carry out projects more efficiently.

The government also implemented the Nine-Year Water Resources Development Plan for all-weather agriculture, which was

Sin-gog Pumping Plant

inaugurated after the serious drought in the western provinces in 1965. The Plan aimed to raise the ratio of fully irrigated and drained paddy fields to 85 per cent by 1973. Under the Plan, five large-scale pumping plants were established in the spring of 1966, and a total amount of 12.9 billion won was invested for development of 65,000 hectares of paddy fields into fully irrigated and drained fields during the period from 1965, the beginning year of the Plan, to 1968.

The year 1968 marked a new turning point in the development of water resources. The three southern provinces had suffered unprecedented droughts during both 1967 and 1968. In this circumstance a new water resources development plan was established as a permanent countermeasure against drought. The enormous amount of 83.6 billion won was invested for implementation of this plan during 1968–73, thereby enabling 83 per cent of all addy fields to be fully irrigated. Furthermore, the government lans to irrigate 90 per cent of all paddy fields by 1976.

Moreover, during both 1969 and 1970, efforts were concentrated n developing underground water in order to raise the efficiency 1 use of limited resources. Despite all difficulties, results were atisfactory, thereby converting 270,000 hectares into fully rigated and drained paddy fields during the period.

The amount invested in projects for water resources development lone reached 27.6 billion won during the same period, exceed-1g the combined amount invested during the previous ten years, f this amount 10.8 billion won was invested in exploitation of nderground water resources. As a result of these efforts, newly rigated and drained paddy fields reached 1,050,000 hectares by 973.

Land Consolidation

As projects for water resources development were carried out at full speed, the need became urgent to establish the foundation for overall agricultural modernization, including irrigation, drainage, land reclamation and field exploitation. The Law on Promoting Rural Modernization was enacted for this purpose in 1970 and the Agricultural Development Corporation, which absorbed the Union

of Farmland Improvement Associations and the Underground Water Development Corporation, was established in order to implement projects for modernization of agriculture more efficiently.

Along with these measures, in 1971 the government modified the Plan for Agricultural Water Resources Development. Under the new plan greater emphasis was placed on projects for ex-

Namyang tidal dike

ploitation of ground water rather than those for exploitation of underground water resources which was almost completed.

Therefore, since 1971 the numbers of reservoirs, embankments and water-pumping plants have been increased and the government has undertaken projects for developing multipurpose large-scale farming areas. These projects include overall programs such as the Four River Basins Development Plan, establishment of irrigation facilities, expansion and consolidation of farm fields and the mechanization of farming.

The integrated plan for Four Major River Basins was set out in 1971 in order to construct 13 dams and power plants, and also to achieve many other works including river conservation, irrigation projects, afforestation, and erosion control on watershed areas of the Han, Geum, Nagdong, and Yeongsan Rivers. The government planned to spend 560 billion won for those purposes during 1971-81, of which 164.7 billion won was earmarked for agricultural projects on areas of 215,000 hectares.

By 1981, this plan will bring about modernization of watershed areas of the four rivers which embraces 64 per cent of the total land area and accounts of 61 per cent of the total population.

The projects for developing multipurpose large-scale farming areas were started in the Geum River and Pyeongtaeg Areas, whereby artificial lakes, water pumping and draining plants, tidal dikes, reservoirs, and water courses will be constructed at a cost of 47.9 billion won by 1976.

The two tidal dikes completed at Asan and Namyang Bays in May 1974 are the biggest and most monumental projects in Korean agricultural history. By 1975, 11,000 hectares of new land will be brought under cultivation, and 16,000 hectares of existing farmlands will be fully irrigated, and thus the farmland in these areas will be immune from flood or drought damage.

Other projects are now under way on the basin areas of Yeongsan River, whereby 100,000 hectares of farmland will be newly reclaimed by 1980. During the first stage, which lasts until 1976, 56.7 billion won will be expended in the construction of four separate dams and 35,000 hectares of farmland will be formed.

Expansion of Farmland

The average acreage per farm household in Korea is not more than 0.9 hectares, which is smaller than in Japan even though Japan is not considered an agricultural country. Although efforts had been made to increase farmland by reclaiming wasteland, the results in the past were insignificant.

At the beginning of the 1960's the government actively started to enforce policy measures to expand cultivated land. In

Consolidation of farmland (*Boeun County, Chungbug Province*)

1962, the Reclamation Promotion Law was enacted and reclamation work by farmers, which had been neglected before, was furthered with the aid of goverment loans and subsidies.

Stimulated by these measures, reclamation work boomed and efforts were made to reclaim mountain slopes and seashores as arable land. As a result of these efforts, during the period of the First Five-Year Economic Development Plan a total of 110,000 hectares of farmland was newly formed.

Since 1972, the method of land reclamation was changed from small-scale to large-scale development. The same year the government selected four areas as model cases and initiated projects for large-scale hillside development. In 1973, a fifth project, embracing 4,000 hectares, was begun at Gochang, Jeonbug Province. Along with these reclamation projects, utilization of idle land in the Restricted Areas north of the Civilian Control Line was also commenced and 'Tong-il' villages were constructed on an area of 700 hectares.

With these government measures, agricultural area increased by 170,000 hectares, from 2,050,000 hectares in 1961 to 2,220,000 hectares in 1973. But there still remain more than 320,000 hectares of convertible forest lands as well as much other idle land. Therefore, the government plans to enact the Law on Promoting Farmland Expansion and Development and to reclaim an additional 110,000 hectares of land during the period from 1975 to 1981.

Water utilization and reclamation in Dongjin River basin

Mechanization of Agriculture

Until the 1950's, Korean agriculture had depended heavily on manpower or draft cattle, while machines were rarely used for farming. Production of farming equipment had also been limited to traditional or small-scale tools for use by men or draft cattle. This situation created many difficulties in increasing agricultural production and hindered the popularization of new farming techniques, such as deep-plowing or intensive fertilizing.

Ownership of Farm Implements

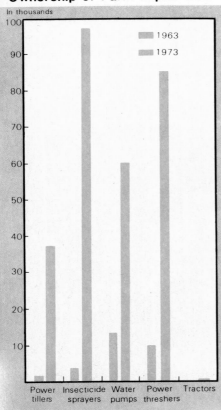

In thousands

Legend: 1963, 1973

Categories: Power tillers, Insecticide sprayers, Water pumps, Power threshers, Tractors

Moreover, in the 1960's agricultural employment declined owing to rapid growth of employment opportunities in non-agricultural sectors. This led to a sharp increase of wage levels in the agricultural sector, and made the mechanization of agriculture an urgent task.

This began with the distribution of equipment for damage control. The government supplied motorized insecticide sprayers and motor pumps through agricultural bodies in 1962 and 1963, when the nation suffered seriously from insect damage and drought.

In 1967 agricultural mechanization for food production started at full speed. The government has promoted the spread of power tillers as well as equipment for preventing drought and exterminating insects, providing farmers with subsidies and loans for lessening their burdens, and has also pushed the domestic production of power tillers through technical cooperation with foreign countries.

Meanwhile, the consolidation of farmland has also been pursued actively. As most farmlands in Korea were divided into small plots and not suitable for mechanization, since 1965 the government has launched consolidation projects in order to establish the foundation for agricultural mechanization by uniting those fragmented farmlands into large-scale fields and widening roads for farming.

During the period from 1967 to 1971, 16,000 power tillers, 68,000 insecticide sprayers, and 22,000 water pumps were supplied. Through these measures, mechanization of farming was estab-

lished in Korea and equipment for preventing damage by harmful insects and drought were popularized on a large scale.

Subsequently, the First Five-Year Agricultural Mechanization Plan was established in 1972, under which cultivation, damage control and threshing would be fully mechanized by 1976. In order to achieve these aims the government set up policy measures to encourage the cooperative use of farming machines among farmers through the organization of 'Gye', and to supply funds at low rates of interest and on a long-term basis. The government also enforced various other measures for the domestic production of agricultural machines.

153

Promotion of the Farm Machinery Industry

The government has made efforts to nurture the farming machinery industry. Specialization and systemization have been pursued on the principle of two firms for each kind of machinery so that they might contribute to improving quality and reducing price.

The proportion of domestic parts of farming machinery has gone up conspicuously since 1972, so that more than 97 per cent of parts of tillers and all parts of power sprayers are now produced at home.

Mechanization of farming has made rapid progress by these diversified measures of the government. The number of power tillers increased from 400 in 1963 to 38,000 in 1973. In addition, the mechanization of tilling, breaking up of soil and transporting, all of which are fundamental to paddy cultivation, has also made remarkable progress.

Power tillers are about three times more efficient than draft cattle but the cost of using power tillers is not more than one-third that of raising draft cattle. Reflecting growing demand for tillers, it was decided to support farmers with funds from the National Investment Fund in order to supply an additional 100,000 tillers by 1976.

In addition, the number of hand-operated and power sprayers increased to 770,000 in 1973, an increase of almost nine times over 1963. In particular, the number of power pesticide sprayers increased rapidly to 80,000 in 1973. Now, every third farm household has a pesticide sprayer. In the case of power thrashers, every fifth farm household has one. At the same time sophisticated farming machinery such as tractors, combines, etc. have become more popular.

Technical training has been intensified to keep pace with popularization of farming machinery. 151 technical training centers have been established in the Office of Rural Development and its subordinates, the provincial offices of rural development, and the rural guidance offices, so that farmers, rural youths and village workers can be educated. This training program began in 1970 and has become full-scale since 1972. 33,000 farmers participate in training every year.

In order to reinforce after-service to the farms that use machinery, the National Agricultural Cooperatives Federation and the manufacturers have established repair centers all over the country, offering year-round responsible repairs.

Mobile repair service for farming machinery

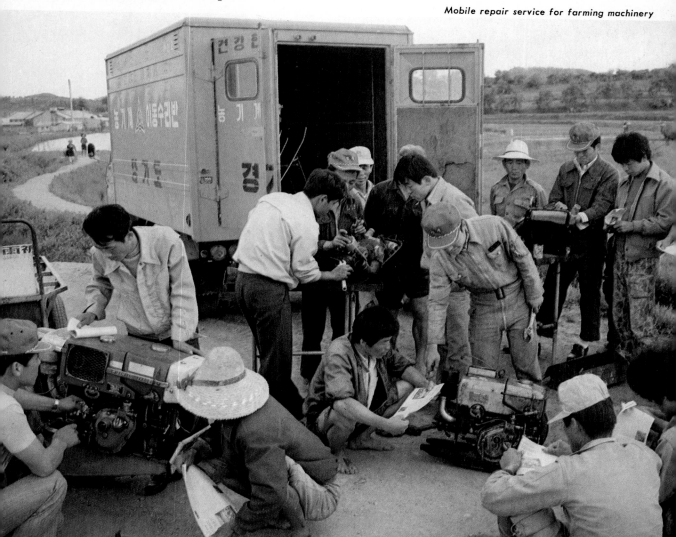

Increasing Farm Income

Poverty had been an ancient legacy in Korea's rural communities. Food was always in short supply just before the barley harvest season. Moreover, farmers borrowed money at high interest in order to pay off old debts.

In the 1950's, grain prices were kept down to low levels by voluminous imports of surplus food grains from the United States. The seasonal fluctuations of grain prices, which declined sharply during the harvest season and soared in the off-season, were repeated yearly. Such a phenomenon became aggravated in a bumper harvest year, so that farmers paradoxically suffered drops in revenues in good years. In 1958, when the largest harvest of the 1950's was recorded, surplus food grains were imported from the United States in large quantities so that prices of food grains declined by 16.4 per cent and farmers' proceeds decreased by 10 per cent.

In order to eliminate such undesirable price fluctuations the government established the Farm Products Price Support Law in 1961 and thereafter enforced a policy of supporting prices for principal farm products.

Particularly for rice, the government enlarged its purchasing quantity, sharply raised its purchase price to support rice prices, and also provided large amounts of farming funds. With these measures such evils as pre-harvest sale of rice, caused by debts, have been eliminated.

As mentioned above, since the 1960's the government has carried out positive policies in order to increase farm household income. Large-scale investments and loans have been provided agricultural infrastructure projects and the high-price policy for rice has been maintained. Also, the marketing structure of farm products has been improved. Farm households no longer have to live in debt but can even enjoy savings.

Particularly from 1968, the high-price policy for rice has been intensified in order to reduce the income gap between farming and urban households, since the latter's income had increased conspicuously due to the rapid economic growth.

Rice prices, which had lagged behind prices of manufactured products, increased by an annual average of 25.0 per cent in the years since 1969 and by an exceptional 35.9 per cent in 1970, and even more exceptional 38.5 per cent in 1974.

In addition, government purchase of grains has been greatly enlarged in order to stabilize grain prices. Purchases of autumn-harvested grains had been only 361,000 kiloliters before 1971, but increased greatly to 617,000 kiloliters in 1971, and to 635,000 kiloliters in 1972 and 902,000 kiloliters in 1974.

Such measures by the government prevented the annually repeated phenomenon of sharp drops in grain prices during the harvest season and sharply moderated fluctuations in rice prices.

Implementation of the Dual Price System

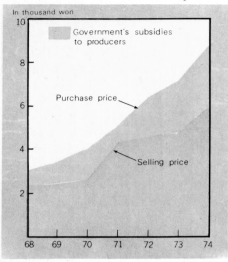

Effect of the Dual Price System

In thousand won

Government's subsidies to producers

Purchase price

Selling price

68 69 70 71 72 73 74

Since the early 1960's a purchase policy has also been carried out to support barley and wheat prices and in 1968 a dual price system was implemented. This system, under which the government purchases barley and wheat from farmers at high prices and sells to consumers at lower prices, aims at promoting farmers' income, stabilizing the consumers' economy, and substituting barley and wheat for insufficient rice.

The government has raised the purchase prices of barley and wheat at an annual average rate of 20.6 per cent since 1968, and has enlarged the scale of purchase to 378,819 kiloliters (300,000 tons) in 1973.

On the other hand, the selling prices of barley and wheat have been set below their purchase prices. In 1968 barley and wheat were sold at 90.3 per cent of the purchase prices and since then the gap has widened every year, bringing the selling prices of barley and wheat to only 68.6 per cent of the purchase prices in 1973.

In order to implement such a dual price system the government has spent 23.2 billion won so far, 8.9 billion won in 1973 alone. This system has resulted in a rise in farmers' income as well as enhancement of farmers' willingness to produce barley and wheat.

In the past, fluctuations in grain prices were severe and grain markets were not in good order, forcing farmers frequently to dump grains or be cheated in selling them. Various measures for improving the marketing structure have been taken in order to remove such defects in transactions of grains. First of all, the joint marketing function of the National Agricultural Cooperatives Federation was extended to increase joint shipments. Collection centers have been established in producing areas, and large-scale joint marketing centers have been opened in principal cities. Gathering centers for farm products were established alongside expressways, thereby forming a nationwide joint sales network. Groups of farmers were formed to facilitate for joint shipments and the standardization of farm products was promoted. As a result, joint shipments accounted for 17 per cent of total sales in 1973, and losses occurring in individual shipments were reduced remarkably.

The government established the Farm Price Stabilization Fund in 1970 in order to stabilize markets of staple crops and to smooth transactions, and also carried out a stockpiling system for farm products. Farm products which normally experience severe fluctuations in prices, such as red pepper, sesame, garlic, apples, eggs, etc., were selected for stockpiling. This stockpiling system aims at stabilizing the annual prices of these products, and preventing farmers' losses by buying and stockpiling items during the harvest season and selling them when out of season.

Also, the government established the Agriculture and Fishery Development Corporation in 1967 in order to support the processing of farm products, develop new projects, and introduce and extend new techniques. Spurred by such assistance, the farm products processing industry, which had remained stagnant, has developed rapidly, so that commodities have been diversified and the chain from the production region to the consumer has been stream-

Improving the Marketing Structure for Farm Products

Systematic shipment of farm products

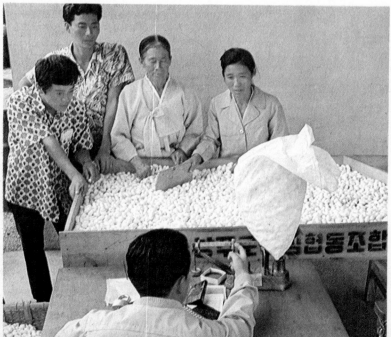

Farm products collection center along expressway

Trend of Grain – Fertilizer Exchange Ratios

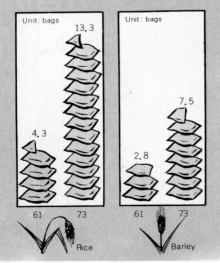

lined so that fresh farm products can be promptly supplied.

Along with these measures, grain warehouses have been expanded since 1967. Large-scale storage facilities such as six low-temperature warehouses, 27 heatproof warehouses, etc., have been constructed in the principal cities and in collection centers while 1,590 small-scale warehouses have been built in the producing regions.

The Agricultural and Marine Products Wholesale Market Law was implemented in 1973 in order to modernize the outdated marketing system and improve the marketing structure. Pseudo wholesale markets, which had been a principal cause of unfair transactions, have been removed and, in addition, improvement of facilities of public markets, publication of transaction prices, and rigorous execution of transactions by weight, have been enforced in order to establish good marketing order.

The terms of trade of farm households have been ameliorated by positive price support policies and remedial measures for the marketing structure. The prices of commodities other than farm products rose at an annual rate of 14.4 per cent during 1961–73, while prices of farm products rose at an annual rate of 17.6 per cent.

As for rice prices compared with fertilizer prices, with one straw bag of rice, 4.3 bags of nitrogenous fertilizer could have been bought in 1961, but 13.3 bags of nitrogenous fertilizer could have been bought in 1973, more than three times as many as in 1961. Similarly, the quantity of fertilizer which could have been bought with one straw bag of barley increased from 2.8 bags to 7.5 bags during the same period.

Special projects for increasing the income of farmers and fishermen have made a significant contribution in enhancing the level of earnings of farm households. The programs are designed to develop prospective agricultural products on a commercial basis, thereby boosting income. Specifically, cultivation estates have been built for silkworm cocoons, button mushrooms, and citrus fruit, all items with a high degree of both profitability and marketability. Considerable amounts of subsidies and technical assistance have also been provided for intensive cultivation, processing, and marketing in these fields. The projects can perhaps be characterized as consolidating tracts of land into comprehensive cultivation estates, thereby replacing previous individual and random efforts with a collective and centralized program.

The first four-year project was successfully completed between 1968 and 1971, and the second plan was initiated in 1972, with particular emphasis on cultivating fruit trees, industrial crops, seaweed (miyeog), and chestnuts for domestic use; and cocoons, button and pyogo mushrooms, oysters and laver for export purposes.

During the period 1968-1971, 90 cultivation estates were newly established with 410,000 farm households participating in the special projects, whereas during the second project period, the number of estates and the participating farm households substantially increased to 137 and 750,000 respectively. The amount of investment in the projects totaled some 86 billion won between 1968 and 1974.

In particular, these programs have been considerably reinforced by the Saemaul Undong (New Community Movement) since 1974, so that the number of farm households participating in the projects marks 820,000 which constitutes 30 per cent of total farm households.

The special projects have borne fruit of unprecedented magnitude during the last five years. Korea's agricultural industry, which formerly dealt primarily with grain production, has been developed into an advanced commercial sector centering on profitable agri-

Special Projects for Increasing the Income of Farmers and Fishermen

cultural products. Increased production of industrial crops ha
resulted in boosted incomes for the participating households, toge
ther with dramatic development of related manufacturing industries
The current situation of industrial crops is as follows:

In the case of silkworm raising, huge sericulture estates have been constructed in regions close to the silk processing factories located at Seosan, Dangjin, Eumseong and Jincheon. Vigorous efforts have been pursued to increase mulberry orchards and to

Button mushroom processing

Production of Major Commercial Agricultural Products

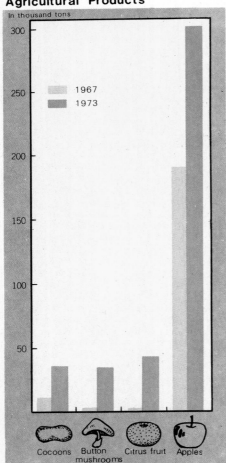

In thousand tons

- 1967
- 1973

Cocoons | Button mushrooms | Citrus fruit | Apples

enhance their productivity, while facilities and techniques have been improved with the introduction of a collective silkworm breeding system.

Thus, since 1968, 9,000 hectares of mulberry orchards have been newly established, and production per unit area has doubled, with a resultant tripling of cocoon production.

As a consequence, farm household income per unit area has risen six times over 1968.

Button mushroom culture, which began in the 1950's, was by and large unsuccessful at first chiefly due to insufficient know-how in this field. However, since this product was selected in 1968 as one of the promising development items, production has been on the increase. This owes a great deal not only to the establishment of cultivation estates and processing factories but also to the high degree of technological improvement.

During the period 1968-1973, the area of cultivation estates was expanded two and a half times to 1,388 thousand square meters while processing factories increased to 62 in number. In addition, actual production per unit area rose seven times over 1968, mainly due to improvements in technique. The total production of button mushrooms stood at a mere 1,700 tons in 1968, but grew to 32,000 tons in 1973, which represents an increase of almost twenty times the output of 1962. Twenty million dollars worth of button mushrooms was exported in 1973; consequently, this product is regarded as one of the most promising export items.

The output of citrus fruit, chiefly produced on Jeju Island, rose to 39,000 tons in 1973, compared with a meager 1,600 tons in 1968. Such a significant production performance is primarily ascribed not only to formation of large citrus groves and installation of windbreaks but also to various supports provided for price stability, including storage and processing facilities.

In the past, apples were cultivated almost exclusively in Gyeongnam and Gyeongbug Provinces. In order to avoid such overconcentration in one area apple cultivation has been diversified into Chungbug, Gang-weon and Gyeong-gi Provinces, and the introduction of new strains has been aggressively implemented. Storage facilities have been expanded in order to maintain prices and processing equipment has been modernized.

As a result, between 1968 and 1973 apple orchards recorded a sevenfold expansion in acreage while production increased by more than 50 per cent. When the new strains begin producing, apple production is expected to turn sharply upward.

As regards livestock breeding, 210,000 calves were distributed under the target of ''one cow for each farm household''.

Ranches have been founded in the regions of Weolseong in Gyeongbug Province and Goseong in Gyeongnam Province with the aim of raising 60,000 head of beef cattle. Total farm households concerned in livestock breeding number 190,000 and one head of beef cattle earned approximately 52,000 won in 1973.

Dairy farms have also been established in the regions of Pyeong-taeg, Anseong, Changweon, Daejeon and Gwangsan, where 15,000 head of milk cows are being pastured.

Consequently, milk production quintupled, and the value of the yield of one cow averaged 145,000 won in 1973.

Success in Increasing Farm Household Income

Special projects to increase the incomes of farmers and fishermen have obviously served not only to boost yields of farm products but also to multiply incomes of farm households, partly due to coordinated assistance in the fields of processing and marketing. Total income of farm households taking part in the programs tripled between 1968 and 1973, which means between a 10 to 20 per cent higher rate of increase than other farm households.

Mostly owing to the government's diverse and concerted efforts in this direction, incomes of farm households have tremendously improved. Average farm household income, a mere 68,000 won in 1962, increased to 481,000 won in 1973, and the chronic deficits in farm family budgets turned into a surplus of 125,000 won. Now that farmers can afford savings and reinvestments with their ordinary income, farming on a large scale is getting on the right track.

The enhanced standard of living has resulted in a sharp rise in expenditures for education, conveniences, and recreation, whereas the ratio of food to total living costs has been cut to 48.2 per cent

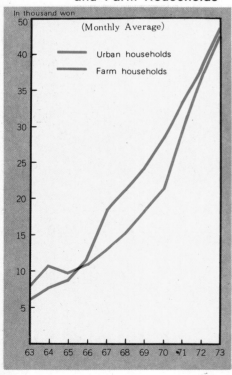

Income of Urban and Farm Households

In thousand won

(Monthly Average)

— Urban households
— Farm households

50
40
35
30
25
20
15
10
5

63 64 65 66 67 68 69 70 71 72 73

from the previous 58.6 per cent.

Such a phenomenon perhaps demonstrates the gradual improvement in life of farm households, as the income discrepancy between urban and rural households becomes narrower. The rapid economic growth has led to a considerable increase in the incomes of urban households which, in turn, would have relatively reduced farm household income. The government, however, has continued to direct its policies towards improving farm household incomes so that, in fact, the gap between rural and urban areas has been significantly narrowed. Thus, average farm household income in 1973 equalled 71.2 per cent of an average Seoul household, compared with 42.5 per cent in 1962. Meanwhile, the ratio of farm household income to that of an urban worker was elevated from 60.1 per cent in 1967 to 87.4 per cent in 1973. Taking into account the fact that farm household incomes form somewhat less than 70 per cent of those for cities in most countries except Japan, this ratio is considered rather high.

Livestock Breeding Industry

In the past, the percentage share of livestock breeding in agriculture industry was negligible. Cattle were bred only for farm work, while chickens and pigs were raised on a small scale as a part-time job. Livestock farming did not satisfy the requisites for an enterprise at all.

However, Korea's livestock breeding entered a new phase during the 1960's. Since the beginning of the First Five-Year Economic Development Plan in 1962, the government has attached major

importance to the industrialization of livestock farming, parallel with the positive fostering of processing firms. The dairy industry started with nothing, so cows had to be imported and milk processing plants and pastures established. In addition, loans on concessionary terms have been granted to those who wish to enter the livestock raising business. A mutual aid system for livestock breeding has been evolved and artificial insemination and improved breeds have been introduced.

In consideration of the rising demand for livestock in the latter half of the 1960's, the government selected livestock farming as a major special agricultural sector worth nurturing. Thus, loans for investments in livestock raising have been expanded.

Government investments for livestock promotion stood at a meager 300 million won in 1967, even then an elevenfold increase over the previous year; thereafter it has expanded by 5 billion won every year.

In conjunction with the intensive investment there has been an urgent need for establishing pastures to provide sufficient space for livestock raising. Lack of interest in the past in utilizing meadows for grazing and heavy dependence on silage inevitably required considerable amounts of foreign exchange for importing animal feed. To stimulate livestock breeding, regulations for furthering livestock farms were instituted in 1969, and in accordance with these regulations various sorts of assistance have been actively provided for cattle ranches.

Between 1968 and 1973, the government invested 3,500 million won to set up 58,000 hectares of pastures. These pastures supply 1,450,000 tons of forage, sufficient to raise 150,000 head of cattle.

Number of Domestic Animals

		(In thousand head)	
Beef cattle	0.2		1961
	7		1973
Draft cattle		1,095	
		1,486	
Milk cows	1.1		
	52.4		
Pigs		1,262	
		1,595	
Chickens	11,000		
	23,000		

Improving Indigenous Breeds

Vigorous measures were also adopted with a view to improving indigenous breeds. Breeding stock has been imported on a large scale from 1968 onward: 15,000 head of cattle during the period 1968–1973, 1,600 head of swine in 1973, and 200,000 chickens every year. Artificial insemination stations have been set up in 172 districts and counties, and at the same time an official approval system for breeding stock registration has been strengthened to upgrade the quality of livestock. Furthermore, nationwide champion cattle contests have been held since 1974 with the government purchasing the champion cattle for breeding purposes.

Comparison of improved breed and Korean indigenous cattle

Animal Feed Supply

In the past, Korea was dependent on foreign countries for most of the raw materials for feed, but feed grain has been partly producible at home following the development of green fodder and sweet potato silage. In particular, the purchase of fish meal processing boats has made it possible to attain self-sufficiency in fish meal, one of the important protein feeds which had previously been entirely imported.

The shortage of animal feed has been intensified by the increasing demand for fodder arising from the remarkable growth in the livestock population in recent years. Furthermore, the worldwide animal feed crisis triggered in 1972 has increased the current feed difficulties. Under this situation, Korea should devise proper measures for increasing the yield of feed grain. On the other hand, the number of formula feed manufacturing factories increased from three in 1963 to 71 in 1973, and production capacity has expanded from 7,000 tons in 1962 to 909,000 tons in 1973.

Modernization of Livestock Breeding

Since 1969, a national livestock breeding station and three demonstration meadows have been established in an effort to stimulate modernization of livestock raising. These selected pastures are expected not only to devise and teach livestock breeding techniques and management skills, but also to play a leading role in industrializing stock raising.

There were only about one thousand head of dairy cattle in Korea in the early 1960's. Thereafter, some 10,000 head were imported from the United States, Canada, New Zealand and Australia, and by 1973 this herd had been increased to 52,000 head. Thus, each of 5,500 dairy farming households possesses on average ten head of

dairy cattle. The number of farms engaged in dairy farming with 40 animals or more in their own pastures is 189. Industrialized and specialized dairy farming has made an invaluable contribution to the development of the dairy product industry. Entering the 1970's, various dairy products ranging from condensed milk, powdered skim milk, and powdered whole milk, to ice cream, yoghurt and butter have been produced domestically. Though all milk was imported in the past, Korea became self-sufficient in condensed milk by 1963 and in powdered milk by 1965.

In addition, breeding of Korean native cattle is also in the process of industrialization. In the early 1960's the total number of Korean cattle was slightly over one million head. However, the vigorous government policies and concrete projects established in

1968, aimed at promoting cattle breeding, have brought about a substantial increase in cattle of more than 5 per cent yearly. Thus, cattle reached a total of 1,480,000 head in 1973.

Along with an increase in breeding cattle, industrialized and specialized cattle raising became popular. In 1973, farm households with more than three head of cattle marked as many as 20,000, while the number of beef cattle ranches with more than 40 head reached 20. This demonstrates the drastic change in cattle breeding patterns from the previous draft cattle to beef cattle raising.

Large-scale poultry farming began to increase rapidly during the 1960's. To meet mounting domestic demand, production of meat and eggs increased three times, while the number of chickens being raised more than doubled.

The poultry industry experienced fierce market competition in the late 1960's due primarily to the commercialization of chicken raising. Chicken farming developed into large-scale operations, parallel with a significant improvement in chicken raising skills. The average number of chickens per farm household grew to 25 from the previous ten, while full-fledged poultry farms with more than 3,000 chickens numbered 1,151. In this situation, small-size chicken farms with less than 1,000 birds have substantially decreased in number, while large-size farms with more than 1,000 birds have increased remarkably. As a result, the poultry industry is likely to expand to an international scale.

The history of breeding swine as a side job of farm households goes back many years, but advanced swine rearing was not realized until the late 1960's. Swine farming has made considerable progress since the resumption of live swine exports to Hong Kong in the early 1960's and pork to Japan in the 1970's. Swine raising has been accelerated by special government assistance for building commercialized pig farms, import of breeding swine, and also enforcing standardized sizes of hogs. During the period 1962-1973 the number of swine being bred increased from 1.2 million head to 1.6 million head. Pig farms with less than ten head have dwindled considerably, while those with more than 100 head have reached 515, reflecting the swift upturn in the scale of operations.

The government worked out a long-term livestock promotion plan in 1973. The objective of this scheme lies not only in satisfying demand for meat but also in increasing the number of domestic animals on a nationwide scale, with a view to multiplying the income of farm households by fully utilizing land. The plan is also aimed at attaining a twofold increase in meat production. To accomplish these objectives, concrete measures have been taken. More specifically, grassland encompassing 250,000 hectares has been formed, and at the same time various kinds of assistance have been provided to farm households which intend to raise animals. These measures include not only the inducement of private capital to develop large tracts, but also the improvement of breeding stock.

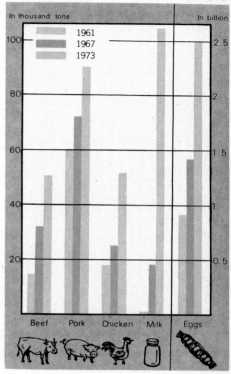

Production of Livestock Products

173

Mountains occupy 67 per cent of the national territory, and forests are the largest single endowed natural resources. In spite of the fact that forest resources are considered very important for daily life, to the extent that they provide water and lumber, mountains have become denuded mainly because of reckless deforestation during the last half century.

It is indeed fortunate, however, that concerted efforts for reforestation have been pursued from the early 1960's. Laws concerning preservation of forests have been instituted. There are mutual financing associations for reforesting mountains in every village and forestry cooperatives have been established in every city and county, with particular emphasis placed on reforestation and erosion control.

In 1967, the Office of Forestry was established with the aim of strengthening forest administration, and in particular consolidating the previous random assistance for reforestation and erosion control in an organized manner. Upon completing a forest land classification survey in 1969, all forest lands have been designated as absolute or relative.

A forest development plan, covering 14 forestry estates, was set up on the basis of the results of the forest land classification survey, and this has spurred collective reforestation of usable forest lands. The

Steady Progress in Reforestation

fourteen forestry estates are primarily absolute forestland and are located in secluded mountains considered important for watershed protection. These estates account for 48 per cent of total forest lands, and one estate covers 200,000 hectares on average. Some of the timber species being grown in the estates are: Cryptomeria japonica, Chamaecyparis obtusa, Larix leptolepsis, and Pinus densiflora Forma Erecta. These trees have been planted in accordance with the principle of the right tree for the right land, in an effort to establish forests for special uses. Especially propagation maintaining seedling beds, planting and tending of forests, and processing of forest products have all been systematized.

Erosion Control

Erosion control projects have been expanded in order to prevent further damage from denuded woodland, as well as to conserve the topsoil. Villagers have voluntarily taken part in the projects, thereby enabling them to be carried out successfully. Projects were previously concentrated on mountain erosion control and were carried out in hit or miss fashion. To coordinate such activities in such a way as to prevent flood damage, 14 erosion control estates were established in 1968 in regions throughout the country considered most flood-prone. Since 1969 strenuous attempts have been made to establish pastures for erosion control purposes, so that the previously devastated mountains around villages have been turned into meadows, thereby resulting in rapid development of livestock.

As part of efforts to forward these projects, a Unification Garden Movement was launched in 1971. This movement reflects desire for unification and is expressed by planting trees on denuded mountains around villages. Unification gardens are divided into two categories: those of each city, province and township; and those of schools. Each garden encompasses more than ten hectares where trees are planted with voluntary participation from various social circles such as soldiers, government officials, villagers, students and teachers. More than 2,180,000 persons across the country joined in the movement and planted 26,000 hectares in 1971 and 1972.

Reforestation received a new spur in 1973. President Park pointed out that the reason for lackadaisical reforestation in the past is attributable to the fact that there were no clear and definite objectives of reforestation, as well as to mismanagement following planting. In this context, he urged the authorities concerned not only to enlighten people as a whole as to the basic government policy aimed at beautifying the national territory through love of trees, but also to evolve policies motivating farmers near mountains to take good care of forests, as well as to plant trees with enthusiasm on their own. In accordance with the President's instruction, a Forestry Development Law was enacted and promulgated to the effect that forestry development should be achieved in a comprehensive and efficient manner. According to the Law, forest lands are divided into three types: for development purposes commercial timber forests, aesthetic forests and agricultural forests. As prescribed in the Law, the owner is obliged to develop as well as to tend his own forests in an efficient manner. In case an owner does not sincerely perform his duties and responsibilities, proxy performance is allowed. Subsidies and loans are provided for forestry development.

Along these lines, the first ten-year national forest plan was launched in 1973. The plan is primarily aimed at nationwide reforesting of mountains and fields covering 6,670,000 hectares. According to the program, between 1973 and 1982 fruit trees will be planted on 300,000 hectares, fast-growing trees on 300,000 hectares, slow-growing trees on 200,000 hectares, and fuel forests on 200,000 hectares, together with reforestation for erosion control purposes on 80,000 hectares. Concrete measures consisting of 31 items have been carried out in such a way as to help implement the plan effectively. Natural conservation, entrance control, responsible timber inspection system, delineation of responsibility for protecting forests, and measures for growing fuel forests around farm villages are particularly noteworthy. About 300 million trees were planted in the spring and fall of 1973, the first year of the ten-year forest plan. The strengthening of forest administration has been augmented by establishment of a forestry bureau in each province and a forestry division in every city and county. These new organizations have given impetus to the early realization of natural conservation and post-planting protection.

First Ten-Year National Forest Plan

Growth in Seafood Cultivation

Clam cultivation site

The Shift from Fish-Catching to Fish-Raising

Although Korea has many suitable places for shellfish and seaweed cultivation, including shallow areas and tidal flats off the west and south coasts, except for traditional laver and oyster raising in Jeonnam Province little had been done until recently. Since the early 1960's, however, interest in shellfish and seaweed cultivation began to increase unprecedentedly. This is partly because of definite limits to developing profitable fishing grounds in offshore areas and partly because of the government's desire to increase income of fishermen.

During the period of the First Five-Year Economic Development Plan, appropriate stations for shellfish and seaweed cultivation were selected and technical skills were developed.

Positive measures have been devised to nurture shellfish and seaweed cultivation, as part of special projects for boosting incomes of farmers and fishermen. Items selected as being worthy of intensive development because of their profitability are oysters,

clams, laver, seaweed, short-necked clams, etc. Some 3 billion won was appropriated for their development during the four years from 1968 to 1971. A number of cultivation estates have been established in appropriate tidal areas off the west and south coasts in which many fishermen have been able to participate. Newly-developed seeding and tending techniques have been fostered among fishermen. while joint cultivation stations have been constructed with funds from mutual financing fishermen's associations. Integrated assistance in the fields of producing, processing and marketing has been improved so as to promote a mass production system.

Great progress in developing tidal flats was made on a large scale between 1972 and 1973. Consequently, seaweed farms have been established off the east coast, oyster beds off the south coast, and grounds for laver, clams and major shellfish off the west coast. In the meantime; inland fisheries have been initiated since President Park revealed keen concern over this matter in 1974.

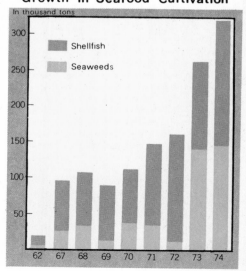

Growth in Seafood Cultivation

Remarkable Progress in Shellfish and Seaweed Cultivation

Output of the shellfish and seaweed cultivation industry stood at a mere 20,000 tons in 1962, but grew to more than 260,000 tons in 1973. The 1973 figure represents an increase of 13 times the yield of 1962. Perhaps more important is the fact that shellfish and seaweed cultivation has become big enough to rank as an industry. Shellfish and seaweed cultivation contributes 15 per cent to total yield of the fishery industry, in sharp contrast with the previous 3.8 per cent, and has become one of the important components of the fishery industry.

Production of 'miyeog' seaweed has increased at the fastest rate among marine products. 'Miyeog' production of a mere 370 tons in 1962 grew 300 times to 110,000 tons in 1973. Such success in

'miyeog' raising is attributed to enhanced productivity and development of a mass production system utilizing improved skills which were obtained through the period of the first and second special projects for agricultural industry.

The yield of clams ran to only 314 tons in 1962, but rose to 7,000 tons in 1973, which represents an increase of more than 20 times the output of 1962. In the past, clams picked up by fishermen on the beach constituted total production. However, along with the construction of joint cultivation stations with funds from mutual financing fishermen's associations in the early 1960's, clam cultivation in artificial beds, created in tidal flates off the west and south coasts has been intensively fostered from 1966. Since 1968, special

Modern laver cultivation site

aquiculture projects have received coordinated support, cultivation estates have been constructed and shellfish and seaweed cultivation beds have been promoted on a commercial basis.

In the early stage, most of the production was consumed domestically, but by 1973 production had increased sufficiently so that exports of fishery products to Japan alone added 5 million dollars to Korea's foreign exchange holdings.

Oyster cultivation started in the early 1960's with the construction of oyster beds in tidal flats off the west and south coasts financed with funds from fishermen's mutual financing associations. The downward tendency of fish production in industrialized countries has emerged mainly from the development of seaside industries and devastation of fishing grounds, while demand for fish has increased at a rapid rate. In response to the increasing export demand for fish, oysters became one of the most promising export items, so that beginning in 1966 the previous extensive stone oyster cultivation method has been replaced by intensive raft oyster culture, with a view to improving productivity. As part of the efforts to commercialize oyster cultivation the producing, processing and exporting of oysters have been dealt with comprehensively rather than independently.

The agreement made in 1972 on shellfish sanitation between the Republic of Korea and the United States enabled Korea to have free access to the American market, which in turn brightened the prospects for export of this product. In an attempt to cultivate oysters on a large scale, the government worked out an oyster development plan in 1972 which calls for developing oyster cultivation in an integrated manner. The program, aimed at enabling Korea to become the largest oyster producing country in the world, set production and export targets for 1976 at 190,000 tons and 25 million dollars respectively.

Oyster production rose from 8,000 tons in 1962 to 80,000 tons in 1973, a tenfold increase over 1962 output. The export amount of oysters expanded from 90 thousand dollars in 1962 to 9 million dollars in 1973, and can be expected to continue rising.

Laver, which constitutes a handsome share of total exports to Japan, had been cultivated relatively earlier as it is easy to raise as a side business with a small investment during farmers' slack season. Rising import demand for laver by Japan in the 1960's required even more vigorous measures for bolstering laver cultivation. In the early stage, particular importance was attached to the development of new cultivation stations. In recent years, strenuous endeavors have been exerted not only to elevate productivity but also to upgrade quality by disseminating cultivation skills with a view to mechanizing the process of manufacturing. Production of laver increased at a phenomenal rate, from 4,000 tons in 1962 to 35,000 tons in 1973, while a mere 1.3 million dollars in exports in 1963 jumped to 10 million dollars in 1973.

EXPLOITATION OF ENERGY
AND MINERAL RESOURCES

Oil: Pivot of the Energy Industry

We are living in Petroleum Age. Vinyl, nylon and other commonly known petrochemical products are essential to our daily life, finding uses ranging from footwear and clothing to wrapping materials and cloches for farm crops. Moreover, vehicles such as automobiles, diesel locomotives, airplanes, and ships depend entirely upon petroleum in Korea. Petroleum also furnishes half the power, light and heat in Korea.

In view of this, it is quite natural that industrial countries having a developed petroleum industry play a leading role in the world economy.

If Korea is to join the advanced countries, there exists a need to promptly develop petrochemical industries even though there are no known crude oil resources in the country.

Not much attention was paid to petroleum, nor was there a high demand for petrochemical products, in early years. But at the beginning of the 1960's, the government launched an ambitious industrialization scheme as a major focus of its development planning effort, which included the expansion of the social over head sector, and the construction of express highways. The necessity for fostering the petrochemical industry has been particularly

Night view of Ulsan Refinery

stimulated by the desire to hand over a modernized country to future generations.

Demand for petroleum has been rising since 1962, the year when a coordinated economic development plan was first evolved. The Ulsan refinery, constructed in 1964, supplied domestically-produced petroleum products for the first time in the nation's history. At the same time, energy policies which put emphasis on petroleum consumption instead of coal increased the demand for petroleum. Demand for petroleum grew at an annual average growth rate of 27.8 per cent during the period between 1962 and 1973, and far exceeded that for other energy resources.

The share of petroleum in primary energy resources, which consist of coal, petroleum-related products, hydroelectric power, and wood and charcoal, rapidly expanded from only 9.5 per cent in 1962 to 40 per cent in 1969. As a result, it outgrew the share of anthracite in total primary energy resources, exceeding 50 per cent in 1971. According to the composition of primary energy resources as of the end of 1973, petroleum constituted a predominant share of 53.3 per cent, coal 31 per cent, wood and charcoal 14.4 per cent, and hydroelectric power 1.3 per cent.

Increasing Petroleum Demand
(In thousand kl)

Year	Oil for Energy	Other Uses	Total
1962	1,064	35	1,099
1966	2,301	44	2,345
1971	11,434	1,065	12,499
1973	14,344	2,036	16,380
Annual Average Growth Rate (1962~1973)	26.4	44.7	27.8

Self-Sufficient Production of Petroleum Products

As Korea depended entirely upon imports of refined petroleum products in the past, many difficulties arose in trying to meet the increase in demand. Moreover, imports of finished petroleum products required substantial amounts of foreign exchange.

In this situation, the government vigorously began to build oil refineries as one of the major types of industry to be emphasized under the First Five-Year Economic Development Plan.

In April 1964, the Ulsan refinery was finished. Jointly constructed by the government and the Gulf Oil Corporation of the United States, the refinery began with a daily production capacity of 35,000 barrels, and petroleum products thus started to be produced domestically.

To meet mounting demands for these products, the government has continued to expand oil refinery facilities; in 1969 the Yeosu plant of the Honam Oil Refinery Co., Ltd. was jointly constructed with the cooperation of the Caltex Company of the United States, and in 1971 the Incheon refinery of Kyungin Energy Co., Ltd.

Honam Oil Refinery Co., Ltd.

was built jointly with Union Oil Company of the United States.

As a result, in 1971, when the Second Five-Year Economic Development Plan was successfully finished, the total daily production capacity of the three refineries reached 265,000 barrels.

During the 1970's the refinery facilities of the Ulsan Plant of the Korea Oil Corporation were more than doubled, with total daily capacity reaching 215,000 barrels. In the meantime, the capacity of the Yeosu plant of the Honam Oil Refinery Co. was increased to 160,000 barrels, and the Incheon plant of Kyungin Energy Co. to 60,000 barrels. By 1974, the total oil refinery facilities had expanded twelve times over 1964, and capacity reached 435,000 barrels.

The domestic production of oil-related products increased, mainly due to the enlarged refinery facilities. In 1964 when the first oil refinery commenced operation, output was only 770,000 kiloliters. By 1970 it had risen to slightly over 10 million kiloliters and further to 16 million kiloliters in 1973.

The share of light oils such as kerosene and gasoline has decreased whereas the share of bunker-C oil, naphtha, and other products has increased. In an effort to satisfy the ever-increasing demands both for fuel oils such as bunker-C and for oil products like naphtha, which is one of the essential raw materials for producing petrochemical products, production has been adjusted to meet the changed pattern of demand.

With boosted production, no petroleum products have been imported at all since the restructuring of the output in 1971.

The petroleum products left over after satisfying domestic consumption have earned considerable foreign exchange, either from direct exports or selling to the United States forces stationed in Korea, or supplying oil to foreign vessels.

Such foreign exchange earnings reached at approximately 200 million dollars in 1974.

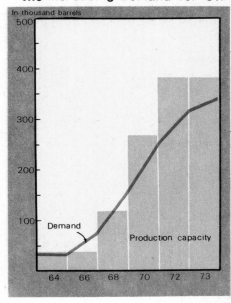

Refinery Facilities and the Increasing Demand for Oil

Production of Petroleum Products				
				(In thousand kl)
	1 9 6 4	1 9 6 7	1 9 7 0	1 9 7 3
Gasoline	93 (12.1)	428 (15.8)	894 (8.2)	1,034 (6.4)
Kerosene	50 (6.5)	216 (8.0)	517 (4.8)	478 (3.0)
Diesel	183 (23.7)	649 (23.9)	1,785 (16.4)	2,854 (17.6)
L.R.F.O.	421 (54.7)	349 (12.9)	596 (5.5)	710 (4.4)
Bunker-C Oil	12 (1.6)	810 (29.9)	5,308 (48.9)	8,308 (51.3)
Jet Fuel	—	134 (4.9)	734 (6.8)	582 (3.6)
Naphtha	—	69 (2.5)	743 (6.8)	1,703 (10.4)
Others	11. (1.4)	59 (2.1)	282 (2.6)	536 (3.3)
Total	770 (100)	2,714 (100)	10,859 (100)	16,209 (100)

Note: Figures in parentheses represent composition ratios.

Construction of Central Terminal Station

The volume of imported crude oil has been steeply increasing in proportion to the expanded domestic demand for petroleum products. Import quantity of crude oil grew from 928,000 kiloliters in 1964 to over 10 million kiloliters in 1970, and again to 16.4 million kiloliters in 1973.

Accordingly, foreign exchange payments became heavier. Furthermore, the sudden upsurge in petroleum prices that was enforced by the oil-producing countries in 1973 has aggravated Korea's foreign exchange burden, thereby creating further difficulties. The foreign exchange spent in importation of crude oil amounted to 300 million dollars in 1973 and came close to 1.2 billion dollars in 1974. This figure seems almost unbelievable compared with the 12 million dollars spent in 1964.

International oil problems are likely to be severe in years to come. Petroleum expenditures in 1974 registered an unprecedented increase of four times over the previous year. The uncertainties have been intensified because the oil-producing countries have been using their oil production and supply as a vehicle for politics.

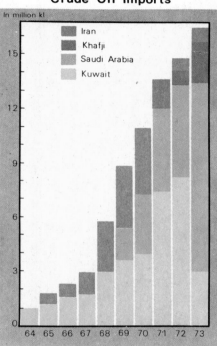

Crude Oil Imports

In million kl

- Iran
- Khafji
- Saudi Arabia
- Kuwait

64 65 66 67 68 69 70 71 72 73

The government is currently seeking to secure oil by pursuing an open door policy to solidify diplomatic relations with Middle East oil-producing countries. A number of concrete measures have been devised to overcome current difficulties. These measures involve the joint construction with oil-rich countries of refineries, the expansion of oil storage facilities, and the enlargment of tonnage of Korean ships.

It is notable that the government plans to build a central storage facility for crude oil with a view to insuring smooth supply.

If this program proceeds as scheduled, the facility is expected to expand to three million kiloliters capacity by 1977, a quantity sufficient for 35 days, the year scheduled for completion of the first construction, and further to 6.5 million kiloliters, which will perhaps satisfy 50 days of consumption by the year 1981 when the second construction phase will be completed.

To build the central terminal station for crude oil at this juncture has great significance in view of current oil storage capacity of only 1.1 million kiloliters.

Development of Undersea Oil Resources

Undersea Oil Exploration Map by Area

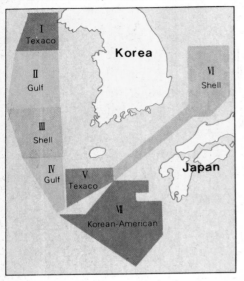

It is anticipated that oil will continue to be in great demand, which in turn will require a huge volume of crude oil in years ahead.

Notwithstanding the rapid growth of Korea's exports, the vast amount of foreign exchange needed to import crude oil will bring marked and mounting pressure on the balance of payments, primarily from the skyrocketing of petroleum prices. As part of effort to secure crude oil, the government intends to undertake joint exploration and exploitation of the undersea continental shelf. Multilateral contracts for developing undersea petroleum resources were made with Gulf, Shell, Texaco, and Korean-American companies between 1969 and 1970, and continental shelf drilling has been continuing in seven sectors off the west and south coasts. Minor differences emerged as to results of exploration of the continental shelf among the companies. Upon the completion of surveys, several companies have embarked on drilling in a few places since 1972.

In the light of the exploration so far, it will be proved perhaps in early 1976 whether the continental shelf is endowed with oil. If oil of economic value for development should be discovered, Korea's economy as well as its petroleum industry would enter a new, prosperous phase.

Undersea oil exploration site

Abundant Electric Power

Increase in Power Generation Facilities

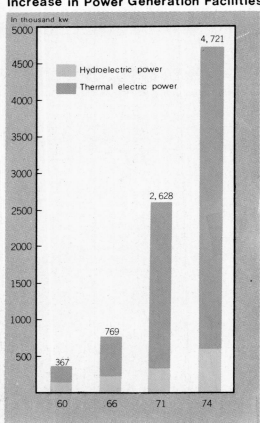

In thousand kw

	Hydroelectric power	Thermal electric power

- 60: 367
- 66: 769
- 71: 2,628
- 74: 4,721

Sufficient Power Generation Facilities

In 1945, total installed power generation capacity in Korea was no more than 199,000 kilowatts and average power generation capacity under the circumstances remained far below the required amount, not only for industrial purposes but also for general use. As part of efforts to increase power generation facilities, the government constructed several thermal electric power stations in Masan, Dang-inri and Samcheog as well as repairing the Hwacheon Hydroelectric Power Plant which was the largest of its kind in the early 1950's. Despite concerted efforts there remained a long way to go in order to ease the chronic shortage of power. No concerted attempts to develop power sources were made until the 1960's.

In 1961 the government merged the three then existing electric companies into the Korea Electric Company. The First Five-Year Power Development Plan, launched in 1962, saw power generation facilities newly installed and expanded so that total capacity reached 402,000 kilowatts including the Busan, Samcheog, and

Paldang Hydropower Dam

Yeongweol thermal power plants and Chuncheon hydroelectric station. Unlimited power supply was realized for the first time in 1964.

Meanwhile, rapid progress in industrialization caused partial curtailment of power supply again in 1967, chiefly due to high demand by the manufacturing sector for electric power. Under this situation, with the aim of coordinating power development, the government greatly enlarged the investment in generation machinery and equipment by the Second Five-Year Power Plan, and encouraged private capital to participate in electric power projects. During this period, the Cheongpyeong and Hwacheon hydroelectric power stations were enlarged, and the Euiam and Namgang hydroelectric power plants were built. The Gunsan, Yeongnam, Incheon, and Donghae thermal power plants, together with a gas turbine plant in Ulsan, were established and the facilities of existing thermal power plants in Seoul and Busan greatly expanded. The installed generation capacity in 1971 totaled 2,628,000 kilowatts of which

Electricity Reserve

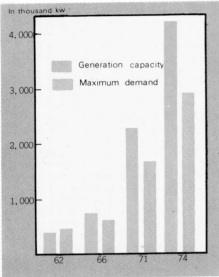

In thousand kw

Generation capacity
Maximum demand

341,000 kilowatts was generated by hydropower stations and 2,286,000 kilowatts by thermal power plants. This total represents a sevenfold increase over the early 1960's and thirteen times the capacity of 1945.

During the 1970's, additional projects for developing electric sources have continued to be carried out and several power generation plants have been added since 1972, including the Kyungin Energy, Yeongdong and Yeosu thermal power plants. Also, the Honam thermal power plant, whose generation capacity is 600 thousand kilowatts was completed in 1972 and the Paldang and Soyang River hydropower stations have been dedicated. The generation capacity of the Soyang River plant, the largest hydroelectric plant in Korea, is as much as 200,000 kilowatts.

The total power generation capacity of 4,721,000 kilowatts in 1974 can be broken down into hydropower plants of 621,000 kilowatts, whose share of total capacity stands at 13.2 per cent, and thermal power stations of 4,100,000 kilowatts whose share takes up the remaining 86.8 per cent.

In this situation there appears plenty of surplus electric power. The feasible generation capacity totals 4,311,000 kilowatts so that electric power of 1,438,000 kilowatts is left over even after meeting maximum demand. In other words, electric power amounting to 50 per cent of maximum demand is held in reserve.

The tremendous expansion of generation capacity has increased available electric power to a significant degree. The mere 1,978 million kilowatt hours in 1962 rose seven times to 14,826 million kilowatt hours in 1973, which represents an annual increase rate of 19.3 per cent during the period.

It is noteworthy that none of the other developed or developing countries has yet experienced such a high rate of increase in power generation.

The government concentrated upon thermal power plants for developing electricity sources mainly due to the fact that thermal power plants cost less to construct than hydroelectric power stations. Accordingly, between 1962 and 1973 electric power generated by thermal power plants rapidly increased at an annual average rate of 23.1 per cent, whereas hydropower stations grew moderately at an average annual rate of 5.8 per cent. This, in turn, markedly altered the ratio of power generation between hydro and thermal electric power plants. Hydropower, occupying one-third of total power generation in the early 1960's, declined relatively to 8.7 per cent in 1973.

On the other hand, consumption of electric power soared. Power used per person expanded 6.5 times from 58 kilowatt hours in the early 1960's to 376 kilowatt hours in 1973. This figure is about average for developing countries.

Increased Power Generation

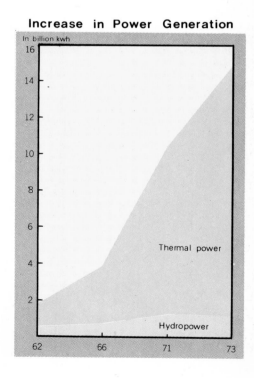

Increase in Power Generation

In billion kwh

Thermal power

Hydropower

View of Danginri Thermal Power Plant

Expansion of Transmission and Distribution Facilities

The expansion of transmission and distribution facilities to connect power plants with end-users was required to handle the increased development of electric power. Transmission cables of a meager 6,232 circuit kilometers in 1961 attained a length of 9,377 circuit kilometers in 1973, an annual average increase rate of 3.5 per cent, while distribution cables of only 9,171 kilometers in 1961 reached a length of 38,658 kilometers, representing an increase of more than four times the length of 1961.

On the other hand, the metropolitan loop system which is a circular transmission grid has been introduced in the Seoul-Incheon area in an attempt to ensure supply of electric power. A massive transmission network in the Honam district has been constructed to link the power grid for the central region with the Yeosu thermal power and Honam hydropower plants. There have also been circular transmission systems established both in Busan and in the Yeongdong district.

The enlarged and modernized facilities for transmission and distribution have enormously reduced electric power loss incurred in the process of transmission and distribution. The rate of electric power loss fell to 11.4 per cent in 1973, as compared with 29.3 per cent in 1961.

Rural electrification projects were launched in 1965. Only 12 per cent of total farm households benefitted from electric lights until 1964, when power supply curtailment was first removed. At present, more than half the farm households can take advantage of electric power. Complete electrification will probably be attained in the near future, as the government plans to realize 100 per cent electrification in rural areas, except for mountain regions and remote islands, by 1977.

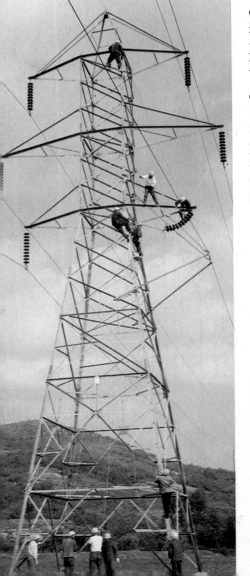

Fuel consumption for thermal power generation increased rapidly, to the degree that electric power generated by thermal power plants sharply expanded. If different kinds of fuel are calculated in calories, fuel consumption of a meager 4,951 billion kcal in 1962 rose six times to 30,165 billion kcal in 1973. In the early stage, coal was used as the means of generating electric power.

Improved Efficiency of Thermal Power Generation

Yeosu Thermal Power Plant

Since the late 1960's, coal has been replaced by oil. In 1962, the volume of coal used in power generation was 722 thousand tons, which accounted for three-fourths of total fuel used for power generation.

Oil consumed for electric power grew vastly to take up four-fifths of total fuel so used in 1973.

Such a heavy dependence on oil was caused by cheap international petroleum prices in the 1960's. Apart from uncertainties in supply and demand outlook for oil, the upsurge in petroleum prices in the 1970's has caused very serious problems in all fields. In this situation, extreme importance has been attached to minimizing the volume of fuel per kilowatt hour as much as circumstances permit. As a result, the efficiency of heat used was raised from 22.6 per cent in 1961 to 33 per cent in 1973.

On the other hand, to minimize the impact occurring from a possibly aggravated oil situation, research has been conducted to devise a method by which electric power can be generated from low-grade anthracite produced domestically and pilot plants have been constructed. Examples are the No.1 Yeongdong thermal power plant (125 thousand kilowatts) completed in 1972, and the No.2 Yeongdong plant now under construction.

Fuel Consumption by Thermal Power Plants

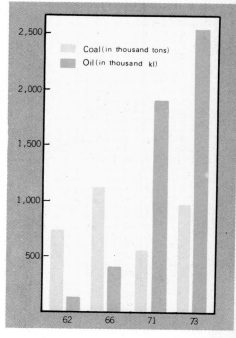

Coal (in thousand tons)
Oil (in thousand kl)

Atomic Power for the Future

It is expected that demand for electricity will be ever-increasing. However much surplus electric power we have now, the development of electricity sources should be continued.

The maximum utilization of domestic natural resources, the curb on domestic oil consumption, and enlargement of power generation facilities underlie the electricity source development plan which was set up in 1974. Along these lines, efforts are likely to be exerted to construct additional atomic power, anthracite and hydroelectric power plants. In an attempt to diversify electricity sources, and to introduce advanced skills with respect to generating electric power, Korea embarked on construction of its first atomic energy plant in 1971 which will have a generating capacity of 595,000 kilowatts. When this plant is dedicated in 1976, Korea's power generation projects will probably enter a new stage. Moreover, the government plans to build an atomic power plant each year after 1979. If the atomic power plant projects go

smoothly, the share of atomic-power-generated electricity in the total generation capacity will rapidly increased.

Projects for Electricity Source Development and Outlook on Generation Facilities

	Generation Stations (To be Constructed between 1975–86)		Total Power Generation Facilities		
	Number of plants	Generation capacity (thousand kw)	1976	1981	1986
Hydropower	8	713	711	1,061	1,334
Thermal Power	8	3,313	4,400	5,495	7,067
Atomic Power	9	6,595	595	2,395	6,595
Pumped Storage Power	4	1,420	—	1,020	1,420
Total	29	12,041	5,706	9,971	16,416

Gori Atomic Power Plant

The enlarged scale of the economy and the improved industrial structure have been accompanied by sharp increases in energy demand. The demand pattern has also changed, from the previous preference for traditional fuels such as wood and charcoal to advanced energy resources such as coal and petroleum.

Mining of coal, which is the only fossil fuel source in Korea, began to develop rapidly in the early 1960's, when energy demands started to increase. Its share of total energy consumption continued to rise from 37 per cent in the early 1960's to 46 per cent in 1966.

Nevertheless, since the late 1960's demand for coal has decreased relatively, while that for oil has progressively expanded with the expansion of the oil refinery industry.

In this situation, the ratio of coal to total energy sources started on a downward trend, and major energy source has been changed from coal to oil. Eventually, oil becomes the major energy source in Korea.

However, the importance of coal has been reaffirmed and augmented by the oil crisis of late 1973. Coal development programs, therefore, have been initiated with the aim of minimizing dependence on imported energy sources.

Rising Coal Production

Coal gondolas

Abundant Coal Reserves

It is roughly estimated that coal resources in Korea run to as much as 1,451 million tons, of which some 545 million tons is expected to be minable, in view of the current mining techniques, prices and deposit status. If only 15 million tons of coal are mined every year, the amount produced in 1974, the coal reserves will perhaps last for as long as 35 years before depletion. Even though the current ratio of recoverable reserves to the total stands at only 38 per cent, it can be enlarged to some extent, provided that mine exploration activities are expanded and mining techniques improved, together with revised price structure of energy sources. From this standpoint, the time when coal will be depleted can be more or less extended.

Changes in Consumption Structure by Energy Source

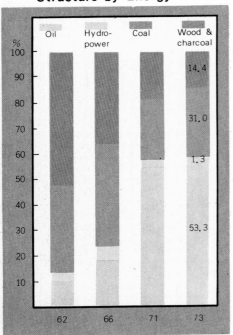

Coal Reserves		
		(In million tons)
	Identified Reserves	Recoverable Reserves
Samcheog	431.7	232.7
Mun-gyeong	72.5	40.1
Gangreung	61.5	40.6
Jeongseon	383.8	40.1
Pyeongchang	101.4	33.1
Danyang	77.4	31.0
Chungnam	146.4	83.2
Hwasun	43.3	27.3
Bo-eun	10.1	7.0
Others	122.4	9.8
Total	1,450.5	544.9

On the other hand, deposit status by coal field shows that the Samcheog and Chungnam coal fields possess more than half the minable coal. The former occupies 42.7 per cent and the latter 15.3 per cent of the total. Other major coal fields are Mun-gyeong, Gangreung, Jeongsun, Pyeongchang, Danyang, and Hwasun.

Mine exploration should be carried out to discover not only the extent of natural resource endowment but also the feasibility of developing the resources. Coal mine exploration activities have been energetically pursued since the 1960's when the First Five-Year Economic Development Plan was initiated. During the period of the first plan, an accurate geological survey of the Samcheog coal field was concluded. The survey produced data on drilling and underground excavation, whereby deep coal seams located 300 meters in depth could be identified through drilling total exploration probes of 71,000 meters. During the period of the Second Five-Year Economic Development Plan, an accurate survey was completed on the Honam and other coal field under the control of the Daehan Coal Corporation, with boring explorations totaling 72,000 meters, carried out.

The strenuous mine exploration activities starting from the early 1960's have made an invaluable contribution to the development of coal sources. Nonetheless, the ratio of proven and probable reserves to the total identified reserves stands at only 25 per cent. Naturally, basic policy should be directed towards creating favorable conditions for developing undeveloped coal seams by rigorous mine exploration. The government, realizing this fact, has decided to complete accurate geological surveys of all coal fields in Korea with boring explorations and underground excavations.

Coal sorting piles

Coal Production Exceeds 15 Million Tons

Coal production of less than five million tons annually in the late 1950's dramatically rose in the 1960's and exceeded ten million tons in 1965.

The output of coal temporarily declined in the late 1960's, mainly due to the government's fuel policies encouraging oil consumption instead of coal. Coal mining, however, was again activated by the government's coal mining promotion policy, together with the provision of handsome subsidies, in the early 1970's.

Coal production has been increasing tremendously, spurred by the energy crisis in late 1973. Despite all the adverse circumstances, coal production in 1974 marked 15 million tons. Private mines led the rapid expansion of coal production. In the 1950's the Daehan Coal Corporation produced as much as 70 per cent of total production, but the share gradually decreased to 31.3 per cent in 1973. Instead, private mines accounted for the major share of coal production, reaching almost 70 per cent in 1973.

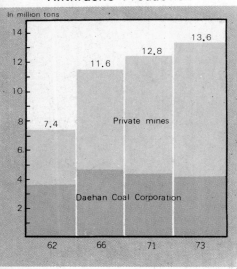

Anthracite Production

In million tons

7.4 — 11.6 — 12.8 — 13.6

Private mines

Daehan Coal Corporation

62   66   71   73

As regards anthracite, most of the production was used in satisfying civilian needs for use in houses and other buildings. The substitution of oil for anthracite in regard to power generation and industrial uses cut demand but with the recent upsurge in petroleum prices the government is now pursuing every avenue to ensure an adequate supply since it is anticipated that private consumption will rise sharply.

In this connection, it is noteworthy that one to two per cent of total domestic production of anthracite has been exported recently. The total export quantity of high-grade coal for industrial uses marked 221,000 tons in 1973.

The government, aiming at forestry conservation and modernizing the structure of fuel consumption, has been encouraging the replacement of wood and charcoal by coal. Accordingly, the government instituted the Extraordinary Law for Coal Development in 1961, which calls for marginal private mines to establish large consolidated mining corporations.

Nine consolidated coal mine firms have been brought into existence over a period of several years, of which some companies such as Samcheog and Mun-gyeong have grown to major size.

In 1962, the Law for Mining Development Promotion (later replaced by the Korea Mining Promotion Corporation Act) was legislated, which not only calls for supplying to private mines funds required for the enlargement and development of coal mines, but also enables the government-run Daehan Coal Corporation to provide intensive support for exploration and development by private mines.

The severe slowdown in coal mining in the late 1960's arose

Intensive Promotion of the Coal Mining Industry

Coal conveyer belt (*Mugho Harbor*)

chiefly from the increased volume of oil supply, which sharply reduced coal demand. To cope with the slump in coal mining, the government exerted vigorous efforts toward stirring up demand for coal, and also instituted and brought into force the Extraordinary Law for Coal Mining Promotion in 1969. According to the law, a commodity tax of 10 per cent shall be levied on bunker-C oil, and the proceeds was invested in the development of coal mines and marketing. Financial assistance for coal mining has been greatly increased in this manner.

Financial Assistance to Coal Mining

(In million won)

Year	Financial Loan Funds	Loans for Coal Stock	Subsidies	Total
1 9 6 2	268	—	—	268
1 9 6 6	200	—	—	200
1 9 7 0	600	2,300	2,084	4,984
1 9 7 1	930	3,000	2,868	6,798
1 9 7 2	930	4,250	3,517	8,697
1 9 7 3	930	4,500	3,701	9,131

Three different kinds of financial assistance available for coal mining are currently provided:

Firstly, the Korea Mining Promotion Corporation operates the government loan funds, including the provision of operating funds for mining, in such a way as to enlarge and develop coal mines. Since 1970, the scale of government loan funds provided has increased significantly as most of the marginal private mines have been in the process of gradual development from open pit into deep coal mining.

Secondly, in an effort to secure smooth supply and demand of coal, and to avoid seasonal fluctuations in production, financing for coal stockpiling during the off-season was instituted in 1970. Total financing reached 4.5 billion won in 1973, 3.5 billion won or 78 per cent of which was granted as loans to private mines.

Thirdly, in accordance with the Extraordinary Law for Coal Mining Promotion, subsidies have been furnished to every aspect of coal mining, including production and marketing, since 1970. Total subsidies provided as of the end of 1973 reached 3.7 billion won, four times the amount of financial loan funds disbursed.

Apart from such financial aids, various sorts of support have been rendered to facilitate the development of coal mining. The assistance involves facilities and freight rebates of railway transportation, preferential treatment in transmission and distribution facilities, and other special supports related to mine exploration activities.

Even though Korea is endowed with very poor natural resources, minerals are numerous enough to be classified into 200 types. As many as 59 among them have been designated for development by law because they are deemed to have economic value.

According to results produced by exploration activities carried out so far, reserves of metallic mineral products such as iron, gold and silver, lead, zinc and copper ores are estimated as relatively plentiful. In particular, tungsten ore reserves represent one of the richest sources of tungsten in the world. Limestone is perhaps the most abundant in Korea among nonmetallic mineral resources, while Korean kaolin has gained world recognition for high quality. In addition, nonmetallic minerals like talc, pyrophyllite, and silica, which are regarded as essential industrial raw materials, are available in good supply.

Development of Natural Resources

Yangyang Iron Mine

Active Mine Exploration Program

Mine exploration activities to identify resources have been actively carried out. The government completed geological investigation of the Taebaeg mountain region on a large scale in 1961, locating iron ore of 1.5 million tons, coal of 34 million tons, and limestone of 34 million tons. In 1962 the Law for the Promotion of Mining Development was enacted and in 1967 the Korea Mining Promotion Corporation was established, which is assigned to take full charge of promotion of mining.

The mine exploration activities performed up to now can be summarized as follows:

The Geological and Mineral Institute of Korea finished a survey for a geological map of 1/250,000th scale across the country, and is more than halfway to completion of a map of 1/50,000th's. Great progress in investigating the nature of soil and mineral deposits has been achieved.

In addition, the Korea Mining Promotion Corporation has proceeded with mine exploration through boring and underground excavation. Drilling costs have been generally financed by the government, whereas in the case of underground excavation, non-interest bearing, long-term loans which account for 60 per cent of total required costs have been provided to the mining corporations in question. In view of the high degree of risk which mining investment involves, and in an attempt to advance mine exploration, repayment of loans will be exempted in case no mineral has been found at all following a ten-year underground excavation.

As geological surveys indicate that potential reserves of minerals will exceed proven reserves, the government plans to continue intensive exploration for mineral deposits.

Mineral exploration site

Reserves of Major Minerals

(In million tons)

	Mineral	Concentration	Estimated Reserves	Potential Reserves
Metallic	Iron	24~50%	121.4	200.0
	Copper	0.6~ 1	11.2	11.2
	Lead & Zinc	3~10 //	10.8	16.0
	Tungsten	0.5~ 1 //	12.7	16.0
	Gold & Silver	10~50	7.1	50.0
	Manganese	20~30%	0.4	2.0
	Molybdenum	0.3% above	2.6	4.5
Nonmetallic Mineral Ore	Talc		9.1	9.1
	Kaolin		11.3	40.0
	Pyrophyllite		1.8	10.0
	Graphite		38.0	70.0
	Fluorite	45~70%	1.0	3.0
	Silica Stone	98 //	51.4	100.0
	Limestone	45 //	4,199.3	40,000.0

The government has provided intensive support for developing mines since early 1960. Government loan funds have been available for the development and operation of mines. And at the same time government-run enterprises like the Korea Tungsten Mining Company, which possesses advanced skills and equipment, have helped develop private mines which are small in size and backward in skills and technique. Mine development promotion activities have been intensified since the Korea Mining Promotion Corporation emerged to assume all business concerning mine development.

Idle mining licenses were thoroughly readjusted several times from 1968 onward in an effort to speed up development.

Mining licenses under which no production has occurred for

The Supply and Demand for Mineral Products

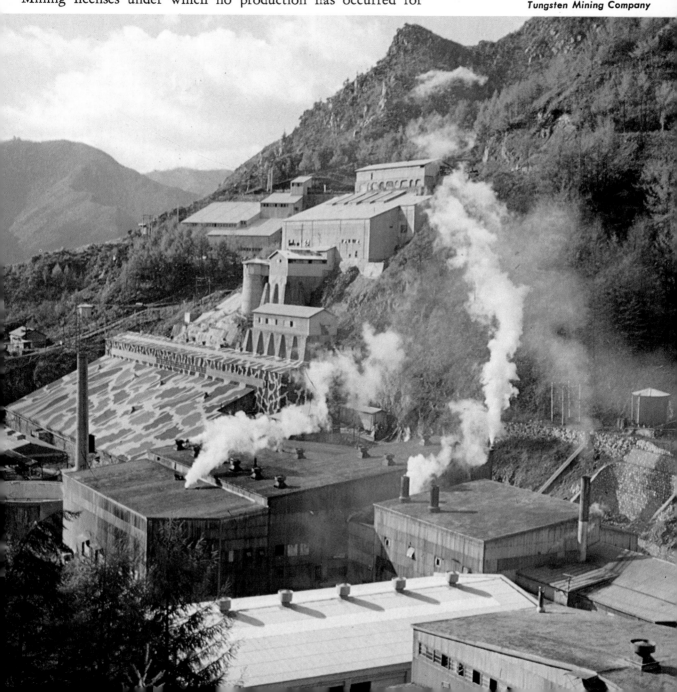

Sangdong Mine of Korea Tungsten Mining Company

Production of Major Minerals

	Concentrate		Unit	1962	1966	1971	1973
Gold	Au	99.9%	tons	3.3	1.9	0.9	0.5
Silver	Ag	"	"	12.8	15.5	48.0	46.4
Copper Ore	Cu	6 %	thousand tons	10.7	21.1	29.6	38.7
Lead Ore	Pb	50 %	"	2.8	13.9	33.1	25.7
Zinc Ore	Zn	50 %	"	0.9	23.4	56.3	96.3
Iron Ore	Fe	56 %	"	470.7	789.4	503.6	595.4
Tungsten Ore	WO_3	70 %	"	5.8	3.7	3.7	3.9
Graphite	FC	75 %	"	185.1	130.9	72.5	43.6
Pyrophyllite	SK#	32	"	18.1	54.7	142.3	304.8
Talc			"	28.4	53.6	70.1	113.1
Kaolin	SK#	34	"	38.2	112.3	191.2	377.3
Limestone	CaO	50 %	"	1,259.0	2,926.0	10,617.0	12,903.0

Mineral Exports and Imports

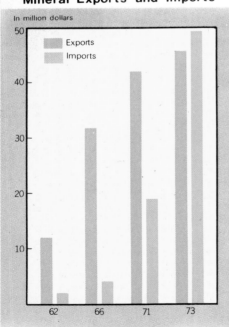

In million dollars

Exports
Imports

three years are cancelled and reissued to a third person.

In 1973, the development-oriented mine licensing system was introduced and has been put into effect. This system was originated to provide that mines be efficiently developed.

The main rule of the system is that if mines remain undeveloped in spite of promising conditions, the holder of the mining license will be instructed to develop them, and unless the holder follows the instruction, then a third person capable of doing so will be authorized to undertake development. It is expected that the new system will be much more effective than the idle mine licensing readjustment system which was put into operation previously. In addition to these measures, the government is now preparing an act which stipulates that inefficient small-size mine lots should be consolidated to optimum size.

The increased demand for mineral products arising chiefly from industrialization and the government's mining promotion measures account for the sharp expansion of mineral production. Especially lead, zinc, copper and silver ores have been vastly developed, whereas output of tungsten ore has remained constant, mainly due to production adjustments in consideration of international tungsten prices. The production performance of nonmetallic mineral products such as talc, pyrophyllite, kaolin and limestone has risen notably as well.

Until the middle of 1960's, about 60 per cent of total mineral production was exported and only 40 per cent was taken up by demand at home. However, domestic demand started to rise from the late 1960's due primarily to the expansion of iron refining facilities in tandem with the development of refining facilities and ceramics. The share of exports in total production thus fell to 44 per cent in 1973. Mining should perhaps no longer be regarded as an export industry, since it provides raw materials for domestic industries, and far more than half the production serves as raw materials for domestically-produced manufactured products.

During 1973, export volume of Korean mineral products recorded 46 million dollars while imports marked 50 million dollars.

The figures indicate that imports are slightly in excess of exports. The export amount of tungsten totaled 12.5 million dollars, which accounted for 27 per cent of total mineral exports. In addition, there are a handful of other mineral products considered as promising export items, namely, zinc, talc, kaolin, and silica sand.

Some 15.6 million dollars worth of asbestos was imported, which accounts for 32 per cent of total mineral imports. Other major imported minerals are copper, iron and phosphate ores.

Yeonhwa Zinc Mine

UTILIZATION OF LAND AND EXPANSION OF INFRASTRUCTURE

Yeongdong expressway construction
(Daegwanryeong)

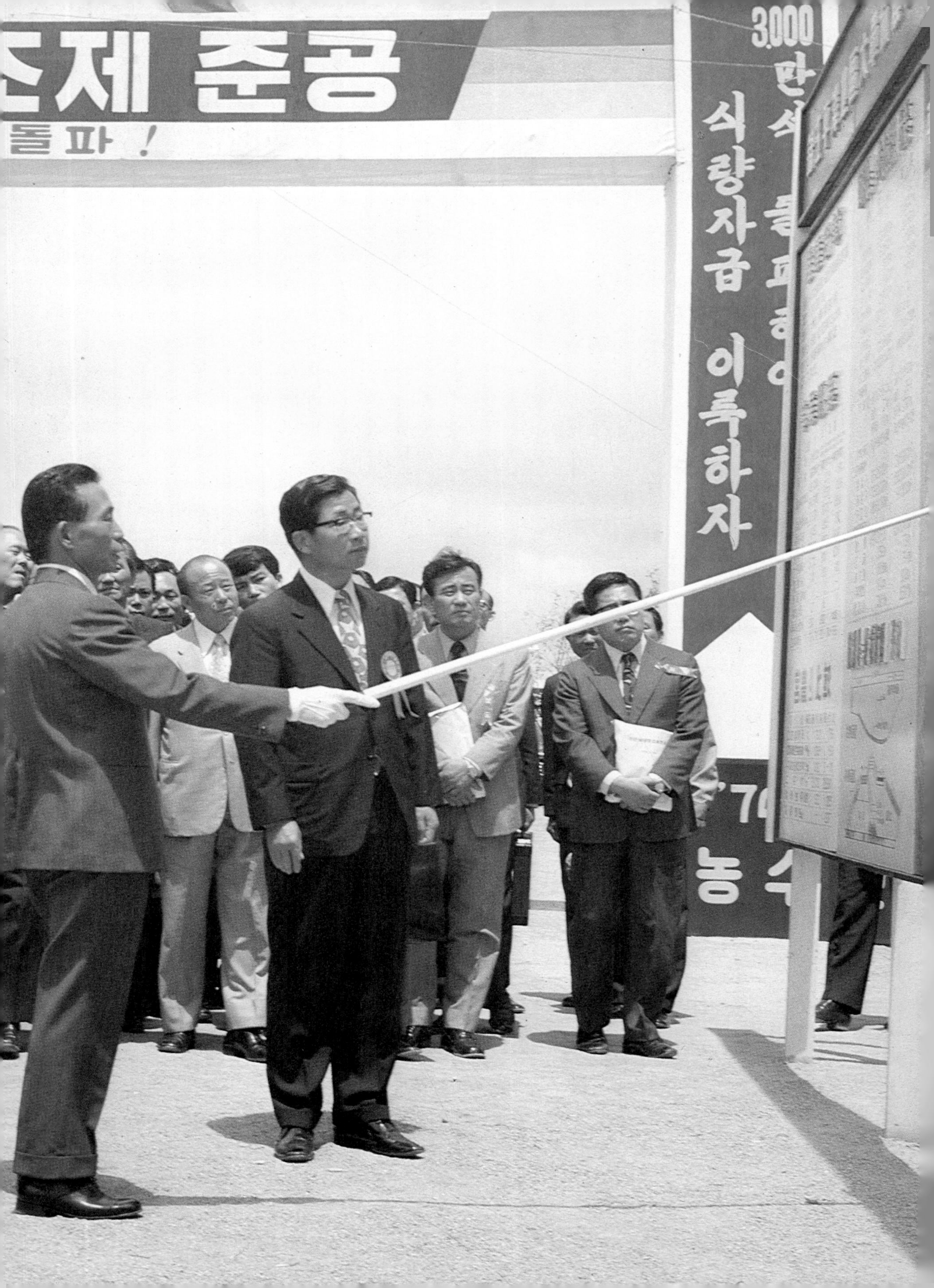

조제 준공
돌파 !
3,000
식량자급 이룩하자
'76
농

The Korean peninsula is approximately 1,000 kilometers in total north-south length. It has an area of 220,000 square kilometers, and a total of some 3,000 offshore islands. Korea had a population of 48 million (including the northern half of the country) and population density of 208 persons per square kilometer as of the end of 1973. After the national territorial partition along the 38th parallel in 1945, south Korea held two-thirds of the total population in an area of 98,000 square kilometers; thereby, the population density per square kilometer reached over 334 in 1973.

In a country where land is small in area and natural resources scarce, the best way to overcome such a restriction is to make the best use of the land. Since many new factories and industrial estates have been constructed, the Korean peninsula has seen a great transformation. This was a natural result of economic development, but some kind of rational planning was necessary for more efficient utilization of national land. It was only at the beginning of the 1960's when a comprehensive and concrete design for national land development was set forth.

After the Military Revolution in May 1961, the government initiated a series of land surveys in some specific areas, and the Law on Integrated National Land Development was enacted in 1963. The basic plan for land development in six specific areas — Seoul, Incheon, Ulsan, Taebaeg Mountains, Jeju and Asan Bay — was established. After reviewing the land development plans carefully, the government finalized the plan in 1971 and made a blueprint for the nationwide development which would be implemented by 1980. Under this plan the national land was divided into four main areas according to the basins of major rivers, and further divided into eight areas according to administrative districts. The ultimate goal of the plan is to establish a foundation for effective utilization of national land, development of physical resources, and preservation of natural environment. To achieve the goal, the government divided the national land into six areas by role in economic function: agriculture, forestry, industry, urban areas, cultural assets and continental shelf. Upon this foundation the government established and implemented construction of heavy chemical industrial estates, overall development plans for four major rivers, and enlargement of highway transportation.

In 1972 the government enacted the Law on Management of National Land, and restricted free utilization of private land, aiming at more efficient utilization of national land, announcing a basic land price pattern to share equally the profits accruing from land development. The government also provided the legal foundation for a water resources development plan and heavy chemical industrial estates through the enactment of Law on Promotion of Industrial Estates in 1973.

Before launching the overall development plan, the government had already made every endeavor for the intensive development of large-scale industrial estates at Ulsan, Pohang, and elsewhere, con-

Preparation for the National Land Development Plan

Construction of tidal basin of Incheon Port

struction of a superhighway linking Seoul and Busan, construction of a nationwide network of highways and railroads, electrification of industrial railroads, and large-scale expansion of harbor facilities.

A nationwide rearrangement of urban areas was envisaged to decentralize densely populated urban areas resulting from industrialization, and efforts were made to expand communication facilities. Since 1960 the appearance of the Korean peninsula has been changed with unprecedented rapidity with the construction of large-scale water resources development projects such as the Soyang Dam.

Construction of Industrial Estates

The government has devoted itself to the construction of industrial estates since the early 1960's in an effort to curtail the cost of production and strengthen international competitiveness by increasing external economies resulting from the common use of facilities. The Export Industrial Estates Assistance Law was enacted in 1964, and the first such estate encompassing 462,800 square meters was completed in Guro Dong, Seoul. The estate has since been enlarged in scale and remarkably good results have been obtained.

Thus the government continued to construct further estates, including an export estate in the Seoul-Incheon corridor, a petrochemical estate at Ulsan in 1969, and the Gumi Industrial Estate. In 1970, a free export zone was established in Masan. Consequently the number of industrial estates increased from one of 462,800 square meters in 1964 to 27, with a total of 4,958,700 square meters and the number of tenant firms exceeds 1,200.

As the scale of industrial estates became larger, their character diversified. A free export zone was established in Iri after the one at Masan, and the number of export industrial estates increased from one (Korea Export Industrial Estate) to six in the Seoul-Incheon corridor. The Gumi Industrial Estate, the largest in Korea, is the electronics industry estate. Besides these, there are many special industrial complexes by industry: petrochemical industrial complex in Ulsan, iron and steel-related industrial complex in Pohang, and eleven complexes in Daegu, Daejeon, Jeonju, Gwangju, Seongnam and elsewhere, constructed by local authority. There are also three private industrial complexes. At present the Changweon Machinery Industrial Estate and Yeocheon Chemical Industrial Estate are under construction.

The availability of suitable land and facilities has increased investment by tenant factories sharply, and foreign investment, inducing foreign capital and technical knowhow, has increased conspicuously too. As of 1974 the number of tenant firms in the major industrial estates reached 1,211, of which 823 factories were in full operation and 178 under construction.

The compounded effects of the industrial estates have been reflected in great increases in exports and employment. Exports in 1973 by the Masan Free Export Zone, Korea Export Industrial Estate, Gumi Industrial Estate and local industrial complexes amounted to 496 million dollars, thus constituting 15 per cent of the total export of 3.2 billion dollars in the same year, and contributing to employment by creating about 130,000 jobs.

Such remarkable results are not only attributable to the tenant firms' efforts, but also to the fact that industrial estates provide all social overhead services such as roads, harbors, stevedoring, electricity, and water supply for industrial use. Also customs offices, banks and post offices are located on the estates to provide convenient services for tenant firms.

Location of Industrial Estates

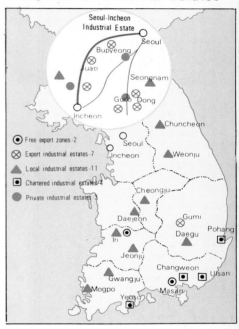

219

Construction of Yeocheon
Industrial Estate

Present Status of Industrial Estates

Division	Constructed Area thousand m²	Tenant Firms	Operating Firms	Period of Construction
Free Export Zones (2)	1,864	112	96	
Masan	942	111	96	70~73
Iri	922	1		73~74
Korea Export Industrial Complexes (6)	3,732	300	235	64~74
Gumi Industrial Estate	10,528	81	24	69~73
Local Industrial Estates (11)	9,180	510	335	67~73
Private Industrial Estates (3)	1,035	150	106	68~70
Pohang Iron & Steel Industrial Estate	4,010	35	17	70~74
Ulsan Petrochemical Industrial Estate	3,355	10	10	68~69
Changweon Machinery Industrial Estate	3,693 (12,562)	13	—	73~74
Yeocheon Chemical Industrial Estate	2,314 (4,264)	—	—	74~75
Total (27)	39,711 (50,529)	1,211	823	

Note: Figures in parentheses are planned construction areas.

The Korea Export Industrial Complex was established to strengthen the foundation of export industries and thereby contribute to export promotion and industrial development. Since 1965, when the construction of industrial complexes began, six industrial complexes encompassing 3,732,200 square meters have been built.

As of 1974, 235 factories had been built in these six complexes and 54 were under construction. These firms receive favors of bonded area and are privileged to sell 30 per cent of their products in domestic markets.

Export-Oriented Industrial Complexes

Masan free export zone

The free export zones were established by the Law on Establishment of Free Export Zones in an effort to promote exports, improve technical skills, and increase employment by inducing foreign capital.

The entire zone is bonded so that enterprises may import necessary raw materials tax-free for reexport purposes. Besides this privilege, they could enjoy further preferential treatment in the application of laws.

The Masan Free Export Zone, the pioneer one in Korea, was constructed on an area of 942,200 square meters. Standardized factories with 69,400 square meters of total floor space were built, and thereby the inducement of foreign enterprises was accelerated. As of 1974, 111 firms were located here, of which 96 firms were in operation.

In 1973, the second free export zone was established in Iri, Jeonbug Province. The highway linking Iri and Gunsan harbor will be completed by 1975 in an attempt to increase the transportation capacity for exports and imports for this complex, and construction of the harbor at Gunsan is well under way to increase stevedoring capacity.

Free Export Zone

Ulsan Industrial Estate

Ulsan, as a coastal industrial estate, is conveniently located. The plan for the development of the area began in the early 1960's, and development moved into full swing from 1966, when the area was designated as a specific development district. During the decade 1964–73, 18,181,900 square meters of land was prepared, and a harbor with berthing capacity for 40,000 ton vessels and 1,440,000 tons of stevedoring capability was developed. Basic infrastructure such as a highway linking Ulsan and Eonyang was constructed and additional water facilities for industrial use will be completed by 1976.

Sixteen large-scale factories are now in operation and many new factories will be built in accordance with the expansion plan for petrochemicals. The Ulsan Industrial Estate has become the center of heavy industry such as oil refining, fertilizer, petrochemicals, shipbuilding, automobiles and aluminum smelting.

Ulsan petrochemical industrial estate

The government secured an area of 11,702.5 square meters at Yeong-il County, Gyeongbug Province for the construction of an integrated steel mill and began construction of support facilities in 1968. The first stage of work was completed in 1972 with a total investment of 11.5 billion won. The estate has a berthing capaciy for 50,000 ton vessels and stevedoring capability for 1,548,000 tons; 100,000 tons of industrial water can be supplied daily.

The Pohang Iron and Steel Company, with an annual production capacity of 1,030,000 tons, and its subcontract firms are now operating in the estate. The company plans to expand its capacity to 2.6 million tons and harbor facilities will be expanded to enable 80,000 ton vessels to berth.

Pohang Industrial Estate

Gumi industrial estate

The Gumi Industrial Estate is a large-scale integrated industrial estate composed of electronic plants and other industries, encompassing 10,528,900 square meters. It is adjacent to the Seoul-Busan Highway, and the Nagdong River nearby supplies enough water for industrial use.

Eighty-one companies will occupy the estate, of which 24 are now in operation and 30 are under construction. The estate was designated by the government as an industrial development area in August 1973, and privileges for exemptions from various taxes were given to tenant firms in accordance with the Law on Tax Exemption. The estate has contributed greatly to the development of export industries such as electronics.

Gumi Industrial Estate

Construction of Multipurpose Dams

Average annual rainfall amounts to about 1,000–1,200 millimeters. There is little precipitation except during the rainy season, in June, July and August. Therefore, the supply of water differs greatly according to weather conditions; rivers flood in the rainy season, but dry up in the dry season, and this makes generation of hydroelectric power and supply of water for industrial use difficult.

Appropriate management and development of water resources

Soyang Dam

has great significance as a means of preventing floods and droughts, and leading to the development of energy and a higher yield of crops.

But before 1961, development of water resources, including irrigation, was at an early stage. The utilization of water was confined to the drawing of natural waters from rivers or underground.

225

There were no systematic flood control programs in most rivers, and even minor floods brought great losses.

The demand for industrial and agricultural water has sharply increased since 1962, due mainly to the full-scale drive for economic development and the increase in use of water for daily living, resulting from the improvement of living standards. Because of these increases, natural water resources could not fully meet demand and shortage of water in dry seasons was a common occurrence.

Total precipitation amounting to 114 billion tons was sufficient, but with 51 billion tons vaporized and 63 billion tons going into rivers, there remained only 12.8 per cent (8.1 billion tons) for use. To find a way out of this situation in which there was enough precipitation but it could not be utilized fully, the government began to develop water resources at the beginning of the 1970's.

Chuncheon Dam

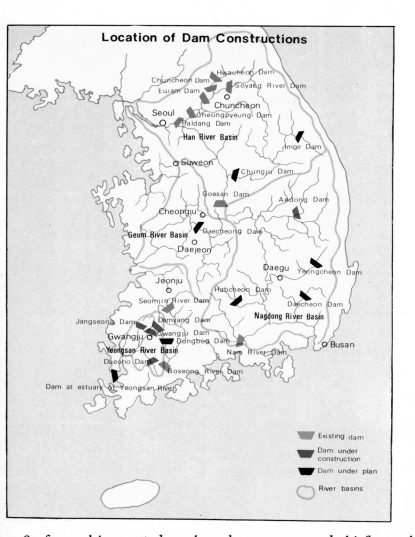

Location of Dam Constructions

Hwacheon Dam
Chuncheon Dam
Euiam Dam
Soyang River Dam
Chuncheon
Seoul
Cheongpyeung Dam
Paldang Dam
Han River Basin
Imge Dam
Suweon
Chungju Dam
Goesan Dam
Andong Dam
Cheongju
Daecheong Dam
Geum River Basin
Daejeon
Daegu
Yeongcheon Dam
Jeonju
Habcheon Dam
Seomjin River Dam
Daecheon Dam
Jangseong Dam
Damyang Dam
Nagdong River Basin
Gwangju
Gwangju Dam
Dongbog Dam
Yeongsan River Basin
Nam River Dam
Busan
Daeoho Dam
Boseong River Dam
Dam at estuary of Yeongsan River

Existing dam
Dam under construction
Dam under plan
River basins

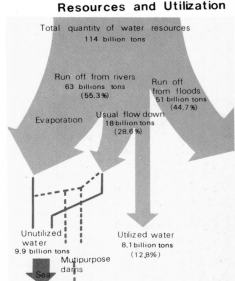

Present Status of Water Resources and Utilization

Total quantity of water resources
114 billion tons

Run off from rivers
63 billions tons
(55.3%)

Run off from floods
51 billion tons
(44.7%)

Evaporation

Usual flow down
18 billion tons
(28.6%)

Unutilized water
9.9 billion tons

Utilized water
8.1 billion tons
(12.8%)

Sea

Multipurpose dams

power generation

Water for agricultural use
Water for industrial use
Water for daily life

High utilization of water

Development of Water Resources

So far multipurpose dams have been constructed chiefly on the Han River, which runs through the Seoul metropolitan area and which has many places suitable for generation of hydroelectric power. During Japanese rule, great emphasis was given to the construction of hydroelectric power plants, but they were constructed mainly in the northern part of Korea because of its favorable geographical situation. In South Korea only three dams were built: the Hwacheon and Cheongpyeong Dams on the Han River and the Boseong Dam on the Boseong River. Even after the liberation in 1945, no multipurpose dams were built except for the Goesan Dam on the Han. The construction of multipurpose dams has increased with the implementation of the economic development plans since the 1960's.

The Chuncheon Dam and Seomjin River Dam were completed in 1965, and Euiam Dam in 1967. The Nam River Dam was completed in the early 1970's after a long period of work. The Chuncheon and Euiam Dams are mainly for power generation, but the Seomjin River Dam, Nam River Dam and the newly-completed Soyang Dam are multipurpose dams.

227

Soyang Multipurpose Dam

The Soyang Dam, the largest earth embankment dam in Korea, impounds the Soyang River at a spot 13 kilometers northeast of Chuncheon. It has a height of 123 meters, a breadth of 530 meters and, total pondage of 2.9 billion cubic meters. The dam was completed in 1973 after six years of construction work. The dam meets the increasing demand for water in the Seoul-Chuncheon metropolitan areas. It also has one of the biggest hydroelectric power generation capacities: 200,000 kilowatts.

The dam contributes to a stable supply of power for domestic consumption and prevention of damage from floods. It is capable of lowering the water level of the Han River at the Han River bridge in Seoul by 70 centimeters as it has the capacity to hold back reserve 500 million cubic meters of flood water.

It can also meet the demand for water in metropolitan areas by supplying 1.2 billion tons a year. Water reserved in time of flood is used to generate power in plants such as Euiam, Cheongpyeong and Paldang power plants on the lower reaches of the river. Therefore, it has the same effect as constructing an additional power-generation plant with a capacity of 34,000 kilowatts.

Seomjin Dam

Seomjin Multipurpose Dam

The Seomjin Dam is located on the upper Seomjin River, in Jeonbug Province. It is made of concrete and has a height of 64 meters, a breadth of 344 meters, and total pondage of 466 million tons. The construction was begun in August, 1961 and completed in December, 1965. The dam supplies water for irrigation to 30,000 hectares of the Dongjin River Plain in time of drought and irrigates the Honam Plain by discharging stored waters to the Dongjin Plain through 6,215 meters of tunnel. It has a generating capacity of 31,000 kilowatts.

Nam River Dam

Construction of the Nam River Dam and Other Multipurpose Dams

The Nam River Dam is located at Jinju City on the upper reaches of the Nam River, a tributary of the Nagdong River. The dam is made of earth, and has a height of 21 meters, a breadth of 975 meters, and total pondage of 136 million tons. The construction of the dam was begun in March, 1962 and was completed in October, 1969. The dam supplies water for various purposes to the Nam River Basin, and prevents damage from salinity on the Gimhae Plain. The Nagdong River is saved from flood by dint of a diversionary canal which has a total length of 11 kilometers and links with Sacheon Bay. The dam also has the capacity of 12,000 kilowatts of power generation.

Construction of the Andong Multipurpose Dam was begun in 1971 and will be completed in 1976. Upon successful completion of the dam, which has a height of 73 meters and total pondage of 1.2 billion cubic meters, it will be equipped with power generating and water pumping double purpose facilities, the first of its kind in Korea, and will have a capacity of 90,000 kilowatts.

Construction of four dams of Jangseong, Damyang, Daecho and Gwangju in the Yeongsan River Basin was begun in 1973 and is now under way. Upon successful completion of these dams, they will contribute to supply of water for agricultural use and to flood control in the Yeongsan River Basin.

In addition, by the early 1980's the government plans to complete construction of the Chungju and Imge Dams on the Han River, Habcheon, Yeongcheon and Daecheon Dams on the Nagdong River, the Daecheong Dams on the Geum River and the Dongbog Dams on the Seomjin River.

Present Status of Dam Construction

Division	Name of Dam	Construction Period	Location		Height (m)	Length (m)	Pondage (million m³)	Effect Power-generation (thousand kw)	Water-supply (million m³)	Flood Control (million m³)
Han River Basin										
(Constructed)	Hwacheon	39~44	Gang-weon, Hwacheon, Gandong		78	435	1,018	108		
"	Chuncheon	61~65	Gang-weon, Chunseong, Sinbug		40	453	150	57		
"	Cheong-pyeong	39~43	Gyeong-gi, Ga-pyeong, Oeseo		31	407	185	79		
"	Goesan	52~57	Chungbug, Goesan. Chilseong		29	171	15	2		
"	Euiam	62~67	Gang-weon, Chunseong, Sindong		23	224	80	45		
"	Paldang	66~73	Gyeong-gi, Yangju. Dongbu		32	500	244	80		
"	Soyang River	67~73	Gang-weon, Chunseong, Sinbug		123	530	2,900	200	1,213	350
(Planned)	Imge	77~80	Gang-weon. Jeongseon, Imge		90	300	428	150	287	100
"	Chungju	77~81	Chungbug, Jungweon		89	390	3,080	210	2,002	600
Nagdong River Basin										
(Constructed)	Nam River	62~69	Gyeongnam, Jinyang, Naedong		21	975	136	12	300	43
(Under-construction)	Andong	71~76	Gyeongbug, Andong, Waryong		73	525	1,243	90	926	110
(Planned)	Habcheon	76~80	Gyeongnam, Hab-cheon, Daebyeong		93	464	1,070	80	450	80
"	Yeongcheon	74~76	Gyengbug, Yeong-cheon		42		90		90	10
"	Daecheon	78~81	Gyeongbug, Chyeongdo		45		123	5	124	10
Geum River Basin										
(Planned)	Daecheong	75~79	Chungnam, Daedeog		71	560	1,490	90	865	200
Yeongsan River Basin										
(Under-construction)	Jangseong	73~76	Jeonnam, Jangseong		36	613	90		85	6
"	Damyang	73~76	"	Damyang	46	317	67		65	4
"	Daecho	73~76	"	Naju	31	496	91		88	6
"	Gwangju	74~76	"	Damyang	25	505	17		15	
(Planned)	River banks	76~81	"	Mogpo	17	4,300	253		253	188
Seomjin River Basin										
(Constructed)	Seomjin	61~65	Jeonbug, Imsil, Gangjin		64	344	466	31	150	38
"	Boseong	36~39	Jeonnam, Boseong, Deugnang		12	904	5	3		
(Planned)	Dongbog	77~80	Jeonnam, Hwasun		46	240	126	3	92	15

In 1970 the government drew up a project for the development of four major river basins, including dam construction for agricultural water resources, river improvement for installation of flumes, development of river banks, forestation and water supply.

The four rivers related to the above project are the Han, the Nagdong, the Geum and the Yeongsan. Total area covered by the project comprises 62,762 square kilometers, equivalent to 64 per cent of the total national territory, of which 12,330 square kilometers represents agricultural land, corresponding to 54 per cent of

Comprehensive Development Project for Four Major River Basins

Asan sea-dike construction

Asan sea-dike completed by strong
will and assiduous effort.

From left: Before construction,
final construction of water
interception, and the completed dike-gate

232

total area under cultivation, and 61 per cent of total inhabited area, respectively. These areas may be called the heart of the country.

This project, requiring the investment of over 560 billion won, is unprecedented in its magnitude. The plan includes the construction of 13 multipurpose dams, including the Soyang Dam, river improvement of 2,487 kilometers, improvement of irrigation for 215,000 hectares in 98 selected areas, water supply of 3,140,000 cubic meters to 79 cities, industrial water supply of 1,590,000 cubic meters to nine areas, drainage facilities, and forestation. In line with this mammoth project, the development of Geum River·Pyeongtaeg Area and Yeongsan River Area is being actively expedited.

With the completion of the project in the 1980's, there will be no more suffering from floods, due to flood control of 2.2 billion cubic meters of water every year, and food grain production is expected to increase by 458,000 tons owing to the protection of 1,338 square kilometers of agricultural land, the reclamation of 30 square kilometers of agricultural land, and the improvement of irrigation facilities. In other words, when the development of the four big river areas is completely implemented it will greatly contribute to flood-free and drought-free utilization of land, increased production of food grains, stabilization of farming, and continuous progress of industry with a sufficient, inexpensive supply of water.

The Plan and Effects of Four Major River Basins Development Project

	Scale of Project		Effects of Project	
River improvement	2,487.4km (859 areas)		Protection of agricultural land	1,338km²
			Protection of housing	108,000 houses
			Production increase of food grains	86,475tons
			Formation of agricultural land	30km²
Dam construction	13 dams		Supply of water	7.12 billion m³
			Power generation	1,718,000 kw
			Flood control	1.77 billion m³
Irrigation		98 areas	Production increase of food grains	351,000 tons
Forestation	Erosion control	414km²	Protection of earth and sand efflux	1,352,000 m³/year
	Stream beds	692km	Production of forestry fuel	1,312,000 tons/year
	Afforestation	4,376 km²	Production of lumber	76.6 million m³
Water supply	Water supply facilities	79 cities	Water supply	3.14 million m³/day
Industrial water supply	Water supply facilities	9 areas	Industrial water supply	1.59 million m³/day
Drainage		72 areas	Production increase of food grains	18,000 tons
Development of river banks		1 area	Water supply	300 millon m³

Andong Dam construction

Yeongsan River Basin

The Yeongsan River Basin project involves construction of five multipurpose dams, one estuary embankment, drainage facilities in the Naju-Yeongsan Area, and river improvement of 439 kilometers.

The five multipurpose dams are the Jangseong, Damyang, Daecho, Gwangju and Dongbog Dams. Of these, the first three have been under construction since 1973 and the fourth since 1974. Construction of the Dongbog Dam, which will be capable of supplying water of the Seomjin River to the Yeongsan Area and generating electricity up to 3,000 kilowatts, is to begin in 1977.

The government has drawn up a project to construct 17 meter river banks in the estuary of the Yeongsan River for prevention of damage from brine and water leakage amounting to 300 million cubic meters. After completion of the project, it will contribute to the improvement of irrigation and increased supply of industrial water.

Development of the Geum River, Pyeongtaeg Area and Asan Bay

The Pyeongtaeg Area Comprehensive Development Project to construct sea-dikes in the estuary of Asan and Namyang Bays, 16 water-pumping stations, and waterways of 900 kilometers, has various purposes including facilitating of all-weather agriculture, prevention of flood damage, and extension of land under cultivation.

The government completed the Asan Sea-dike of 2,564 meters and the Namyang Sea-dike of 2,060 meters in May 1974 after a two-and-a-half-year construction period. These two sea-dikes are capable of preventing brine damage to farms in the Pyeongtaeg Area, and with the creation of an artificial fresh-water lake, will contribute to maximum utilization of agricultural water resources. The Asan Sea-dike, connecting Asan in Chungnam Province and Pyeongtaeg in Gyeong-gi Province has the capability of supplying 107 million tons of agricultural water to this area, and controlling floods by way of drainage of up to 5,000 tons of water per second through the dike-gates. Meanwhile, the Namyang Sea-dike is capable of supplying 20 million tons of water for agriculture and coping successfully with floods, and furthermore has made possible newly-developed arable land of 2,000 hectares. In fact, the completion of these two sea-dikes is a splendid victory over nature in light of its scale and the skill required in advanced engineering techniques.

This area is evaluated as the most promising potential site for the second steel mill project for the development of heavy and chemical industry. Ships of 100,000 tons can berth in this area thanks to the deep water in the bay. The capability of supplying abundant industrial water to this area will be augmented after consruction of the Sabgyo Sea-dike.

The development project of the Geum River basin is designed to construct one multipurpose dam, a water way of 583 kilometers, and 18 water-pumping stations so as to supply sufficient agricultural water to the Og-gu · Seocheon Area and contribute to increased production of food grains. The Daecheong Dam, which is expected to be completed by 1979 as a multipurpose dam in this area, will have reservoir capacity of 1.5 billion cubic meters and electric generation capacity of 90,000 kilowatts.

Asan Sea-dike water-gates

Expansion of the Highway System

Growth of Traffic Volume

In the 1960's, the transportation volume of passengers and freight increased markedly along with the high rate of economic growth and consequent change in industrial structure, as well as the increasing tendency of spending leisure time outdoors, caused by rising income levels. The number of passengers transported in 1973 totaled 4 billion, recording a five-fold increase over 679 million in 1961, and the volume of freight transported increased nearly three times, from 31 million tons to 120 million tons during the same period. The volume of passengers increased from 10.1 billion passenger-kilometer (number of passengers multiplied by kilometers transported) in 1961 to 43.7 billion passenger-kilometers in 1973, a 3.3 fold increase, and that of freight from 3.9 billion ton-kilometers (tonnage of freight multiplied by kilometers transported) to 15.9 billion ton-kilometers, a three-fold increase in the same period. These increase rates are much higher than the 2.6 fold increase in actual production of the agriculture-forestry-fishery and the mining-manufacturing sectors and 2.3 fold increase in per capita income in the corresponding period.

In Korea, public roads and coastal marine transportation witnessed little development in the past. During the Japanese occupation, public transportation relied mainly on railroads which had been constructed for the purpose of expediting Japanese invasion of the continent. But in recent times, facilities for public transportation such as roads and marine transportation have been developed and modernized, thus decreasing dependency of the public on railroads. In 1961, railroads accounted for 90.8 per cent of total freight transportation and 53 per cent of total passenger transportation; by 1973, the corresponding rates had decreased to 53.9 per cent and 24.5 per cent, respectively. In case of public roads, composition ratio in freight transportation increased from 8.1 per cent in 1961 to 19.8 per cent in 1973 and in passenger transportation from 45.5 per cent to 73.6 per cent during the same period.

Meanwhile, the share of coastal marine transportation has also been augmented because of the great advantages of bulk transportation, especially for owners of factories located in the coastal areas with better access to imports of foreign raw materials and exports of products, and for coal mines and cement producers in the Taebaeg Mountain Area.

In the near future, it is expected that the volume of transportation will grow more rapidly and the structure of transportation will be significantly modernized as the Korean economy, especially heavy and chemical industry, develops further.

The vicinity of Singal Interchange on Seoul-Busan Highway

Enhancing Transportation Facilities

To meet the increasing need for transporation, the government spared no efforts in accelerating road and highway construction. Building of expressways between Seoul and Busan, with a length of 428 kilometers, and between Seoul and Incheon, with a length of 30 kilometers, were completed in 1970, thus linking the two main ports, Busan and Incheon, with the capital city, and integrating the two major economic districts, the Han River and Nagdong River Areas, into one-day travel times. In 1973, the government completed two additional highway networks, the Honam Highway (260 kilometers) and Namhae Highway (177 kilometers) which pass through the main grain-producing area of Honam and the south-coast industrial region. In 1974, construction of the Yeongdong Highway and Donghae Highway was launched to remedy the delay in economic and social development in the Yeongdong and Donghae Area due to geographical remoteness and to facilitate access to mountainous areas. The government is geared to complete the project in 1975, and has already finished the 104 kilometers

The Highway Construction Plan

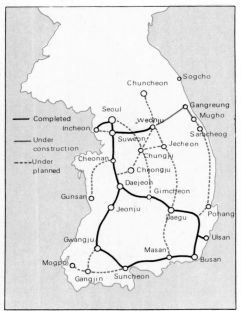

between Sin-gal and Saemal, a substantial part of the highway.

Since 1968, many highways have been constructed by Korean technicians, thus marking a new era in the construction industry and forming a basis for the participation of Korean technicians in the construction of highways abroad. It cannot be ignored that the highways have been constructed at a lower cost and in a shorter time than in other countries. It took only 100 million won to construct each kilometer of the Seoul-Busan Highway, which is equivalent to one-seventh of construction costs of the Tokyo-Nagoya Highway in Japan.
The latter required seven years for completion, while the former took only two and a half years, even though it was longer by 100 kilometers than the latter.

In this regard, the completion of the Seoul-Busan Expressway has provided not only economic benefits but confidence and pride, the conviction that nothing is really impossible, provided one does his best for the achievement of the set goal.

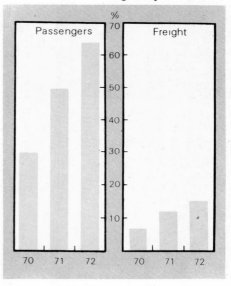

Increase in Highway Traffic

View of Geum River resort along Seoul-Busan Highway

The Impact of Highway Construction

The construction of the highways has had a considerable impact on the socio-cultural and economic aspects in Korea.

Highways have speeded up changes in the structure of transportation. Between 1970 and 1972, the share of highways in total freight transportation increased from 24.7 per cent to 47.5 per cent, and in the total passenger transportation from 8.9 per cent to 21.2 per cent.

In earlier days, highways were used more for passenger transportation than freight transportation. But the role of highways as industrial roads is growing year by year due to increasing reliance on highways for freight transportation.

Highways have the advantage of saving both time and money. From 1970 to 1972, total social benefits derived from the use of highways amounted to 30.5 billion won, an excess of 19.1 billion won over the tolls of 11.4 billion won paid, reflecting 62.7 per cent of the total social benefits returned to the people.

An increase in employment and income in areas adjacent to highways was experienced due to dispersed construction of factories in these areas, the total number of which increased about threefold, from 82 in 1969 to 226 in 1973. The construction of highways thus made a substantial contribution to expansion of production and employment in rural areas adjacent to highways.

Highways also engendered substantial changes in farming. The opening of highways gave an impetus to rural areas, and brought about widened markets and more convenient transportation and

Jinryang collection point
for agricultural products

communications, thereby allowing farmers to initiate profitable farming. Highways also contributed considerably to the efficient distribution of agricultural products by excluding middlemen, shortening the distribution channels of agricultural products, and reducing the distribution profit margin of agricultural products.

Highways also had a positive effect on sightseeing and international balance of payments. Exports by firms located near highways constituted 81.8 per cent of total exports of industrial products. This was partly due to the building of highways serving existing export industries, and partly to the inducement of new export industries to areas adjacent to highways, with better access to cheaper land and labor markets.

Finally, by shortening travel time, highways narrowed the gap between urban and rural areas, and supported the Saemaul Undong (New Community Movement) which places emphasis on the strengthening of social and cultural identification.

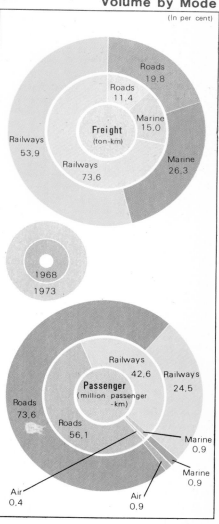

Change in Traffic
Volume by Mode
(In per cent)

Highway Utilization by Type of Vehicle
(In per cent)

	1 9 7 0	1 9 7 1	1 9 7 2
Passenger cars	52.7	49.7	41.3
Trucks	34.8	37.3	42.3
Buses	12.5	13.0	16.4
Total	100.0	100.0	100.0

National Road Paving Program

If highways are likened to main arteries of the human body, national and local roads may be compared to capillary blood vessels which should be mutually developed along with the former.

The government has paved a total of 1,193 kilometers of roads, 488 kilometers during the First Five-Year Economic Development Plan, and 705 kilometers during the Second Plan period, including the main national roads between Seoul-Busan, Seoul-Incheon, Seoul-Chuncheon, Jeonju-Gunsan, Busan-Masan, and Seoul-Munsan. During the Third Five-Year Plan period, the government paved 328 kilometers of main roads including Jeonju-Namweon in 1972 and 288 kilometers including Cheonan-Janghang in 1973.

Since 1962, the additional pavement and improvement of roads reached 1,809 kilometers, and accordingly the ratio of paved roads rose from 15 per cent in 1962 to 35 per cent in 1973. Together with the construction of highways, the government has placed high priority on the paving of national roads for citizens' convenience and formulated a policy to pave completely all national roads by 1981.

National Roads and Pavement Ratios

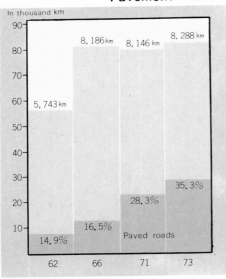

Since more than 60 per cent of the Korean railways suffered destruction during the Korean War, reconstruction of the railways was too slow to meet effectively the growing demand for railway transportation. However, since the beginning of the 1960's, measures for the development of railways, such as construction and electrification of industrial lines, have been implemented to promote the development of resources and the formation of industrial sites.

The construction of new railroads of 469 kilometers, the electrification of 334 kilometers of industrial and metropolitan lines, use of heavier tracks, replacement of ties, motor cars, acquisition of additional lightening of weight of passenger and freight cars and improvement of signal facilities have been pursued as means of modernizing railways.

The implementation of the Taebaeg Comprehensive Development Project and the remarkable success in constructing 375 kilometers of industrial lines consisting of the Yeongdong Line (199 kilometers), Taebaeg Line (103 kilometers), Jeongseon Line (39 kilometers) and Mungyeong Line (34 kilometers), have greatly contributed to the development of underground resources such as coal, cement, graphite and tungsten in these areas. In October, 1973, one

Railroad Modernization

Construction of Industrial Railways

Taebaeg electric railway

more industrial railway network, the Gohan Line of 15 kilometers, penetrating the 855 meter-high Taebaeg Mountains and linking the Yeongdong and Yeongseo Districts was completed.

In view of the increasing demand for bulk transportation of products of large-scale plants constructed in various areas, the government constructed 40 kilometers of industrial estates and harbors during the 1968–1974 period. Include the Honam Oil Refinery Siding, Pohang Iron and Steel Mill Siding, Petrochemical Siding, and Incheon Port Line.

Meanwhile, the industrial Jung-ang Line, Taebaeg Line and Yeongdong Line had been instrumental in the development of the Taebaeg and Yeongdong areas, transporting around 80 per cent of total nation-wide freight. Since these lines were constructed in mountainous regions, there were many difficulties, such as abrupt curves, slopes, tunnels and bridges, were encountered. Reinforcement of transportation in these areas for the development of industry and energy resources emerged as a most urgent problem.

In light of this, the government began to construct the Jung-ang Electric Railway in May, 1968, and completed the 155 kilometer line between Cheongryangri and Jecheon in June, 1973. The Taebaeg Electric Railway, 80 kilometers between Jecheon and Gohan, has also been completed, thus electrifing the most important 235 kilometer route—Seoul-Jecheon-Gohan. During the 1960's, construction of the Gyeongjeon, Gyeongbug and Chungbug Lateral Lines also contributed to the formation of regional economic spheres and the development of industries.

To relieve the congestion of urban traffic, in April 1971 the government launched a program to electrify metropolitan railways as a means of providing mass transportation.

Finally opened on August 15, 1974, the network includes 38.9 kilometers between Seoul and Incheon, 41.5 kilometers between Seoul and Suweon (part of the Gyeongbu Line), and 5.6 kilometers between Cheongryangri and Seongbug, linking them with the newly-constructed Seoul Subway Line.

The construction of the metropolitan subway between Seoul central station and Cheongryangri, a length of 10.3 kilometers, serves not only as a means of mass transportation but for dispersing the congested population of the city, developing satellite cities, and reducing traffic pollution.

Electrification of Railways in the Seoul Area

Improvement of Facilities and Domestic Production

Railway operations are in the process of being modernized. Steam locomotives have been replaced by diesels and electric locomotives, and electric railcars have come into use for short-distance transportation. The number of diesel locomotives increased from 95 in 1961 to 336 in 1974, while steam locomotives decreased from 356 to 93 in the same period. Electric locomotives and electric railcars have been in operation since 1973; at present, the number of electric locomotives and electric railcars totals 66 and 126, respectively.

Until 1961, the number of old-fashioned cars, heavier in weight and poorly equipped, was 1,303. But since 1962, domestically manufactured passenger cars, which are lighter by 10–20 tons than the old ones, have been produced. Since June, 1969, modernized passenger cars with air-conditioners and heaters have been imported, and at present the number in use is 65, out of the total of

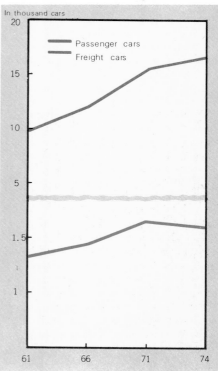

Number of Rolling Stock

In thousand cars

Passenger cars
Freight cars

1,577 passenger cars.

Box cars and gondolas were the only freight cars available in the past, but nowadays specialized freight cars such as tank cars, refrigerator cars, flat cars and gravel cars have been added. In 1974, the freight cars in use numbered 16,269, of which 4,256 were special freight cars, showing an increase of 6,599 cars over the level of 1961. Especially, the container transport line between Seoul and Busan, which came into operation in 1972, and the mechanization of stevedoring contributed greatly to epoch-making progress in safer and faster transportation. At present, there are 100 container cars in Korea.

Meanwhile, since 1959 the government has striven to boost domestic production of passenger and freight cars in order to meet the sharply rising demand. Accordingly, 839 passenger cars and 3,608 freight cars were produced in Korea from 1959 to 1971, and leading manufacturers of passenger and freight cars shipped 2,330 freight cars abroad.

Expansion of Harbor Facilities

Korea is surrounded by sea on three sides and has 1,350 ports along 13,200 kilometers of coastline, or approximately one port for every 10 kilometers of coastline. Most are fishery harbors and 42 ports are under administration of the central government.

Parallel with the recent rapid increase of international trade, great expansion of the facilities of large harbors has been required. Augmented facilities of harbors adjacent to coastal industrial complexes where new industrial facilities are concentrated, have been urgently required as economic development progresses.

The government has expanded the facilities of Busan and Incheon ports under the Harbor Modernization Plan. In line with the construction of coastal industrial complexes, Ulsan, Pohang, Yeosu and Masan ports have been expanded and developed into industrial ports. Furthermore, the government has assisted indus-

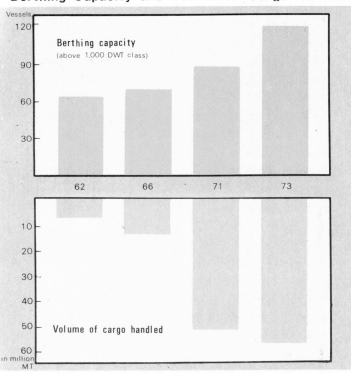

Berthing Capacity and Volume of Cargo Handled

Vessels

Berthing capacity
(above 1,000 DWT class)

62   66   71   73

Volume of cargo handled

in million MT

Incheon Port before construction of tidal basin

trial development in Mt. Taebaeg Area by expanding the facilities of Bugpyeong, Mugho and Samcheog ports. In the ten-year span, 1962–1971, the government invested 38 billion won for the development of harbor facilities, and is scheduled to make an additional investment of 70.8 billion won during the Third Five-Year Economic Development Plan. Total berthing capacity stood at only 63 vessels above 1,000 dead-weight tons in 1962. But due to government efforts to expand port facilities, the berthing capacity doubled, reaching 118 vessels in 1973. Incheon and Pohang were developed into ports large enough to accommodate vessels of the 50,000 dead-weight ton class. Under the government's harbor facilities modernization plan, stevedoring capability more than tripled, from 9,720,000 tons in 1962 to 27,930,000 tons in 1973.

Tidal basin at Incheon Port

Port of Busan

The port of Busan, the largest port in Korea, was opened for ocean trade in 1876. In spite of the important role of Busan, its annual stevedoring capability stood at the low level of 2.1 million tons until 1960. But thanks to the expansion of the port and cargo handling facilities in the 1960's, in line with the rapid growth of imports and exports, the total volume of cargo handled in 1973 was 13.44 million tons, which constitutes 40 per cent of the total volume of cargo handled at the 17 first-class Korean ports that year.

The stevedoring capability of Busan Port increased from 3,950 thousand tons in 1962 to 6,600 thousand tons in 1973, due partly to expansion of container facilities.

In June 1973, the government launched the Port Development Project estimated to cost 52.4 billion won, including a loan of 80 million dollars from IBRD. With completion of this project by 1978, the stevedoring capability will be increased to 13 million tons.

Busan Port

Tidal Basin at Incheon Port

In 1883 the port of Incheon, called Jemulpo at that time, was opened for ocean trade. However, mainly due to the unparalleled tidal range in the Incheon area, it was impossible for large vessels to berth directly at piers, and the only option was to unload cargo on lighters.

Because of this handicap a considerable portion of cargo headed for Seoul and the central districts was unloaded at the port of Busan and then transshiped by road or rail. Thus development of Incheon as a port for the capital and the central industrial region emerged as a most urgent problem to be solved.

To tackle this problem in April 1966 the government launched a massive tidal basin construction project, which was finally completed in May 1974.

This basin, the first in the Orient, is equipped with new, modern large locks and gates, the sixth largest in the world.

Before the construction of this basin, Incheon was able only to accommodate three vessels of 4,500 dead-weight ton class and four vessels of 2,000 dead-weight ton class. With the completion of the basin, the port can hold 25 vessels, including those of 50,000 dead-weight ton class, berthing simultaneously. Also, stevedoring capability has been considerably increased, from 1,420,000 tons to 6,270,000 tons.

Other Industrial Ports

Ulsan Port: Along with construction of the Ulsan Industrial Complex for oil refining, fertilizer and petrochemicals, the government started a project to expand the facilities of Ulsan Port. With the completion of the first stage of the project in 1972, Ulsan Port was transformed into a large industrial harbor whose stevedoring capability stands at 10,722,000 tons for oil and 2,012,000 tons for freight per year, allowing a vessels of 140,000 dead-weight ton class to berth. The volume of cargo handled at the Ulsan Port, which was only a fishery harbor in 1961, recorded 2,734,000 tons in 1973, second only to Busan. In the future this port is foreseen to expand further, keeping pace with expansion of the Ulsan Industrial Complex.

Pohang Port: The government started construction of the Pohang Iron and Steel Mill in April 1968 and of new port facilities in May 1968. After completion of the new harbor in 1973, eight large vessels, including those of 50,000 dead-weight ton class, can berth in this port at the same time. This port is expected to keep on expanding in light of the projected increase in production capacity of the Pohang Iron and Steel Mill, from 1.03 million tons to 2.6 million tons per year.

Mugho Port: The ports of Mugho, Samcheog and Bugpyeong are in character more like one integrated port rather than three separate ports inasmuch as they are strung out only 8 kilometers apart. Situated in the central part of Korea's east coast, these ports play important roles as industrial harbors for the Mt. Taebaeg Region, with its large deposits of coal and iron ore, and have been briskly developed thanks to the growth of the cement industry and increasing marine transportation of anthracite.

During the First and Second Five-Year Economic Development Plan periods, the government carried out a series of measures at Mugho, including improvement of the breakwaters and quays, and expansion of the cement and anthracite transportation facilities, resulting in an increase of berthing capacity to six vessels, including two of 10,000 dead-weight ton class, at one time, and an increase in stevedoring capability from 1.2 million tons in 1961 to 3.25 million tons in 1973. In the future, the government plans to expand facilities of this port with investments equivalent to 4.4 billion won, including a loan from IBRD, to meet the increased demand for faster transportation of resources.

Since Mugho is unable to cope with the increasing demand for transportation through expansion, the government launched a Bugpyeong Port Development Plan in 1974. This port will be changed into a modern harbor with an annual stevedoring capability of 10 million tons and a berthing capacity of seven vessels, including one of 20,000 dead-weight ton class, by the time this plan is completed in 1977. At the moment, the role of Samcheog Port is of less importance. However, the need for development of this port will grow in the near future.

Yeosu Port: Yeosu port has been developing as an industrial har-

Pier No. 2, Ulsan Port

bor since the construction of the Honam Oil Refinery. The expansion of harbor facilities will keep pace with the construction of the petro-chemical complex and the 7th Fertilizer Plant. Yeosu Port is divided into two parts: the old and the new. The old port, which served mainly as a harbor for fishing boats in the past, plays the role of industrial port nowadays with stevedoring capability of 698,000 tons per year as of the end of 1974, thanks to government investments totaling 497 million won during the 1962–1974 period. Meanwhile, the new port will be capable of berthing two 50,000 dead-weight ton vessels, two 20,000 dead-weight ton vessels, six 5,000 dead-weight ton vessels and one 3,000 dead-weight ton vessel by 1981 as an outcome of investments equivalent to 16.6 billion won. The stevedoring capability of the new port will reach 5.07 million tons around 1981.

Masan Port: Masan port also consists of two parts: the old port for commercial use and the new port for the free export zone. The stevedoring capability of the old port stood at 703,000 tons in 1973. Meanwhile, as a result of the investment of 1.3 billion won during the six years ending in 1973 for development of the new port stevedoring capability was increased to 315,000 tons per year and one vessel of 10,000 dead-weight ton class can be accommodated. Stevedoring capability of the new port will reach 630,000 tons, about the same level as the old port by 1976 when the investment of 400 million won is completed. At that time, it will be possible to berth vessels of the 10,000 dead-weight ton class.

Mugho Port

Gunsan outer harbor under construction

Construction of Gunsan Outer Harbor

Gunsan Port is in an estuary with unfavorable natural conditions: a sharp tidal differential of about 7 meters and 18 kilometers of sea lane linked to the inner harbor. Since the silt and sand from the lower part of the Geum River accumulate inside the harbor, giving rise to technical difficulties in expanding inner harbor berthing facilities, the government has mapped out a plan for construction of a large-scale Gunsan outer harbor near Jangsan Island.

In 1974, the government launched a project for building the Gunsan outer harbor facilities, with a berthing capacity of one vessel each of 10,000 dead-weight ton and 5,000 dead-weight ton classes, and expediting the transportation of cargo from inland industrial complexes such as the Iri Free Export Zone, Jeonju and Daejeon. In 1986, the goal year of the project, this port will have a stevedoring capability of 1.8 million tons.

The need for a speed-up in communications has been growing as the degree of interaction between different societies intensifies. A great many innovations through the development of modern scientific techniques in the field of communications have begun to fill the gap.

A modern postal system was introduced to Korea in November of 1884, followed by telegraph and telephone systems and more

Modernization of Communication Facilities

Status of Postal Service

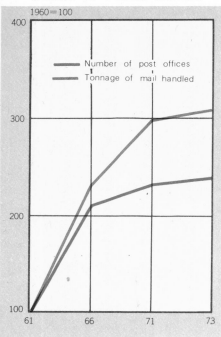

Korea International Tele-
communications Office

recently a microwave network. Nowadays, it is possible for television watchers to see live transmission of landings on the moon and sport games which take place in other parts of the world.

The sophisticated development of communications for a better and more convenient human life requires not only progress in scientific techniques but also active expansion of communication facilities.

Due to the government's intensive efforts for improvement and expansion of postal service during the First and Second Five-Year Economic Plans, the total volume of mail handled by the postal system increased rapidly, from 157 million items in 1961 to 607 million in 1973. As of October 1974, the total number of post offices throughout the country stood at 1,919 in consequence of the considerable increase in the number of post offices established mainly in rural areas to meet the goal of one post office for each township during the First Plan period.

Mailing of printed matter is especially suitable since dozens or hundreds of addresses can be contacted inexpensively at one time. This is why the volume of mail is on the increase despite increased reliance on telecommunications. The government instituted a postal zone number system in 1970 and a standard envelop system in 1972 in order to implement the mechanization of the mail sorting system and to cope with the increasing volume.

Geumsan Satellite Relay Receiving Station

With completion of the Geumsan Satellite Relay Receiving Station in June 1970 news commentaries and on-the-spot broadcasts of events from every corner of the world can be telecasted simultaneously to television watchers in Korea.

The total cost of construction of the Geumsan Satellite Relay Receiving Station, inaugurated in April 1969 under a loan agreement with the American Export-Import Bank in 1968, amounted to 1.84 billion won.

The station is connected with the satellite relay receiving stations in many Pacific countries via communications satellites located above the Pacific Ocean.

The station initially had 20 circuits but the number has since been increased to 57.

The government has launched a project for constructing a Second Satellite Relay Receiving Station and when completed, early in 1977, it will connect with satellites over the Indian Ocean.

Modernization and Expansion of Communication Facilities

In Korea, a steady and growing demand for telephones was created in the process of urbanization during the rapid economic development of the 1960's. Respective increases of 190,000 lines and 311,000 lines occurred during the First and Second Five-Year Economic Development Plans and further expansion took place in 1972 and 1973. The number of telephone lines at the end of 1973 totaled 846,000, a sixfold increase over the 123,000 telephone lines in existence in 1961. The average number of telephones per 100 persons increased to three in 1973 from less than one in 1960. Such a rapid expansion of telephone facilities is almost unprecedented in the world.

In major cities antiquated systems have been replaced by automatic dialing, which now encompasses 591,000 circuits, a tenfold increase over 1961.

The government has also drawn up a plan to expand telephone facilities in farming and fishing areas to speed their modernization. Thanks to this plan, the number of installed magnetic-type telephones, which are cheaper than the automatic type, increased to 157,000 in 1973, an increase of 100,000 over the 1961 level.

The installation of trunk lines, consisting of microwave and coaxial cable networks between major cities, is a revolutionary

The tropospheric scatter communication system between Korea and Japan

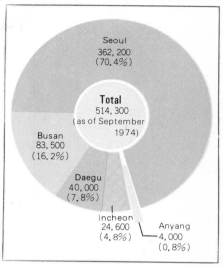

Microwave station

Status of Long Distance Automatic Telephone Network

Seoul
362, 200
(70. 4%)

Total
514, 300
(as of September 1974)

Busan
83, 500
(16. 2%)

Daegu
40, 000
(7. 8%)

Incheon
24, 600
(4. 8%)

Anyang
4, 000
(0. 8%)

innovation in Korea. The coaxial cable network has operated since 1967, and makes it possible for hundreds of people to communicate simultaneously. Meanwhile, microwave networks for wireless communication facilities have existed since 1968, and permit thousands of people to communicate at one time, and radio and television broadcasts to be relayed.

In consequence of the installation of microwave and coaxial cable networks, the operator call system between major cities such as Seoul, Busan, and Incheon was replaced by the direct-dialing system, thereby decreasing the usual waiting time from 30 minutes to five minutes. This system will be installed extensively in industrial complexes, tourist resorts and provincial cities until the five-minute-service extends to all cities and towns.

The benefits derived from the direct dialing service June 1974 five cities— Seoul, Busan, Daegu, Incheon and Anyang— are shared by 470,000 telephone subscribers in these cities. In view of the convenience of this system, it is anticipated that direct long-distance dialing will be extended to the whole country in the near future.

Revolutionary developments have also been experienced in the field of international telephone service. The installation of the Korea-Japan tropo-scatter communications system in May 1968, and the establishment of the Geumsan Satellite Relay Receiving Station in June 1970 have greatly enhanced the capacity and efficiency of Korea's international telephone service.

Number of Urban Telephone Lines & Subscribers

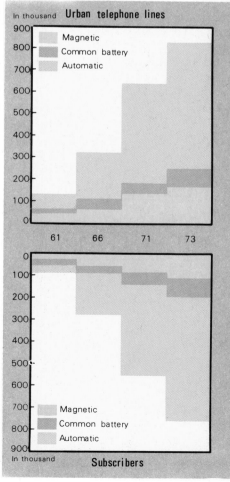

In thousand   Urban telephone lines

Magnetic
Common battery
Automatic

61   66   71   73

Magnetic
Common battery
Automatic

In thousand   Subscribers

259

Cultural and Tourism Resources

Korea is a country which is proud of her unmatched scenery and the abundant historical relics inherited from her 5,000 year-long history. The development of tourism has manifold significance. It facilitates preservation of the nation's scenic beauty, historical relics and cultural assets, contributes to the people's recreational and cultural life, and increases foreign exchange earnings.

The government has directed considerable effort towards developing tourism resources and expanding and improving tourist facilities.

The National Park Law, promulgated in 1967, provides for scenic areas to be reserved as national and provincial parks. In

accordance with the Law, Mt. Jiri was designated a national park in December 1967. Since then Gyeongju, Jeju, Mt. Seolag, Mt. Sogri, Mt. Naejang, Mt. Gaya, Mt. Gyeryong and the Hanryeo Waterway have been designated as national parks.

The government also established a Historical City Development Plan to repair and maintain cultural properties located in old cities such as Gyeongju, Buyeo and Gongju. Under the plan, the government launched the Gyeongju Tourism Project in 1972.

The government began research on landscaping from 1970 in order to develop national lands in harmony with the natural environment. The Korea Landscape Development Corporation,

Dabo Pagoda

Bulgug Temple

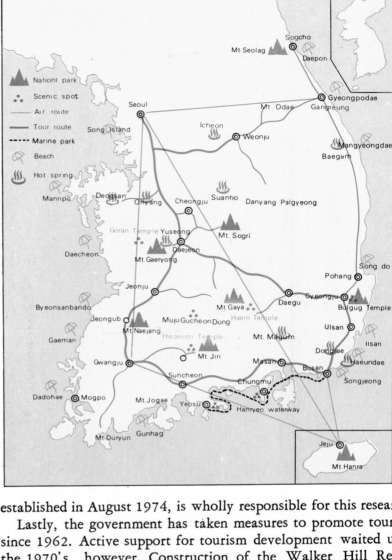

Gyeonghoeru

established in August 1974, is wholly responsible for this research.

Lastly, the government has taken measures to promote tourism since 1962. Active support for tourism development waited until the 1970's, however, Construction of the Walker Hill Resort was carried out in the early 1960's and the Tourism Promotion Law was promulgated in 1962.

The government's financial assistance to tourism amounted to 9.2 billion won in 1972 and 1973, contributing to an increase in the total number of registered hotel rooms from 907 in 1960 to 8,465 in 1974.

In addition to this, tourism transportation facilities were also expanded, including construction of express highways and airports, operation of the deluxe express train "Saemaul Ho" and a car-ferry for tourists to and from Japan.

Accordingly, in 1973 foreign visitors to Korea numbered 679 thousand, an increase of 44 times over the 15,000 who came in 1962. Foreign exchange receipts from tourism amounted to 269 million dollars in 1973, an increase of 60 times over the 4.4 million dollars earned in 1962.

Night view of Namdaemun (South Gate of Seoul)

Integrated Development of Gyeongju

Gyeongju, with its cultural relics and beautiful scenery, is a prime tourist center in Korea. The ruins and remains of Sinra culture give the visitor the feel of past history, since for a thousand years this city was the splendid capital of the Sinra Dynasty (B.C. 57~ A.D. 935). As part of the government's rehabilitation program to develop historic cities, this area was designated a national park in 1968 and the Gyeongju Development Office was set up in January 1972 to carry out projects in line with the master plan drafted in November 1971.

The plan, including restoration of historic spots, rehabilitation of Bulgug Temple and its surroundings, road construction projects for sightseeing, and the Bomun Lake resort project, has been carried forward with an investment of 10.8 billion won in the two years up to 1973.

The restoration program was aimed at finding relics of the brilliant Sinra Dynasty culture buried in scattered ancient tombs, and classifying these chronologically, so as to exhibit and preserve them permanently for posterity. Precious relics of great value, such as a golden crown, and a rare painting of a flying horse, have been found in Tombs Nos. 98 and 155, and many other relics have been discovered in various historic ruins. In the meantime, work was begun on the new Gyeongju National Museum as well as on the careful rehabilitation of seven historic spots: Toham Mountain, Five Tombs, the tomb of general Kim Yu Sin,

Panoramic view of Bulgug Temple

the tomb of King Mi Chu, a crescent shaped wall and the Buddhist carvings on South Mountain.

Bulgug Temple, a main attraction of Gyeongju tourism, has been restored to its original appearance, while shops and inns around the temple have been consolidated and beautified, along with construction of a new parking lot of 16,529 square meters, establishment of lodging facilities and the opening of souvenir stores for tourists.

The road connecting the main highway with Bulgug Temple. was expanded to four lanes, and the path between the temple and the famous mountaintop Seoggulam grotto shrine was widened and paved. A forty kilometer road linking the tomb of General Kim Yu Sin, the Poseok Pavilion, an old astronomical observatory tower, and Bunhwang Temple, has been newly constructed.

The Bomun Lake resort development plan is part of the Gyeongju plan for urban renewal and the buildup of Gujeong and the eastern district as a secondary center, with the Bomun Lake district as a new tourist resort complex.

The ten-year master plan for Gyeongju's development from 1972 to 1981 emphasizes constructing infrastructure facilities and rehabilitating historic places in the earlier phases up to 1976, and in the latter stage, the completion of a new downtown area for this cultural sightseeing city. In 1973, purchase of the necessary land for the Bomun resort was completed.

Undersea tomb of King Mun Mu

Seoggulam grotto

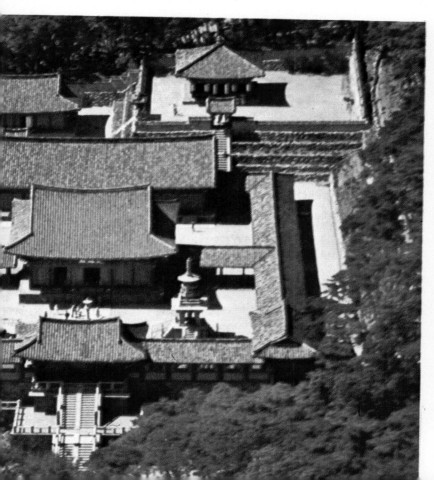

View of Mountain Hanra on Jeju Island

Development of Tourism in Jeju Province

Cheonjiyeon Falls

Jeju, the southernmost province and the largest island in Korea, is entirely distinct from the mainland, with unique natural and cultural characteristics, a subtropical climate, and the geological characteristics of a volcanic zone, together with unique folk customs. The island, often called Samdado (island abounding in three things: rocks, women, and wind), is very famous for its local legends and beautiful landscape, as well as its unique woman divers.

Mt. Hanra, in the center of Jeju, is the highest in South Korea. Lava erupting from the present site of Baegrog Lake, in the volcanic crater at the summit of the mountain, formed the unique soil of the island through thirty recorded eruptions. There are 33 unique species of plants among the 1,565 species found on the island. There are many scenic spots, including Baegrog Lake, Cheonjiyeon Falls, Jeongbang Falls, Yongyeon Lake, Ilchul Peak, Andok Ravine, Samseong Cave, a dragon-head rock, and many lava caves.

By exploiting these unique sightseeing resources, the government plans to develop Jeju Island as a famous resort. In this effort 65 billion won will be invested to build up sightseeing facilities and folk custom exhibits in Jeju City, and to develop the Jungmun area in the south of the island as a sightseeing center fully equipped with tourist hotels, beaches and recreation facilities. The government will facilitate development of beaches and of the Mt. Hanra area, and will choose four villages to be preserved as living folk villages. The plan also includes a car ferry to Jeju, expansion of the airport to accomodate B-727s, and an increase in the number of tourist hotels and other facilities.

National Parks

Beautiful scenery in the seven other national parks must also be preserved and developed. In this context, the government is planning to develop Mt. Seolag, Buyeo and Gongju along the lines of the Gyeongju Plan, and will make strenuous efforts to preserve the natural environment in the other national parks as well.

Mt. Seolag is the most famous tourist spot in Korea, providing grand views in summer, winter, and especially autumn, so that one can hardly describe the loveliness of the scenery. The ridge lines stemming from the summit of Daecheong Peak, 1,708 meters above sea level, stretch to Sogcho City and the surrounding counties of Goseong, Inje and Yangyang in Gang-weon Province. The main road connecting Seoul with Sogcho goes along the the Han-gye-ryeong route, which forms the border between inner and outer Seolag.

Seolag Dong in Sogcho City, a noted tourist resort, belongs to outer Seolag, and is bounded by Dalma Peak to the north, Sinheung Temple to the west, and Daecheong Peak to the south. Cable cars run from Seolag Dong to Gweon-geum Castle.

Seolag Mountain

There are many renowned scenic spots around Seolag and it is said that the more often one visits there the more one comes to love it. There are 25 kinds of animals, 90 kinds of birds, 360 kinds of insects, and 822 kinds of plants that are under protection in the park.

Jiri Mountain is another famous area of Korea and was the first national park specified after the National Park Law was enacted. This park covers 439 square kilometers including the main peak Cheonwang Bong, reaching 1,915 meters above sea level, and many other peaks. Well-known scenic attractions include the so-called Eight Views of Jiri: the cloudscape at Nogodan, the autumn colors at Jigjeon, the sunsets at Banya, the royal azaleas at Seseog, moon-viewing at Byeogso, Bulil Falls, enchanted land of Inha, and the sunrise seen from Cheonwang Peak.

Mt. Sogri, often called the Nine Peak Mountain, lies 1,057 meters above sea level, forming the borderline between Chungbug and Gyeongbug Provinces.

Beobju Temple was erected on Mt. Sogri about 1,400 years ago during the Sinra Dynasty, 26 years after Buddhism was officially

Naejang Mountain

became as the official religion of Sinra in 527 A.D.. The temple holds five national treasures, including Byeolsang Pavilion. Mt. Sogri was designated a national park in March 1970, and is located only three hours' distance from Seoul.

Naejang Mountain, designated as a national park in 1971, is easy to reach via the Honam Highway. The autumn colors are beautiful and the famous Naejang Temple is located at the head of a valley surrounded by many rocky mountains, like folding screens, averaging in height 699 meters above sea level.

Gaya Mountain, 1,430 meters above sea level, is located on the border between Gyeongnam and Gyeongbug Provinces, and is also called Udu Mountain. The famous Haein Temple is located here, where 80,000 carved wooden printing blocks of Buddhist literature are preserved. It was built in 802 A.D. during the Sinra Dynasty, but the existing temple was reconstructed two hundred years ago, after being burnt and rebuilt six times over the centuries. The fact that the wooden printing blocks have been so well preserved in spite of many calamities shows how much esteem the old Koreans held for this unique accomplishment.

Dodam Sambong (three peaks)

Hanryeo Waterway with Namhae Bridge
and the hydrofoil "Angel"

269

Beobju Temple

The eighty thousand wooden printing blocks of complete Buddhist scripture at Haein Temple

Gyeryong Mountain is another famous site of numerous temples, religions, and legends. Among the famous temples are Gap Temple, Donghak Temple and Sinweon Temple. The Eunseon and Yongmun Waterfalls are well-known scenic sights, together with the lovely autumn colors on the mountain sides. Yuseong Hot Spring on the way to Donghak Temple is another nearby tourist attraction. The government plans to develop a national park area including the ancient cities of Buyeo and Gongju, which were successive capitals of the Baegje Dynasty.

Finally, the Hanryeo Waterway is the only maritime national park in Korea. The area, commanding superb views, includes the coastline from Hansan Island to Yeosu, encompassing five cities and seven counties in Gyeongnam and Jeonnam Provinces, and includes 115 inhabited and 253 deserted islands. Haegeumgang, Hansan Island, Samcheonpo, Noryang, Geumsan and Odong Island are scenic spots in the area. The island-dotted sea, calm as a lake, is most suitable for summer vacations. It has become convenient to visit this area by road since the Namhae Highway opened.

In addition to the national parks, there are many other places of great natural beauty in Korea, such as Danyang Palgyeong with its famous eight scenic views, Gwandong Palgyeong, Muju-gucheon Dong, Hong Island and Song-gwang Temple. Panmunjeom, site of the truce talks, should be added as a modern historical spot.

Government's efforts to preserve the national cultural heritage may be found in the purification and restoration program for cultural assets which was launched in 1962. But a far-reaching rehabilitation program involving major projects for whole cities and districts had to wait until the 1970's. The integrated development for Gyeongju was a pilot project and is now showing results. Other integrated development projects for Buyeo and Gongju are also scheduled.

Preservation of Korea's Cultural Heritage

Golden crown from Tomb No. 155 in Gyeongju

National Museum in Seoul

Panoramic view of Admiral Lee's shrine (Hyeonchungsa)

As part of the restoration of cultural assets, various ancient relics and ruins scattered around the country are being rehabilitated to preserve Korea's splendid national heritage for posterity.

The Hyeonchungsa shrine located in Asan County is dedicated to Admiral Lee Sun Shin, known as Chungmugong, a great historical hero. The restoration and expansion of the shrine was launched in 1966 after the area was dedicated in 1962 in accordance with the instructions of President Park. The shrine is composed of many structures including pavilions, memorial gates, a museum, and archery grounds.

The museum holds such relics as the Admiral's War Diary, his sword, and his belt. The surrounding area and roads are beautifully landscaped.

In 1963 the South Gate of Seoul, National Treasure Number 1, was reconstructed. Further government projects are intended to develop tourism resources and to preserve the cultural legacy of Seoul, the capital city for the five hundred years since the beginning of the Yi Dynasty.

Five royal palaces and the remaining parts of the old city wall have been repaired, and the National Museum was moved to new,

Nagseongdae shrine

larger facilities.

The home of General Kang Gam Chan, a famous patriot and warrior of the 11th century, was reconstructed and dedicated as a shrine (Nagseongdae) in November 1973, following President Park instructing that General Kang's relics should be revered in memory of outstanding achievements.

Improvement of the Dosan-seoween (an old Confucian academy) in Andong County, Gyeongbuk Province, was carried out in April 1969 to commemorate the achievements of Lee Hwang, the great Yi Dynasty scholar, and included repairing 31 buildings, constructing a new exhibition hall, and landscaping the surrounding area.

Repairs on Admiral Lee's naval headquarters on Hansan Island, on Haengju Castle, and on a memorial shrine for seven hundred volunteers who died in battle during the Japanese invasion, have been carried out. Statues of great historical figures have been erected in various places. In September 1973 the government also initiated the construction of a Korean folk village on 6,612 thousand square meters of land near Suweon. The village provides a unique opportunity for foreign tourists as well as residents to observe indigenous Korean folk customs.

Dosan-seoweon, an old Confucian academy

KOREA MOVES ABROAD

Highway construction in Malaysia

Expansion of Trade

During the last decade Korea has achieved a high economic growth rate and acquired a good reputation in overseas countries through the rapid expansion of exports. The economic development of Korea in the 1960's was sparked by unprecedented expansion of exports to overseas markets, the inducement of foreign capital and advanced technology, and the diligence of Korean workers overseas. The amount of merchandise exported was only 32 million dollars in 1960, but surpassed 1 billion dollars in 1970 and amounted to 3.2 billion dollars in 1973, a hundred times more than in 1960. Moreover, in 1974 export value exceeded 4.7 billion dollars. We can realize how rapidly Korean exports have expanded by comparison with world export expansion, which rose from 118.4 billion dollars to 510.5 billion dollars during the same period. Accordingly, the share of Korean export value in the world market reached 0.6 per cent and her position among 100 major exporting countries improved from 94th in 1961 to 24th in 1973.

In accordance with this export expansion, the share of merchandise exports grew 2 per cent of gross national product in 1961 to 26.9 per cent in 1973, and total export value, including invisible trade receipts, made up 32 per cent of the gross national product.

There were tremendous changes in the export pattern in tandem with the rapid expansion of export value. Generally, the foreign trade patterns of developed countries are based on the export of industrial goods and the importation of raw materials, while the exports of developing countries are typically primary agricultural, fishery, and mineral products, and imports are mostly consumer goods. Until 1960, Korea maintained a foreign trade pattern that was typical in general of developing countries.

Primary goods like tungsten, iron ore, graphite, silk and fish accounted for 80 per cent of total merchandise exports, which occupied only 2 per cent of gross national product. Each year Korea experienced fluctuations in export volume because of the inflexible trade pattern based on primary goods, and could not cope with international price movements. The nation also had to import large quantities of consumer goods as well as capital goods. Accordingy, import value was ten to twenty times as great as export value. For example, in 1958 imports were 22 times the amount of exports, and eight times as large in 1961. As 80 per cent of these imports were financed from foreign aid, Korea faced a very uncertain situation, since the volume of foreign aid decided the import volume.

Entering the 1960's, the Korean trade structure shifted toward

Exportation of Industrial Goods

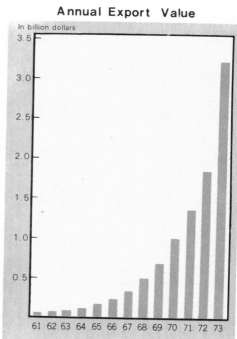

Annual Export Value

In billion dollars

61 62 63 64 65 66 67 68 69 70 71 72 73

Merchandise Export

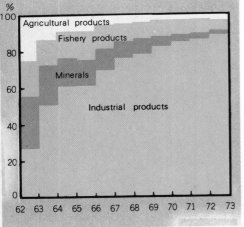

the export of manufactured products, thanks to progress in industrialization. Manufactured products accounted for only 27 per cent of total exports in 1962, but jumped to 88.2 per cent by 1973. The Korean trade pattern was thus transformed into that of a developed industrial country. This expansion in the export of manufactured items brought many benefits, specifically the acceleration of industrialization and increased employment, as well as more flexible adaptation to international market conditions and escape from the intrinsic restrictions on the expansion of primary exports.

The ratio between consumer and producer goods in the export of manufactured products is also very important. In 1960's, the early stages of industrialization up until the middle, Korea had to import producer goods and exported mainly consumer goods. From the latter half of the 1960's, however, the development of the heavy and chemical industries brought about the substitution of domstically produced goods for imported producer goods. During the 1970's Korea even began export heavy and chemical industrial products, such as steel products, machinery and petrochemicals, and such products accounted for 28.9 per cent of total exported manufactured goods in 1973.

Ratio of Exports to GNP				(In billion won)
	1 9 6 1	1 9 6 6	1 9 7 1	1 9 7 3
G N P	297.1	1,032.5	3,151.6	4,928.7
Merchandise export	5.8	70.6	409.2	1,325.9
Ratio of export to GNP	2.0	6.8	13.0	26.9
The Ratio of export including services to GNP	5.3	10.3	16.3	32.0

Korean commodity fair in Jakarta

In 1960, exports to Japan comprised 70 per cent of total exports, and the export market included only 19 countries. Until 1964 Korea exported mostly primary goods and Japan was Korea's most important customer.

By 1973, however, Korean goods were being exported to 116 countries all over the world and the largest Korean export market was the U.S.A.. This was a result of the increased share of industrial goods, rising to 88 per cent of total exports, and efforts at diversifying export markets by the government and export enterprises.

Exports to Europe, Africa and recently even the Middle East, have expanded and every effort has been made to increase the market in Eastern Europe. Entering the 1970's, Korea has made concerted efforts to establish trade with Eastern Europe and the U.S.S.R., following the East-West detente, as well as with other amicable socialist countries.

Diversification of Export Markets

Brussels fair

Korean Manpower and Technology Abroad

In 1961, Korea started exporting manpower and technology overseas. As of the end of 1974, 90,000 Koreans were working in 54 countries all over the world, and on 340 large trans-oceanic vessels. Foreign exchange earned through these activities between 1965 and October of 1974 reached 719 million dollars, peaking in 1967 due to the employment in Vietnam, and aslo in 1973 when manpower export to Guam was active.

After the passage of the Emigration Law in 1962, emigration has increased every year, from 387 in 1962 to 33,537 in 1973. Total emigration during this period was 128,104 persons, 80 per cent of whom settled in North America and 11 per cent in South America, principally in Brazil. Emigrants have played a key role in foreign exchange earnings and remitted 125 million dollars to their native country in 1973. Now Korea plans to shift the emphasis in emigration policy from simple emigration to labor and technology export.

In the early 1960's the government negotiated with labor-short West Germany concerning manpower imports, and in October 1963 the two governments formally signed an Interim Employment Programme (Arrangement) regarding Korean miners. In December of the same year, 247 Korean miners went to West Germany for the first time. By October of 1974, the total had reached 6,496 due to positive government policies. Meanwhile, the employment

Technicians Abroad and Foreign Exchange Earnings

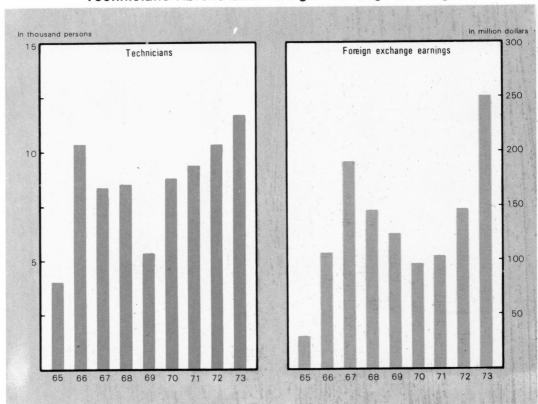

Korean technicians arrive in Japan

Nurses leave for West Germany

of Korean nurses in West Germany was discussed in 1965 on the recommendation of Koreans in West Germany. The Korean government addressed this problem in 1968, and arrangements for Korean nurses to go to West Germany were completed in 1971. The number of Korean nurses working in West Germany is now 9,279, serving at 500 hospitals. Some 946 technicians have been dispatched to West Germany to acquire highly advanced technology with the cooperation of private companies and technical tie-ups between Korea and West Germany. Thus the total Korean labor force working in West Germany has reached 16,721.

After 1965, with the escalation of the Vietnam War, the Korean government dispatched many technicians to Vietnam in connection with military shipping, transportation and maintenance. In 1965, 92 Koreans had jobs with the American company RMK-BRJ in Vietnam.

This increased to 10,097 in 1966, and 25,283 by 1967, but declined after the armistice. Korea then shifted attention to other regions such as Southeast Asia, Guam and the Middle East.

In 1964, 192 Korean crewmen were working on foreign vessels, but in 1974, 9,137 were sailing the five oceans of the world. Presently, highly skilled Korean crews are operating foreign ships under comprehensive contracts owing to wage increases and troubles with labor unions in maritime transportation countries such as the U.S. and Japan. The number of foreign ships employing Korean crewmen totals 342, under 16 flags. Among these 203 are Japanese and 38 American. The ability of Korean crews has been improved and they enjoy a good international reputation. They also enjoy a high level of income, just next to Japanese and American seamen, having earned 550,000 dollars in 1964 and 21 million dollars in 1974, and have played an important role in enhancing national prestige.

The Exportation of Korean Construction Technology

Overseas construction began from 1966. Proceeds of contracts from foreign countries recorded 11 million dollars in that year, and increased to 174 million dollars in 1973, Due to positive government support, the presence of Korean workers in Vietnam subsequently led to the conclusion in 1966 of a contract with the government of Thailand to construct a 96 kilometer highway.

In the 1960's, construction projects were very small in scale and no overseas special technology or heavy equipment. By 1970, however many were large scale, including projects exceeding 10 million dollars in value. In 1973 total proceeds of construction contracts were 17 times that in 1966, and this is expected to increase to 25 times in 1975. This rapid 40 per cent on annual average increase since 1966 corresponds to the increase rate of merchandise exports in the 1960's.

At first the target regions for construction exports were only Thailand and Vietnam, but have since been expanded to 23 regions. Korean technicians are now working in the Arabian desert, the Himalayas and in many places in the Pacific region.

In support of construction exports the government furnishes informations about possible products gathered by consulate officials in the target regions to appropriate companies and maintains resident construction attaches in these countries to carry out market surveys report on competition from foreign companies and assist in dealings with local government offices.

Early in the 1960's the only resident construction attache was in Vietnam. Two more were added in 1968, and three in 1974. Now six attaches are working in Indonesia, Malaysia, the Philippines, Guam and Saudi Arabia. The government will continue support the development of construction business in overseas countries through dispatching of overseas construction dispatches to foreign countries planning public works.

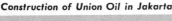
Construction of Union Oil in Jakarta

*Construction of hospital
in Vietnam*

Construction Export by Region (66–74)

(In thousand dollars)

Region	Proceeds of Contracts	Region	Proceeds of Contracts
Guam	87,690	Australia	6,272
Vietnam	82,575	Samoa	5,443
Indonesia	74,112	Bangladesh	6,389
Malaysia	75,669	Singapore	2,758
Thailand	44,813	Hong Kong	2,630
Saudi Arabia	88,011	Ecuador	3,749
Philippines	22,812	Jordan	1,332
Brunei	19,936	Khmer	741
Pacific Ocean	22,055	Japan and Okinawa	502
Taiwan	15,834	Hawaii	876
New Guinea	12,826	Nigeria	143
Nepal	9,509	Others	6,249
		Total	**592,926**

Annual Proceeds of Contracts in Construction Export

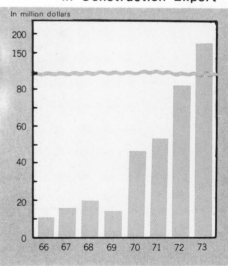

Korean Aviation World-Wide

Interior of KAL Plane

Expansion of International Airline Service

The history of Korean aviation can be divided into three stages from the founding of the Korean National Airlines (KNA) in 19 48 to the emergence of the present Korean Air Lines (KAL). Because of the Korean War, KNA stopped operations shortly after its founding, but reopened in 1954, and closed again in 1962 due to a shortage of capital and irrational management, plus the hijacking of a DC-3 to North Korea in 1958.

Thereafter, from 1962 to 1969, the Korean Aviation Corporation (KAC), which began as a government owned enterprise, performed the principal role in Korean aviation. It opened its domestic

284

business with two DC-3's and one DC-4, but introduced two turbo-prop twin engine F-27's in 1963 and one twin engine DC-9 in 1967. International routes such as Seoul-Tokyo, Seoul Osaka, Busan-Fukuoka and Seoul-Hong Kong were developed. The management of the government enterprise was so rigid however, that KAC could not meet the increasingly fierce competition from international airlines, so KAC was placed under private management in 1969 through sale to Korean Air Lines (KAL).

KAL achieved rapid expansion and a diversification of aircraft thanks to the world-wide travel boom. Air transportation recorded great development through active government support, which included the expansion of international airport facilities at Gimpo and other fields, securement of foreign capital to acquire planes, and the extension of international routing agreements. Korea's international routes developed rapidly with DC-9's on the Korea-Japan route in the latter part of the 1960's and the introduction of large jets in the 1970's, compared with the late 1950's when there were only intermittent runs on the Seoul-Hong Kong route and irregular runs from Seoul to Seattle by KNA.

Now KAL enjoys 50 per cent of the total service on the Korea-Japan route, competing with NWA and Japan Air Lines with B-727's, 707's, 747's and DC-8's on the Seoul-Tokyo, Seoul-Osaka, Busan-Fukuoka, Busan-Osaka and Jeju-Osaka routes.

Since the ambitious opening of the Seoul-Tokyo-Honolulu-Los Angeles service in 1970, this route has been very successful in terms of both passenger and cargo volume. Presently KAL is growing in of international prestige by competing with world famous companies by the use of Jumbo jets.

Since 1973, air cargo service from Seoul to Paris has been possible on KAL thanks to the opening of a North Pole route, and in 1974 KAL made concerted efforts to secure ties with Switzerland, Italy, Finland and West Germany.

Major cities in Southeast Asia have been served since 1969 with the opening of the Bangkok-Seoul line. In order to extend this line as far as Singapore, the central city of Southeast Asia, KAL is seeking to rearrange aviation agreements between Korea and Singapore, and efforts are also being made to open a route linking Manila with this line. It is expected that the formation of an airline network linking Korea with Europe via Southeast Asia will be realized in the near future.

Comparison of International Airline Passengers

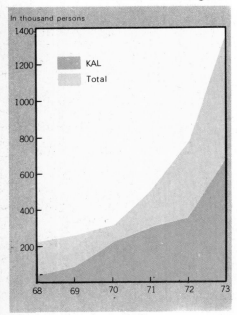

KAL Routes

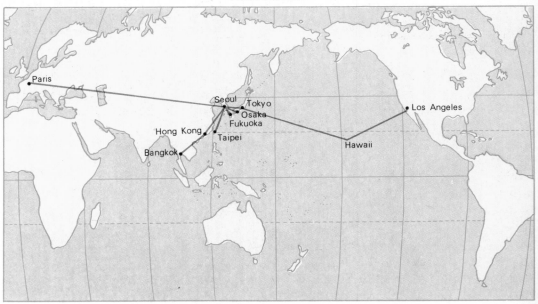

Korean Air Lines possessed only two DC-3's and one DC-4 at the beginning of the 1960's. In the latter half of the 1960's, however, it obtained 13 turbo-prop aircrafts (F-27's and YS-11's), used mainly on domestic routes. In the 1970's jets, including three Boeing 727's, two Boeing 720's, four Boeing 707's and four DC-8's, were added to the KAL fleet, concentrated on international routes.

Moreover, in 1973 KAL acquired two jumbo-jet 747's, the symbol of modern scientific technology; and in 1974, a third was added. With a total of 28 aircraft, including three 747's, KAL has grown into the second largest aviation company in East Asia after JAL and serves 11 cities in six foreign countries.

After acquiring an economical wide-bodied jet aircraft, the DC-10, in 1974 and adding two DC-10's to its fleet in 1975, KAL plans to put them on the America, Europe and Southeast Asia routes.

Improvement of Air Transportation

Carrying more than 7,000 passengers a day, or 2,430,000 per year in 1973, up from 900 passengers a day in 1968, KAL has increased its passenger volume by more than seven times over the 1968 level.

On the Japan route, the most important international run, KAL had only 31 per cent of the business in 1969 while NWA and JAL shared the remaining 69 per cent. By 1973, however, KAL, had secured 50 per cent of the total Tokyo-Seoul business. In 1973 KAL's passenger volume totalled 2,430,000 including 640,000 passengers on the Japan route, 179,000 on the Southeast Asia route, and 93,000 on the American route. Cargo volume amounted to 287,000 tons, the overall number of flights was 40,100, and the total flying distance 31,950,000 kilometers. The amount of foreign currency earned by KAL exceeded 100 million dollars.

Air Cargo of International Airlines in Korea

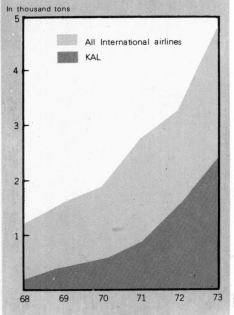

Foreign Exchange Earnings

(In thousand dollars)

Year	Supplementary Revenue (KAL)	Airport Revenue	Freight Revenue (KAL)	Total
1966	241	321	2,129	2,691
1967	308	357	1,831	2,496
1968	469	590	2,636	3,695
1969	550	709	5,994	7,253
1970	859	1,030	14,175	16,064
1971	741	1,351	23,163	25,255
1972	1,034	1,010	43,915	45,959
1973	5,658	1,424	98,186	105,268

Advancement of Marine Transportation

Korea, surrounded by the sea on three sides, finds marine transportation one of the most promising ways to save foreign currency, by carrying trade cargo on domestic vessels.

At the time of independence in 1945, Korea had only five freighters owned by the Chosun Mail Steamship Company. By

A Korean ship cruising oceans

Ocean-going Ships

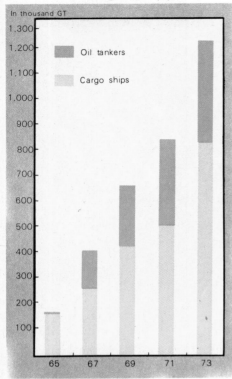

In thousand GT

	Oil tankers	Cargo ships

1,300
1,200
1,100
1,000
900
800
700
600
500
400
300
200
100

65 67 69 71 73

Oversea Transportation by Korean-Flag Ships

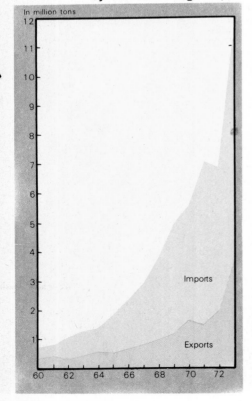

In million tons

12
11
10
9
8
7
6
5
4
3
2
1

Imports

Exports

60 62 64 66 68 70 72

1950, the number of vessels had increased somewhat, but they were much inferior to ordinary merchant ships because most of them had been built hastily during the Second World War.

Most of the vessels acquired in the 1950's were small coastal ships and fishing boats. The nation had few ocean-going ships on international routes. Until the early 1960's, the number of vessels even decreased due to obsolescence. Since then the government has made great efforts to revitalize the marine transportation sector.

Due to lack of both the technology and domestic capital need to construct large ships, the expansion of marine transport was first through the purchase of foreign vessels, mostly second-hand.

In 1965 the state-operated Korea Marine Transportation Co. imported the first four second-hand vessels (47,000 gross tons) from England with a 5 million dollar foreign currency loan.

Since then, Korea has acquired a number of additional second-hand vessels. The country's inventory of merchant ships jumped from a total of only 170,000 tons in 1962 to more than 1,230,000 tons in 1973.

As a result of the expansion of marine transportation, overseas cargo volume increased rapidly and Korean seamen gained worldwide experience, leading to the development of triangular transportation through participation in international marine transportation markets.

In 1961, Korean vessels carried only 862,000 tons of import-export cargo, but in 1973 this had reached 11,007,000 tons, more than 13 times the 1961 level. Freight revenues from the marine transportation business are both a source of foreign currency, and permit savings on charges which would otherwise be paid to hire foreign vessels. The amount of money earned by transporting ocean-going cargo was only 4 million dollars in 1962, but amounted to 81 million dollars in 1973.

Total earnings, including the dollars saved by employing domestic vessels, rose from 8 million dollars in 1962 to 164 million dollars in 1973, making a great contribution to the improvement of the balance of payments. The increase in freight revenues has not yet caught up with the rapid growth of export and import volume. Korean vessels still transport no more than 30 per cent of total

Development of Overseas Marine Transportation

Korean vessel arriving at New York

cargo.

In only ten years Korea has developed a merchant fleet which totals 1,230,000 tons, giving Korea the hope of becoming a major maritime country. The development of marine transport has been indispensable in saving on foreign exchange, and is necessary to the achievement of a self-sustaining economy. Prospects for the marine transport industry have also been brightened by the fact that domestic shipyards are now able to construct large, modern vessels. Modern vessels built to date have totalled 260,000 gross tons.

The government plans to extend its ownership of ocean-going vessels to 6 million gross tons by 1981 four times greater than the present level. This will provide space for carrying 50 per cent of all export cargo.

The government plans to foster the shipbuilding industry and the marine transportation business by constructing half the needed vessels in domestic shipyards, enhancing both employment and income at the same time.

The Korea Marine Transportation Co. and Pan-Ocean Bulk Carriers Ltd. Co. have been selected as principal-size shipping companies by the government and encouraged to specialize in their own respective activities. They will explore the potential of Korean maritime traffic, improving the ratio of cargo shipped on domestic vessels.

Developed countries, in the face of the world-wide food and resource crises, have devoted themselves to research on and development of marine resources.

Korea long neglected the development of marine resource, and active investment in the development of deep-sea fishing was avoided because of the highly speculative nature of this industry. As a result, up until the 1960's Korea short-sightedly limited herself to traditional coastal fishing.

In the 1960's, however considering the value of exporting deep-sea fishery products to improve balance of payments, the government began to promote deep-sea fishery operations in order to improve the balance of payments through the export of deep sea fishery products, resulting in unparalleled progress in this sector.

By 1973, 552 fishing boats plied 21 fishing grounds in the Pacific, Atlantic, and Indian Oceans, netting 361 thousand tons of catch and achieving exports of 120 million dollars.

Modern fishing boats and well-stocked fishing grounds which

Deep-Sea Fishery in Five Oceans

Factory-fishing boat of Korea Ocean Co.

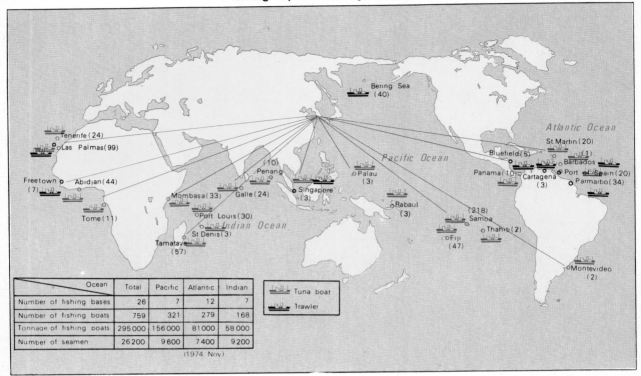

Ocean	Total	Pacific	Atlantic	Indian
Number of fishing bases	26	7	12	7
Number of fishing boats	759	321	279	168
Tonnage of fishing boats	295000	156000	81000	58000
Number of seamen	26200	9600	7400	9200

(1974 Nov)

ensure plentiful catches are indispensable to deep-sea fishing. Therefore, since initiating the First Five-Year Economic Development Plan, the government has taken measures to train fishing experts, establish a deep-sea fishery fund, and expand the number of fishing boats. The number of fishing boats increased to 552 in 1973, many of them modern and specialized. Average tonnage of deep-sea fishing boats increased from 150 gross tons in 1964 to 354 gross tons in 1973, and 17 vessels exceeded the 1,000 gross ton level.

Until 1965, only tuna boats had engaged in deep-sea fishing, but the discovery of the Las Palmas fishing grounds off Africa in 1966 and the successful pollack fishing test operations in the North Pacific marked an expansion of available grounds. Bonito boats went to the South Pacific in 1970 and shrimp boats to South American fishing grounds in 1972, while codfish deep-long-line boats plied northern oceans. Ordinary trawlers were rebuilt into factory ships where the haul could be processed into semi-finished products. In 1974, a mammoth factory-fishing boat of 27 thousand gross ton which is a self-contained marine factory went into operation.

With only 20 tuna boats prior to 1964, the deep-sea fishing industry was in the test phase of exploring fishing grounds and developing new fishing techniques. The number of fishing boats tripled in 1965, and reached 447 in 1973. Only eight trawlers were operating in 1966, but the number increased to 28 the next year and jumped to 105 in 1973.

Beginning with the tuna fishing grounds in the neighborhood of Nicholas Island in the Indian Ocean in 1957, the government developed tuna fishing grounds off Samoa in the next year, while cuttlefish, octopus and other varieties were caught in new fishing grounds off Las Palmas in the Atlantic, pollack in fishing grounds in the North Pacific, tuna at Port Louis in the Indian Ocean, bonito off Palau in the western Pacific in 1967, and shrimp off the coast of Surinam in 1970. As of the end of 1974, 26 overseas fishing grounds were being exploited in Fiji, Tahiti, Samoa, Panama in the Pacific Ocean, Penang, Galle, Mombasa, Tamatave in the Indian Ocean, and Tenerife, Freetown, Abidjan, St. Martin, Bluefields, and Montevideo in the Atlantic. Research is taking place on other fishing grounds around the world.

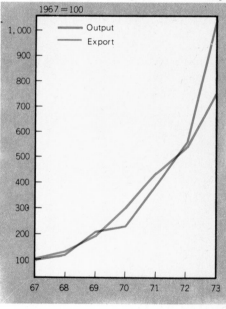

Expansion of Korean Deep-Sea Fishery

Bonito fishing operation

Fishery Exports

The size of the catch and deep-sea fishery exports have increased in proportion to the expansion of the fishing fleet. Between 1957 and 1962, exports totalled only 200,000 dollars, but increased rapidly after 1963, rising to 10 million dollars in 1967 and 120 million dollars in 1973. Consequently, deep-sea fishery has become an important export industry.

Classifying the catch in 1973 by ocean, in volume terms 268 thousand tons or 74.2 per cent of the total was caught in the Pacific, 17.5 per cent in the Atlantic, and 8.3 per cent in the Indian Ocean. In terms of value, however, 44.3 per cent of the total catch came from the Pacific, 36.3 per cent from the Atlantic, and 19.4 per cent from the Indian Ocean, indicating that the catches from the Atlantic and the Indian Oceans were relatively more profitable than that from the Pacific Ocean.

Pollack fishing in the North Pacific

The export of deep-sea fishing products in 1973 earned a total sum of 118 million dollars, of which the Pacific catch contributed 44 per cent (52,500,000 dollars), the Atlantic 36.5 per cent (43,400,000 dollars) and the Indian Ocean 19.5 per cent (23,100, thousand dollars).

Long-line tuna and bonito fishing operations are labor-intensive; 25 seamen are employed in each long-line tuna fishing boat (200~300 tons), and 45 seamen in a bonito fishing boat (400 tons). Trawlers depend highly on mechanical operations and usually require 28 seamen for a ship of 349 tons.

The total of seamen employed in this industry was only 25 persons in 1957, but increased to 3,632 in 1966, to 15,433 in 1973, and to 26,215, in 1974, a 70 per cent increase over the previous year.

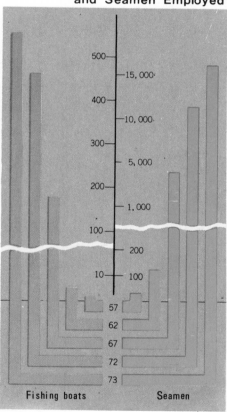

Number of Fishing Boats and Seamen Employed

Fishing boats   Seamen

TOWARDS AN
AFFLUENT SOCIETY

Improving in the Standard of Living

In Korea the low standard of living in the 1950's was due to the slump in production, price instability, and a per capita income of less than 70 dollars. Per capita income increased by only 12 dollars in eight years, from 62 dollars in 1953 to 74 dollars in 1961.

However, gross national product increased at an annual rate of 7.8 per cent during the First Five-Year Plan period and 10.5 per cent during the Second Five-Year Plan period, owing to intensive development efforts beginning in 1962. Per capita income increased rapidly to 110 dollars in 1966, 376 dollars in 1973 and to over 500 dollars in 1974.

Korea was thus transformed into an advanced developing country. Under the headline "South Koreans Like Work," The Economist, a weekly magazine published in England, commented on August 31, 1974, that "After the brief flurry that followed the shooting of President Park's wife two weeks ago, the South Koreans have settled back again into what they are good at — work. The people are poor but visibly beginning to feel their living standards improving. But the Koreans are incredibly industrious, putting in six days a week and 10 to 12 hours a day in factories and offices. Like Japan, South Korea has almost no raw materials. Like Japan used to be, it has plenty of space, unpolluted air and abounding self-confidence, and productivity is still leaping ahead of wages." The magazine also reported that the Korean economy was successfully overcoming

A happy home

Durable Convenience Goods

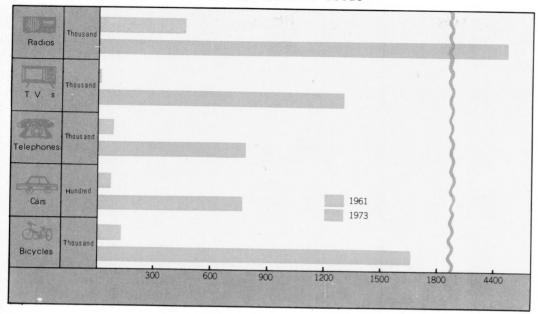

| | | | 1961 |
| | | | 1973 |

difficulties brought on by the worldwide economic crisis.

Korea has achieved rapid growth during the past 12 years. With higher incomes, the pattern of consumption improved in terms of both quantity and quality. Private consumption expenditure recorded a 2.6 fold expansion, from 942.6 billion won in 1960 to 2,415.8 billion won in 1973. Savings recorded a 15.1 fold increase, from 39 billion won to 586.5 billion, during the same period. Looking more closely, 58 per cent of private consumption until 1961 was for food expenses, but in 1973 the figure was only 45.7 per cent.

These figures indicate the improvement in the people's standard of living. Miscellaneous expenses, in particular increased drastically from 16.7 per cent to 23.8 per cent during this period. These changes were brought about not only by higher incomes but also by the abundant supply of cheap, durable goods produced by Korea's developing industrial sector.

Radios, television sets, refrigerators, telephones, electrical appliances, bicycles and cars are produced and in widening use. With the improvement of educational and medical standards, expenditures on these services have increased. Between 1961 and 1973 the number of radios increased from 458,000 to 4,447,000 television sets 543 times from 2,015 to 1,093,000 sets; telephones seven times from 97,000 to 774,000; bicycles 12 times from 130,000 to 1,650,000; cars eight times, from 9,809 to 78,334. Furthermore, numerous refrigerators and pianos were produced. In 1973 there was one radio per household, one television set per five households, one telephone per eight households and one car for every seventy-seven households. Nowadays, living standards of Koreans are among the highest in Asia outside Japan.

Improvement of the Living Environment

The Saemaul Undong (New Community Movement) has changed both the environment of farming and fishing villages and that of the cities. This movement, which initiated by President Park, has spread all over the country, improving living environment and changing old ways of thinking, combined with measures for raising personal income and modernizing the pattern of living. The Movement has laid emphasis on improving roofs, fences, roads, river embankments and sanitation facilities. As time went on, it has spread from rural communities to cities, urban schools and factories.

In 1973 all the villages in the country, totaling 34,665, were classified into three types; underdeveloped, developing and developed. Development projects are undertaken in accordance with each village's need and capabilities. Such projects have emphasized improving the environment, increasing employment in rural areas, thrift, helping neighbors, simplification of traditional family ceremonies, and the modernization of markets in urban areas nationwide.

There have been special activities in factories and support for rural projects. Koreans living abroad have adopted 197 villages and assisted them with contributions totaling 566 million won.

Improvement of rural environment (right) and urban area (left)

Improving
the Marketing System

A sound marketing system which enables consumers to purchase commodities of good quality at a reasonable price is important for the stabilization of livelihoods. Past deficiencies may be attributed to low productivity resulting from merchants' undercapitalization, to the out-of-date family enterprise business management system, and to high prices and instability of the price system caused by complicated marketing channels between producer to consumer.

Following the military revolution, the government legislated the Market Act in August 1961 to provide the foundation for an improved marketing system. In July 1964 the government also instituted the National Cooperative Union of Small Tradesmen to support the organizing of commerce systems. In order to systematize market administration, the government also established the Commission for Market Normalization in April 1965 and transferred the Central Wholesale Market, which was the main distributive channel for agricultural and marine products, to the Department of Agriculture and Fishery.

However, these efforts during the 1960's had no significant effect. Improvements were finally achieved in the marketing system

Inside a supermarket

in the early 1970's. After the Emergency Measures of January 14, 1974, aimed at overcoming the economic crisis caused by the oil shock of late 1973, the government concentrated its efforts on reforming the distribution of necessities for effective stabilization of the economy and protection of the people's livelihoods. Reform measures adopted at that time aimed at:

① Securing stable markets for necessities,
② Operating effectively the system of price controls,
③ Rooting out unfair transactions such as hoarding and price manipulation, and
④ Promoting large, organized distributive mechanisms.

For these purposes supermarkets were introduced in large cities, and authorized distributors of necessities in middle and small cities. Chain stores connected with Agricultural Cooperatives were increased in rural communities.

Supermarkets established in large cities are expected to supply sufficient goods at stable prices to ordinary consumers.

Having sufficient capital they are able to purchase commodities in bulk at stock affiliated supermarkets located in residential areas or at existing market places, thus making it possible for consumers to buy necessities at a lower price. Since the first New Community Supermarket was established as part of the New Community Movement in April, 1971, following the suggestion of the late First Lady, Mrs. Park Chung Hee, who showed deep concern over the people's living situation, supermarkets have increased in number from 8 in 1971 to 21 in 1973. In August 1974 the number reached 61 as a result of strong expansion efforts started that year.

Meanwhile, authorized distributors of necessities have been set up as simplified supermarkets in middle-sized and small cities. These jointly purchase necessities at factory prices for the entire city or province. While supermarkets are limited to large cities due to capital and scale requirements, the authorized distributors are able to operate as individual shops and there is at least one in every middle-sized and small city of over 100,000 population.

In rural communities more chain stores of the Agricultural Cooperatives have been established, operated jointly with the Cooperative collection offices for farm products, and have led to modernization of the distribution of daily necessities and farm products. Products of medium and small industries were also included at the joint marketing offices to improve their distribution.

The government is trying to improve marketing channels by directly supporting arrangements such as:

① Guarantee of joint purchases by the above-mentioned agencies at factory prices,
② Financial aid for the rationalization of industrial enterprises,
③ Higher discounts for commercial bills to finance merchants' operating capital,
④ Special financial support for middle and small industries, and
⑤ Tax concessions.

Shipment by refrigerator car

City Planning and public Housing

Growth of Seoul

Since the 1960's the shape of Seoul, Korea's capital city, has greatly changed. Many new buildings, including the 31-story Samil Building, highest in Korea, lend an air of cosmopolitanism. Elevated highways, scenic drives, by-pass roads and traffic tunnels link the outskirts with the city's main traffic network. The opening of the Jongro Line of the Seoul subway, completed 40 months after construction started in 1971, must be recorded as a major step toward solving the traffic Problem of the capital city.

Wretched shacks, previously seen everywhere, symbolizing the

wounds of the Korean War, have given way to modern apartments. Changes in the citizens' mode of life is indicated by the popularity of apartments among both high and middle income groups.

Seoul became the capital city in 1394, and its population was 103,300 in 1428. At the time of the liberation from Japan in 1945 the population was 901,300, but increased rapidly, partly due to an influx of refugees from the north during the Korean War. Seoul had a population of 2,445,400 in 1960, which grew to 6,289,500 by 1973. From 1966 to 1970 the population

Night view of the capital City of Seoul

increased at an average annual rate of 9.8 per cent, of which only 1.9 per cent represented natural increase, the other 7.9 per cent being due to immigration from the provinces.

City authorities have made efforts to prevent unlicensed substandard housing from spreading, and have curbed the construction of new factories within the city, to moderate the concentration of population in the capital. Dispersion of public offices and private enterprises to the provinces has also been pursued, facilitated by the opening of an express highway and improvement of the rural living environment through the New Community Movement. As a result of these efforts the concentration of population in Seoul has eased considerably since 1971, and the rate of increase of the city's population declined to 3.0 per cent in 1973.

The rapid increase of Seoul's population caused serious housing problems. City authorities have sought to expand residential construction, by investing large sums in the vast Gwangju Residential Site and Citizens' Apartments, and by stimulating the activity of private housing construction. The number of dwelling units increased by two and a half times between 1961 and 1973, from 275,

Sejong Ro (1961 and 1973)

Namdaemun Ro (1960 and 1973)

400 units to 700,700 units while the ratio of house owners
total households increased from 56.8 per cent in 1961 to 57.6 per
cent in 1973, despite the rapid increase in population.

The Han River, which flows through Seoul from east to west,
had had only one traffic bridge and one railway bridge prior to the
1960's. In 1965, however, the Second Han River Bridge, 1,048
meters in length and 18 meters in width, was opened, linking
north Seoul with Gimpo International Airport and the Seoul-
Incheon Expressway. In 1969 the Third Han River Bridge, 915
meters long and 27 meters wide, connected with the Seoul-Busan
Expressway and Yeongdong District. In 1970 the city center was
linked to Yeoeui Island by another bridge, 1,390 meters long and
24 meters wide. Two other bridges, one 1,280 meters long and
25 meters wide, and the other 1,230 meters long and 25 meters
wide, were opened in 1972 and 1973 respectively. In 1974 construction of yet another bridge, 1,300 meters in length and 25
meters in width, was started. Thus, including the First Han River
Bridge, six bridges now cross the Han in Seoul, and there are
plans for construction of three more. With the one already under

Cheongge Ro (1965 and 1973)

Toege Ro (1960 and 1973)

The third bridge on the Han River

Yeoeui Island

construction, Seoul will have ten bridges upon the completion of these projects.

The city authorities also constructed highways 16 meters wide along both sides of the Han River, which have helped to prevent floods with their embankments, as well as to ease traffic. With the completion of two more riverside highways, a traffic network serving both sides of the river has been established.

The city has also begun to develop the neglected islet of Yeoeui located in the Han River between Mapo and Yeongdeungpo. A 7.6 kilometer embankment was constructed to secure 2,876,000 square meters of new land. This is the location of the May 16th Plaza encompassing 397,000 square meters, a vast housing site of 1,709,000 square meters and 15 planned public office buildings, including the new National Assembly Building, a consolidated hospital, and a number of mammoth apartments.

The Yeongdong District encompassing 31,736,000 square meters and connected to north Seoul by two bridges, has been developed as a new suburban residential area to disperse the crowded population of north Seoul by resettling some 700,000 people in this area.

In late 1972 the Temporary Measure Act for the Promotion of Development of Special Districts and the Residential Construction Promotion Act were legislated to induce the people's active participation in development by exempting taxes on real estate and home construction in the districts under development.

Yeongdong, Jamsil, Banpo and Cheonho were exempted from seven kinds of taxes including the speculation control tax, farmland tax, registration tax, acquisition tax, permission tax, property tax and city planning tax, and building funds were made available at lower interest rates.

On May 5, 1973 the Children's Grand Park with a capacity of 50,000 visitors was opened to the delight of all children. A total sum of 8.2 billion won was invested for zoos, botanical gardens, playgrounds and recreational facilities in the park area of 721,000 square meters.

On August 15, 1974 the Seoul Subway was finally opened. The construction of the initial Jongro Line began in April 1971 required 40 months to complete. The line is 10.3 kilometers long and represents an investment of 33 billion won, including 23.6 billion won from domestic sources and 9.4 billion won in foreign investment. The whole process from the development of the master plan and specific blueprints to engineering and construction was carried out with domestic skills. From the technological viewpoint, this insures the successful construction of five more planned subway lines. In particular, a special anti-vibration engineering method was developed and applied in order not to cause damage to the nation's historic buildings located beside the subway line, including the South and East Gates. Requiring a total of 2,826,000 man-

Riverside Road

Subway

Metropolitan Electric Railway

days of labor and 2,285,000 unit-days of heavy equipment, it set a new world record for lowest cost and shortest period for construction per kilometer of length. Compared to 22.5 million dollars per kilometer for the Tokyo Subway, 13 million dollars per kilometer in London, 16 million dollars per kilometer in San Francisco, and 11.5 million dollars per kilometer in Toronto, The Seoul subway cost no more than 7.5 million dollars per kilometer.

Seoul became the forty-first city to have a subway, and Korea the twenty-first country. Three electric railway lines covering the extended metropolitan area connect with the subway: the 38.9 kilometer Incheon line, the 41.5 kilometer Suweon line, and the 18.2 kilometer Seongbug line. These were opened simultaneously increased traffic capacity per day by more than three times, from 86,000 persons to 270,000 persons.

In addition, Seoul has invested an enormous sum social overhead capital projects such as the Samil Elevated Highway which is 5,761 meters in length and 16 meters in width, five city tunnels, the Nagseongdae Site of 20,000 square meters, and several scenic skyways.

The city waterworks capacity has been expanded by 13.8 times, from 128,000 tons in 1955 to 1,770,000 tons in 1974, which increased the daily water supply per capita from 126 liters to 304 liters despite a 5.8 times increase of population during the same period.

Environmental improvements through investment in street paving and cleaning and other public works are being pursued as well.

Seoul, at present the eighth largest city in the world with more than six million population, has thus made rapid progress as the heart of the nation's growing economy and continues its efforts to achieve further improvement.

View of Children's Grand Park

Development of other Cities

Since 1962 the rapid growth of the national economy has spurred urban development and brought about an increasing concentration of population. The ratio of urban to total population, which was 39 per cent in 1960, increased to 42.6 per cent in 1966, to 50.2 per cent in 1970, and reached 52.1 per cent in 1971, indicating a steady increase.

Faced with this problem, the government promoted a national city planning program and broadly amended the City Planning Act in 1971 to combat overcrowding in urban areas.

The cities to which the City Planning Act was applicable totaled 404 in 1973. When classified by population, the three largest have populations of more than one million persons; two are large cities with more than 500,000 persons; 19 are medium-sized cities with more than 200,000 persons; 22 are small cities with more than 50,000 persons; 105 are towns with more than 20,000 persons; and 253 are small towns with less than 20,000 persons.

According to the City Planning Act, the government designated areas adjacent to large cities, totaling 5,062 square kilometers (five per cent of the national territory), as green belts (development restriction zones), to prevent the disorderly expansion of these cities and to secure a healthier living environment for the citizens.

Such designated zones will be covered with woods to provide citizens with recreational areas, and are expected to help prevent atmospheric pollution.

Urbanization
(In thousand persons)

Year	Total population	Urban population	Urban percentage
1949	20,188	5,885	29.0 %
1960	24,989	9,784	39.0
1966	29,208	12,440	42.6
1970	31,469	15,800	50.2
1972	32,669	17,033	52.1

View of Busan City

Private housing construction has shown a remarkable increase over the past 12 years. During the period from 1962 to 1973 housing construction reached 1,116,103 units, an increase of 18.1 per cent. Of these, 201,675 units were in the public sector and 81.9 per cent or 914,428 units in the private sector. While housing construction increased by only 29.2 per cent or 325,935 units

Housing Construction

Panoramic view of the Seoul riverside apartments

during the First Five-Year Plan period, from 1962 to 1966, it showed a rate of increase of 48.4 per cent during the second development plan, from 1967 to 1971. An increase of 250,000 units was recorded during 1972 and 1973, which is equivalent to a five year rate of 56.0 per cent.

The government supported private housing construction by establishing the Korea Housing Bank in 1967 to take charge of financing and supplying construction funds. In the meantime, the proportion of housing construction in the public sector has gradually increased, particularly after the National Housing Construction Promotion Law for the homeless poor was enacted at the end of 1972. In the past, public sector construction averaged some 10,000 dwelling units annually, but the number jumped to more than 40,000 units in 1973. Furthermore, the government now

Housing Construction

(In units and %)

	1962–66	1967–71	1972–73	Total (Composition Rate)
Public Sector	39,915	102,850	58,910	201,675(18.1)
Private Sector	286,020	437,318	191,090	914,428(81.9)
Total	325,935	540,168	250,000	1,116,103(100.0)
Composition Rate	29.2	48.4	22.4	100.0

lends construction funds at low interest rate and for long-term periods; that is, at an annual interest rates of 8 per cent with a grace period of one year and an installment repayment period of 14 years.

A standard blueprint for houses has been supplied in approximately 52,000 copies at low cost or for free, and the government has simplified the building permit process.

The government has also improved the degree of land utilization in densely populated areas, and has accelerated the construction of apartments to reduce both housing costs and maintenance fees.

The number of households living in government-sponsored apartment buildings increased from 524 in 1972 to 3,608 in 1973.

The state-run Korea Housing Corporation builds and provides rental apartments for poor households without housing. Such rental apartments for 500 households were first supplied to 500 households in 1972, and to 1,500 households in 1973. Nowadays apartments are popular not only among the poor but among the affluent.

Raising the Education Level

Growth of Educational Institutions

Korea is proud of her successful campaign against illiteracy, and of an enhanced educational and cultural level. Rapid progress in education and culture has accompanied growth in the economic sector since the 1960's. Enthusiasm for education is unbounded and school training, on-the-job-training, adults education and New Community Education have progressed remarkably both in terms of quality and quantity.

The number of primary schools increased from 4,496 in 1960 to 6,315 in 1974, up 40.5 per cent; middle schools increased from

*View of Seoul National University's
New Gwanag Campus*

1,053 to 1935, up 83.8 per cent; high schools grew from 658 to 1,089, up 65.5 per cent; vocational training schools, colleges, and universities increased from 85 to 202, up 137.6 per cent; and civic schools and other similar schools increased from 481 to 561, up 16.6 per cent during the same period. The total number of schools therefore grew from 6,773 in 1960 to 10,102 in 1974, an increase of 49.2 per cent. This is remarkably higher than the 33.2 per cent increase in population, between 1960 and 1973.

In particular the rate of increase in primary schools, 40.5 per cent, is higher than the rate of increase in population growth. The increase rate of 83.8 per cent in middle schools reflects improvement of the basic educational level, and the increase of 137.6 per cent in higher educational institutions indicates a broadening of secondary and higher educational opportunities.

Enrollment in primary schools increased from 3,621,000 in 1960 to 5,619,000 in 1973, or by 55.1 per cent; middle schoos enrollment grew from 528,000 students to 1,930,000, a full 265.5 per cent; high school enrollments increased from 273,000 to 981,000, or 259.3 per cent; and enrollments in higher educational institutions grew from 101,000 to 273,000, in 170.2 per cent, during the same period. The enrollment in middle and high schools increased most, which shows the general improvement of educational attainment levels.

Expansion of Primary and Middle Schools

In 1961 pupils in primary schools totaled 618,000 or 84.9 per cent of the 728,000 children of school age. However, as a result of promotion of compulsory education, in 1973 913,000 children entered in primary school, which is 97.6 per cent of the 935,000 children of primary school age.

According to statistics of the Bank of Korea, the growth of household savings has been retarded by excessive spending for education in cities and by excessive expenditures on family ceremonies such as marriages, funerals, and ancestor memorial services in rural areas. Private tutoring costs in 1971 were 39 billion won, or 1.2 per cent of the gross national product. In the future, continual efforts are needed to curb tutoring outside school. Elimination of the entrance examination system will contribute to the abolition of such burdensome outside study. Moreover, after introduction of the no-exmination entrance system, the rate of entrance to middle schools, which was no more than 40.7 per cent in 1961, increased to 67.8 per cent in 1971, and to 72.7 per cent in 1974, because of the increasing number of students aspiring to enter higher level schools.

After the First Five-Year Plan, the policy to expand compulsory primary education facilities was continued because the shortage of 14,135 primary school classrooms in 1961 made double-shift system unavoidable. During the First and Second Five-Year Plans, 53,456 classroom units were built, absorbing the increased number of school children and entirely solving the problem of classroom shortages. The capital invested for building, rebuilding, and expanding of facilities was nine billion won during the First Five-Year Plan (1962–66), and five billion won during the second plan (1967–71). The government plans to invest 117.2 billion won during the Third Five-Year Plan (1972–76). By June, 1974, 40.5 billion won had already been invested according to the planned schedule.

Reform of
Higher Education

Many nominal universities and othe higher educational institutions sprang up in Korea amid the social chaos just before and after the Korean War in the 1950's, leading to many problems. After the military revolution of May 16, 1961, the government consolidated superfluous institutions under the "Extraordinary Act on Education" of September 1961, in order to secure balanced development between the national and local educational system, and to expand vocational and scientific education.

According to the Act, the government cut the number of classes and students in universities, and also reformed college education by reducing the costs of private universities. The government

regulated enrollments according to a degree registration system. In 1969 excessive and unfair entrance competition in the universities was eliminated with the establishment of preliminary entrance examinations. The reform of college education in the 1960's emphasized improvement in the quality of university education.

In the 1970's more positive measures have been taken to improve the quality of college education. Following the recommendations of the "International Academic Seminar on Development" sponsored by Seoul National University in 1971 and the "International Symposium on Higher Education Reform" held under the auspices of Yonsei University in 1972, the government

has pursued a policy of promoting the gradual improvement of higher education through trial and error by individual institutions rather than through uniform and unilateral government regulation.

The probationary system for the reform of college education was introduced at leading schools in 1973. Participation in social development by professors and students is encouraged with cooperation between industry and schools. The place of the university in national development is very important, and the role of the university, which used to be "ivory tower," is being changed.

Professors contribute to national development and evaluate government planning within their specific areas. Student social service activities related to the nationwide New Community Movement have been systematized, and participate in the development of their home neighborhoods.

The atmosphere of the universities will thus become conducive to research by professors and study by students.

The expenditures by the government for research at universities has reached unprecedented levels since the beginning of the economic development plans in 1962. It increased by 27.5 times to 468 million won in 1973, from 17 million won in 1963. The number of persons who received research funds increased 12.5 times, to 1,569 persons in 1973 from 128 persons in 1963.

Boy scouts at summer work in Weonseong County, Gang-weon Province

Vocational Education

The government has concentrated its efforts on the improvement of scientific techniques as well as vocational education to assist national economic development.

First, technical schools of each type have been categorized according to the needs of their own community.

Second, practical education in technical schools has been encouraged with the introduction of unit technical training, a practical training course established for each major field.

Third, the government has established a precision instruments experimental school for the training of technicians, and this type of school will be gradually increased in number.

Fourth, technical education courses were introduced into the middle school curriculum in the 1970's to enlarge the pool of skilled manpower and to form a basis for advanced technical education. The Korean Institute for Educational Improvement was established and encouraged to develop the necessary study methods and materials.

Furthermore, the government will reform school curricula related to industrial fields in a way suitable to each university, will increase the number of vocational high schools, and will concentrate on supporting schools whose graduates will participate as well-trained technical workers in industries in their own communities upon graduation.

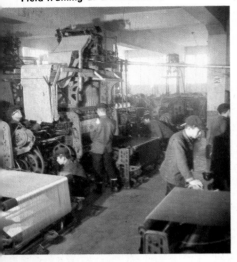

Field training at a technical school

The early risers at the Training Institute of the New Community Movement

New Community Education

In the 1970's New Community Education has been promoted in accordance with the New Community Movement, which seeks to reform the fundamental social substructure of Korea. The goal of New Community Education is to cultivate a spirit of cooperation among students and rural people through school education, following the principles of the National Educational Charter. The purpose of New Community Education is also to train persons who can make practical contributions to the development of provincial areas and thereby establish the basic foundation of the New Community Movement.

New Community Education has been enforced according to educational guidelines throughout all educational courses. New Community Education is concentrated on development of the rural community, reforming the curriculum and guiding study, and also emphasizes practical approaches such as adult instruction and social service activities.

The Training Institute for New Community leaders, which is located at the Institute for Farmers in Suweon, is the center of the New Community Movement. The Institute, established in 1972, has trained 11,977 persons, including New Community Movement leaders, women leaders, executives of companies, and government officials, including ministers and vice ministers, as well as leaders in the religious realm, professors, presidents of universities, presidents of press companies and economic groups, and presidents of individual firms in every field, with good results.

The goal of this education is to endow the trainees with mental discipline, cooperativeness, and a strict and efficient approach to living. The trainees lodge together during the course and have a full schedule of lessons running from 6 a m to 10 p m.

The curriculum is composed of general courses, specific courses and case studies. Besides these courses, the curriculum includes physical training and special events. In particular, the case study hour on successful examples of the New Community Movement, with discussion divided among the group, has proved to be the most impressive time for the trainees.

Through this education, trainees are taught to be leaders of the New Community Movement, and belief in the mission of the New Community Movement is inculcated into their minds and bodies.

Training Center for New Community Leaders at Suweon

Korea has always been a nation of culture, with a long history and a proud tradition. The variety and quality of artistic products, such as the porcelains of the Goryeo Dynasty and white porcelains of the Yi Dynasty, the Seoggulam grotto shrine, Dabo Pagoda and stone observatory dating from the Sinra period, and Buddhist images from the Baegje period are well-known worldwide. The phonetic alphabet called Hangeul and the high level of literature, music and painting show that Koreans are people of culture. This cultural inheritance should be further developed to contribute to the cultural elevation of all mankind.

Cultural Development

Performance of National Symphony Orchestra

In his inaugural address in 1971 President Park said, "I wish to develop our ancestors' glorious traditions and culture. I have special interest in them and will do my best to support a Korean cultural renaissance with the positive assistance for literature and literary studies."

The government transformed the Ministry of Public Information into the Ministry of Culture and Information and started a new policy to assist culture, formerly under educational administration. The government also took the initiative in a long-term project for a national cultural revival in the 1970's.

327

Privately-managed cultural institutes sponsored by U.S.I.S. in districts all over the nation were in charge of propaganda and cultural activities during the Korean War.

The government changed the legal status of the Association of National Cultural Institutions into an incorporated association, and supported the development of cultural institutions throughout the country from 1962. The government institutionalized cultural work as well as cultural institutions with the enactment of the Rural Culture Promotion Law in July 1967. At present, the number of cultural institutions is approximately 133, resulting from the government policy since 1968 of organizing one cultural institution in each county.

Meanwhile, the government has assisted five areas, including culture, literature, fine arts, music and theater arts through an award prize system to stimulate private cultural activities. The Institute for the Promotion of National Culture was established in March 1973, based on the Culture and Arts Promotion Act of 1972. Its goal is to develop the traditional culture of the nation, to elevate the cultural level and popularize national culture through the formation of an independent national spirit, and also to enhance the prestige of the country through international cultural exchange.

Performance of Little Angels at U.N.

Oustatnding cultural activities include those of the Organization of National Folk Arts which held an average of more than ten performances annually throughout the world during the decade 1962–1972, including 78 performances in 23 nations in 1972.

The Little Angels children's singing and dancing troupe established by the Korean Culture Foundation has performed before Queen Elizabeth II of Great Britain and at the UN, as well as three times at the White House in the United States, winning great admiration and enhancing Korean prestige. The Christian Science Monitor complimented them: "As a traditional dancing team, nothing can be more impressive than the Little Angels performances all over the world." Another famous newspaper commented, "Attractive, proud, cheerful, noble, beautiful were the words coming from the fascinated audience that evening."

Korea has produced a number of young prodigies in the international music field. In 1974, pianist Chung Myung Whun achieved worldwide fame as the second-prize winner in the Tschaikovsky Music Contest in Moscow. Two of his sisters, violinist Chung Kyung Wha and cellist Chung Myung Wha, also won positions as leading artists. The violinists Kim Young Uck and Kang Dong Suck and pianist Han Dong Il are also well-known worldwide.

Performance of Korean Traditional Royal Court Music

Korean Folk Fan Dance

The publishing field, which is a barometer of cultural development, barely survived the depression days of 1953–1961, but recovered after 1962 and has become increasingly active since 1972 through enhanced initiative and efficiency.

Since 1966, for purpose of popularizing old classics, the government has supported the rewriting of old literature in the modern language, and also supports work on classical literature by various scholarly organizations.

From 1966 to 1974, the government provided 3,370,000 won for the translation of classical literature into the modern language, and 5,400,000 won for other parallel activities. In particular, translations into the modern national language were a meaningful achievement for preserving and popularizing classical literature.

Traditional arts performance at Munich

Advances in Social Security

Growth of Insurance against Industrial Disaster

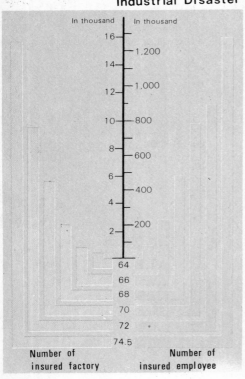

In thousand	In thousand
16—	
	1,200
14—	
	1,000
12—	
10—	800
8—	600
6—	400
4—	
2—	200
	64
	66
	68
	70
	72
	74.5

Number of insured factory   Number of insured employee

Expansion of Social Services

The goal of economic growth is to enhance the welfare of members of society. The welfare society will be achieved when we have fewer poor people and a social security system that benefits all the people. Social security is the goal of Korea's economic growth, but achieving this goal will take time.

Social security in Korea in the form of public support or relief was never feasible. The social security system began to improve with the increase of employment and income in the course of industrialization after 1962.

Social security and health insurance payments to government officials and military personnel, as well as insurance in case of

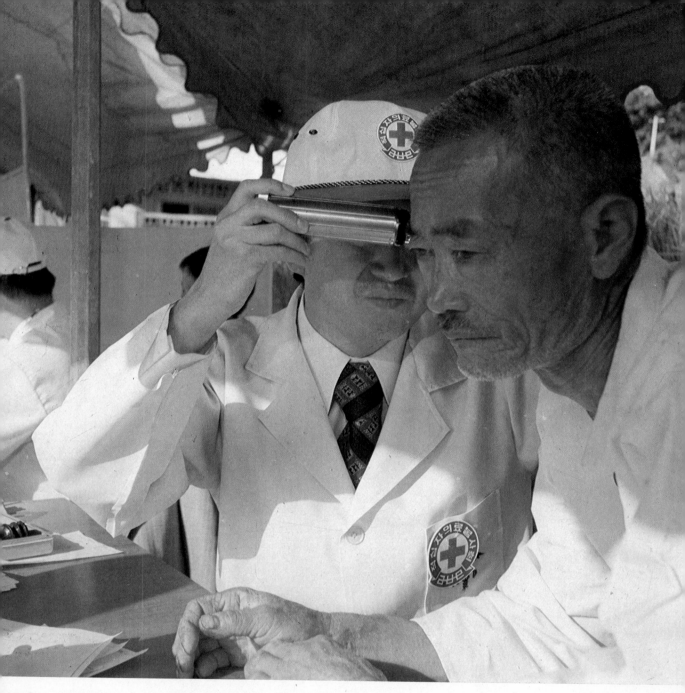

industrial disaster, were established in the early 1960's and have been carried out since then. Pensions are limited only to government officials and military personnel.

Insurance against industrial disaster is a form of social insurance which covers employees of the insured firms and compensates readily and fairly for all injuries occurring on duty. The insurance against industrial disasters is one of the most successful forms of social insurance and has been improved since 1964.

In 1964, this program covered 81,798 employees working at 64 large firms in the field of mining and manufacturing, but was extended to small firms with more than 16 employees or handling construction projects exceeding 10 million won, with the exception of the agriculture, fishing, commerce, finance and stocks brokerage industries.

As of the end of May 1974, the number of insured firms had increased by 234 times over 1964, from 64 to 15,610. The member of insured persons increased 15.4 times, to 1,262,000.

The amount of various insurance payments increased to 4,368 million won in 1973 from 25,211 thousand won in 1964. The total amount paid between 1964 and May of 1974 was 17,850 million won. The breakdown of payments by type was medical treatment, 48.9 per cent, amounting to 8,728 million won; survivors' payments, 19.1 per cent, amounting to 3,415 million won; funeral payments, 1.8 per cent, amounting to 315 million won; payments to disabled persons, 13.6 per cent, amounting to

Trends of Insurance against Industrial Disaster Payments

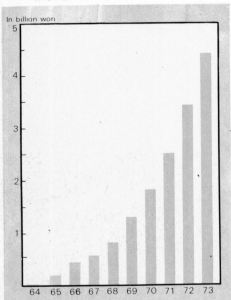

In billion won

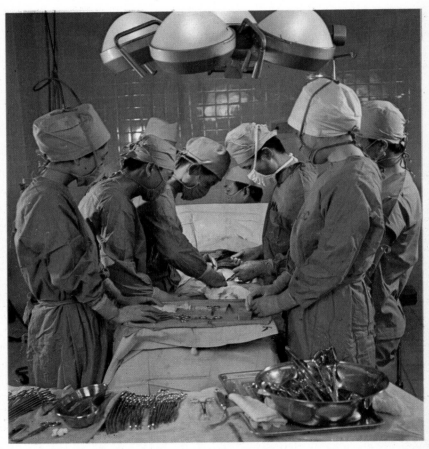

2,432 million won; and lay-off allowances, 16.6 per cent, amounting to 2,965 million won.

The pension system for government officials was established with the passage of the Government Officials' Pension Act in 1960.

This system is financed from contributions by government officials in proportion to their salaries, and by matching deposits by national and local governments. The contribution rate has changed several times, but since 1971 the insured have paid 5.5 per cent of their salaries and the government a matching amount. The number of insured government officials increased to 450,000 at the end of 1973 from 240,000 persons in the year the system was established.

Funds of this pension system now amount to 35,400 million won and constitute one of the largest accumulations among social insurance programs. Pensions for military personnel were established in 1963 according to the Military Personnel Pension Act.

The contributions made by military personnel represent 5.5 per cent of their salaries, and the government contributes an equivalent amount. In 1972 the amount of premiums received reached six billion won, and so the pension fund for military personnel became the second largest after the pension fund for government officials.

Medical insurance has been operating since the Medical Insurance Act was enforced in 1963. The insurance system grew steadily after amendment of the Act in 1970. As of 1973, the amount paid out amounted to only 609 million won. Medical insurance is still in its initial stages, but the insurance system will be improved and expanded. In 1980 all of the nation's citizens will benefit from such insurance. In 1975 pensions for teachers in private schools will be implemented and a national welfare pension system is in the planning stage.

Incheon Sanatorium

Public Relief Programs

Public relief programs are a kind of survival protection system for low-income persons that needs special protection but are not covered by other social insurance.

Korea carries out public relief activities through livelihood protection, self-support guidance, and disaster protection programs. Disaster protection is divided into relief for the victims and relief for military and police personnel.

The core of public relief activity is the livelihood protection program, which is based on the Livelihood Protection Act promulgated in December 1961. The Act covers ① elderly people over 65, ② young people under 18, ③ pregnant women, ④ people who cannot work due to being crippled, having an incurable disease, sickness, handicaps, or other mental or physical troubles, and ⑤ people recognized by the protection institution who have no one responsible for supporting them. The types of protection are ① livelihood protection, ② medical protection, ③ childbirth protection, ④ measures for funeral and memorial services. Also these programs are divided into two parts: one for those living in their own homes, and the other for those living in asylums for the aged or other institutions.

Social welfare expenditures increased 2.4 times to 2.4 billion won in 1973 from one billion won in 1964. The social welfare outlays were made in the form of crops, goods and cash financed from various sources such as national and local government treasuries and foreign aid.

The Livelihood Protection Act covers the poor who are recognized by the relevant agency. The poor as defined by the Act have no members in their family capable of working, but the poor defined by other Acts have family members who can work. The reason for the poverty of the poor defined by other Acts is their laziness or the shortage of jobs, and the government distributes wages through creating working opportunities for the poor.

Support for the poor was previously paid through US farm surpluses under PL 480, relief supplies, cash and financial support from the national treasury. The annual average amount paid from 1964 to 1969 was 4.6 billion won, but the supply of farm surpluses from the United States stopped in 1973. Since then, the government has changed the direction of unemployment measures, according to the business cycle, in order to increase employment opportunities caused by economic development.

The amount paid was only 800 million won in 1973 because the year saw an unprecedented economic boom.

On January 14, 1974, the government announced Emergency Measures for the poor and alloted five billion won on the instruction of President Park; the amount was later expanded to 15

Flood disaster at Yeongsan Riverside (1974)

billion won to combat the recession caused by the oil crisis.

Meanwhile, disaster relief activity has been supported through the Disaster Protection Act enacted in 1962. The purpose of the Act is to repair damage from natural disasters through emergency assistance and the maintenance of social order through the relief of affected people. According to the Act such people are to be provided with: ① lodging, food, clothes, beds and school supplies, ② medical daily necessities such as treatment and maternity aid services, ③ relief for disaster victims, ④ repair for damaged houses, ⑤ livelihood funds and allotments or loans for the purchase of various tools and materials, ⑥ job arrangements, ⑦ funeral expenditures, and ⑧ other necessary cash.

Korea experiences several typhoons and flood disasters each year, since the country is located in the monsoon area. There are relief programs for collective disasters such as flood, fire and disease, according to the Disaster Relief Act. Since 1962 the annual average number of victims has been 391,000 persons, and the annual average amount for relief has amounted to 372 million won. In 1972 the amount of relief for disasters recorded 2.2 billion won, because the disasters were numerous and severe.

The scale of relief projects differ every year according to the level of disaster, and the funds are provided by central and local governments, Red Cross, relief committees and private sources.

Of a total relief expenditure of 3,718 million won for the ten years from 1962 to 1971 the central government supplied 23.0 per cent, or 856 million won; local governments 27.1 per cent, or 1,007 million won; the Red Cross 10.0 per cent, or 373 million won; relief committees 19.0 per cent, or 706 million won; and private sources 17.9 per cent, or 464 million won.

Social security for military personnel has been carried out by the Ministry of Health and Social Affairs since the Korean War. In 1961 this was transferred to the Office of Retired Veterans Administration along with aid for national heroes and refugees from North Korea which was added in 1962, and the name was changed to the Office of Veterans Administration. Relief activities consist of compensation payments, an education protection system for veterans and their families, a military insurance system, and loans for re-settlement.

In 1970 the Social Welfare Act, Children's Welfare Act, Mothers' and Children's Protection Act, Minors' Protection Act and the Extraordinary Act for Self-Sustaining Guidance Activity were put into effect.

Children's welfare and maternity welfare activities are being carried out under the above-mentioned acts.

중단하는 자는 승리하지 못하며
승리하는 자는 중단하지 않는다

He who stops cannot win and he who wins does not stop.

Since the 1960's Korea has seen continuous economic development, overcoming poverty and difficulties with confidence in the modernization of the country. In the 1970's the nation hopes for further industrialization, and to achieve a self-supporting economy under the New Community Movement, to reach an annual export volume of 10 billion dollars and a 1,000 dollars per capita income level through the combined efforts of the government and the people, the city and the village and employers and employees.

A nation's growth depends upon the hard work and the qualities of its people. Koreans have gained confidence and pride through the high economic achievements of the 1960's. The revitalization stemming from the New Community Movement fosters in us the desire to work and the potential to grow.

A diplomat who recently visited Korea reported to the president of his country that "The Koreans were working 24 hours a day," in response to the president's question, "Tell me your impression of Korea in one sentence."

The continuous efforts of the Korean people have produced a miracle of high economic growth. From the president to the worker in the field, all Koreans have been working hard. There is hope for a people who work so hard.

The achievement of a self-supporting economy and an affluent society is a short cut to the peaceful reunification of the country, which is Korea's ultimate goal. At a recent Korean Independence Day Ceremony, President Park stated: "Communists in North Korea! Let's compete in development, construction and innovation, in order to find out which system, democracy or communism, functions better to improve the level of national welfare."

On the day Korea achieves the goal of reunification of the nation, her people will be proud of having created a new chapter in world history. They look forward eagerly to a better future through incessant efforts, faith and pride, expecting a proud new history as a unified country which will be bequeathed to their descendants.

APPENDIX

-Statistics-

CONTENTS

Major Economic

| | Population | Gross National Product | | | Per | Per | Invest- | Domes- | Index Number Industrial | |
	(Midyear)	Current Market Prices	1970 Constant Market Prices	Growth Rate	Capita G.N.P.[1]	Capita N.I.[2]	ment Rate	tic Saving Rate	General Index	Mining
	thousand persons	billion won	billion won	%	dollars	dollars	%	%	1970	
1960	24,695	246.3	1,129.7	1.9	81	71	10.9	1.4	22.7	46.6
1961	25,498	297.0	1,184.4	4.8	83	74	13.1	3.9	24.0	52.9
1962	26,231	348.8	1,220.9	3.1	87	75	13.0	1.6	28.1	62.8
1963	26,987	488.5	1,328.3	8.8	98	87	18.5	6.3	31.7	71.6
1964	27,678	700.2	1,441.9	8.6	102	91	14.6	7.3	34.3	78.8
1965	28,327	805.3	1,529.7	6.1	106	94	15.1	7.5	36.8	82.8
1966	28,962	1,032.4	1,719.1	12.4	126	110	21.7	11.8	45.1	91.0
1967	29,541	1,269.9	1,853.0	7.8	143	124	22.1	11.9	57.1	93.6
1968	30,171	1,598.0	2,087.1	12.6	168	141	26.8	13.6	74.8	88.3
1969	30,738	2,081.5	2,400.4	15.0	208	176	29.8	17.5	89.7	89.6
1970	31,298	2,589.2	2,589.2	7.9	242	203	27.2	16.3	100.0	100.0
1971	31,847	3,151.5	2,826.8	9.2	275	232	25.6	14.5	115.4	103.3
1972	32,416	3,860.0	3,023.6	7.0	304	255	20.9	15.0	132.2	98.5
1973	32,905[2]	4,928.6	3,522.7	16.5	376	313	26.2	22.1	179.4	114.5

Note: 1) *Figures are based on the new parity conversion rate estimated by the Bank of Korea.*
2) *Figures are based on population census.*

Major Indicators

| | Education | | | | | | | Health | | | |
| | Number of Schools | | | | Number of Students | | | Doc- tors | Den- tists | Phar- macists | Death Rate from Epidemics (%) |
	Elemen- tary Schools	Middle Schools	High Schools	Univer- sities[1] (each)	Middle Schools	High Schools	Univer- sities[1]				
1960	4.6	1.1	0.6	63	528.6[6]	263.6	97.8	7.8	1.4	4.7	2.7
1961	5.3	1.1	0.6	66	620.5	278.6	142.5	8.4	1.5	5.0	2.6
1962	4.7	1.1	0.6	86	655.1	323.7	126.5	9.7	1.7	6.0	2.0
1963	4.8	1.1	0.7	103	665.8	364:3	124.2	9.1	1.7	7.2	1.0
1964	5.0	1.2	0.7	123	666.6	399.6	136.2	10.1	1.7	8.5	4.2
1965	5.1	1.2	0.7	131	751.3	426.5	134.7	10.9	1.8	10.0	1.8
1966	5.3	1.3	0.7	128	822.0	434.8	172.0	11.5	1.8	10.7	3.8
1967	5.4	1.3	0.8	124	911.9	441.9	162.0	12.3	1.8	11.5	3.1
1968	5.6	1.4	0.8	122	1,013.5	481.5	161.0	13.2	2.0	12.8	1.6
1969	5.8	1.5	0.9	127	1,147.4	530.1	172.9	14.0	2.1	13.8	0.8
1970	6.0	1.6	0.9	127	1,318.8	590.4	186.9	14.9	2.1	14.6	0.2
1971	6.1	1.8	0.9	134	1,529.5	647.2	199.8	16.2	2.5	15.5	..
1972	6.2	1.9	0.9	141	1,686.4	729.8	213.5	16.4	2.4	16.9	..
1973	7.1	1.9	1.0	147	1,832.1	839.3	236.4	16.4	2.4	17.8	..

Note: 1) *Includes junior technical colleges, junior colleges and junior teachers' colleges.*
2) *Since 1970, libraries equipped with less than 1,000 books are excluded.*
3) *Excludes daily and other similar publications.*

Indicators

of Production		Food Grains Production	Price Index		Deposit Banks		Foreign Transaction			Foreign Exch. Holdings
Manu-facturing	Electric-ity		Whole-sale Price	Seoul Consum-er Price	Deposits	Loans	Export f.o.b.	Import c.i.f.	Invisible Receipts	
=100		thousand MT	1970=100		billion won	billion won	million dollars	million dollars	million dollars	million dollars
21.5	18.5	5,271	31.0	28.6	14.1	11.5	32.8	343.5	79.4	155.2
22.4	19.3	5,933	35.1	30.9	24.7	32.0	40.9	316.1	123.3	205.2
26.2	21.4	5,423	38.4	32.9	39.1	43.2	54.8	421.8	122.3	166.8
29.6	24.1	5,742	46.3	39.7	39.0	49.1	86.8	560.3	91.8	129.6
31.8	29.5	7,066	62.3	51.4	43.1	53.1	119.1	404.4	97.1	128.9
33.9	35.4	7,006	68.5	58.4	78.5	72.1	175.1	463.4	125.8	138.3
42.2	42.4	7,568	74.6	65.4	120.9	102.7	250.3	716.4	238.4	235.8
54.7	53.6	6,836	79.4	72.5	205.9	178.0	320.2	996.2	375.2	347.2
74.3	65.8	6,884	85.8	80.6	373.1	331.2	455.4	1,462.9	424.5	387.7
89.6	84.0	7,737	91.6	88.7	619.2	563.0	622.5	1,823.6	497.1	549.5
100.0	100.0	7,476	100.0	100.0	789.7	722.4	835.2	1,984.0	490.7	583.5
116.6	115.0	7,274	108.6	112.3	977.6	919.5	1,067.6	2,394.3	486.6	534.5
135.7	129.2	7,208	123.8	125.6	1,323.9	1,198.0	1,624.1	2,522.0	579.2	693.8
186.9	161.7	7,163	132.4	129.5	1,753.6	1,587.5	3,225.0	4,240.3	936.3	1,034.2

# of Living Conditions

(In thousands)

Communications		Pictures & Books		Water	Culture					Transportation	
Ordinary Mail Handled (million)	Tele-phone Sub-scribers	Libra-ries2) (each)	Books in Safe-keeping	Supply (m³/day)	News-papers (each)	Com-munica-tions3) (each)	Maga-zines4) (each)	T.V. Sets	Thea-tres5) (each)	Passengers per km (million)	Cars Availa-ble
156.9	86.6	127	3,801	429.2	41	14	606	1.9	273	4,935	31.3
147.1	97.0	291	4,633	450.8	38	12	294	2.0	302	5,372	29.2
174.3	127.7	445	5,239	490.0	39	11	193	31.0	344	5,869	30.8
211.9	157.3	..	..	497.0	34	8	276	34.8	540	6,676	34.2
276.1	191.1	1,171	6,217	540.0	35	9	441	44.8	625	7,353	37.8
367.6	220.6	1,651	7,214	634.0	39	10	620	49.6	671	6,917	41.5
397.0	277.8	2,427	8,692	710.0	42	10	553	51.5	702	8,665	50.2
440.4	339.3	3,232	10,796	814.0	43	10	626	82.0	722	9,557	60.7
480.7	384.5	3,618	12,663	1,041.3	43	10	632	152.1	719	10,590	81.0
522.4	442.5	3,749	12,855	1,310.0	44	7	692	223.7	748	11,077	108.7
540.3	481.2	2,583	13,881	1,649.0	44	7	730	379.6	782	9,819	129.4
551.6	563.1	3,121	16,087	2,001.5	44	7	801	616.4	793	8,750	144.3
564.3	644.9	3,446	18,410	2,164.5	41	7	822	905.4	786	10,062	150.0
569.4	773.9	3,361	19,430	..	37	6	833	1,093.4	745	10,720	170.7

4) *Includes weekly, monthly and other periodicals.*
5) *Excludes theatres in public ownership from 1960 to 1962.*
6) *Excludes normal schools.*

Industrial Origin

	G.N.P.	Agri., Forestry & Fishery	Mining & Manufacturing			Social Overhead Capital & Other Services		
			Total	Mining	Manu-facturing	Total	Social Overhead Capital	Other Services
1 9 6 0	246.3	90.7	38.7	5.2	33.5	116.9	21.5	95.3
1 9 6 1	297.0	119.4	45.2	5.5	39.7	132.3	26.8	105.6
1 9 6 2	348.8	127.7	57.6	6.9	50.6	163.5	33.4	130.1
1 9 6 3	488.5	206.0	81.3	8.1	73.1	201.2	39.7	161.5
1 9 6 4	700.2	321.0	123.1	12.0	111.0	256.0	50.7	205.3
1 9 6 5	805.3	309.1	158.6	14.7	143.8	337.5	70.0	267.5
1 9 6 6	1,032.4	365.1	207.3	16.4	190.9	459.9	102.8	357.2
1 9 6 7	1,269.9	399.2	259.8	20.6	239.1	610.8	139.2	471.6
1 9 6 8	1,598.0	455.1	347.9	20.4	327.4	794.8	202.5	592.3
1 9 6 9	2,081.5	597.4	454.4	23.6	430.7	1,029.6	277.7	751.9
1 9 7 0	2,589.2	724.5	590.7	30.7	560.0	1,273.9	344.8	929.0
1 9 7 1	3,151.5	910.7	719.2	34.1	685.0	1,521.5	400.6	1,120.8
1 9 7 2	3,860.0	1,094.6	940.9	37.9	902.9	1,824.4	478.3	1,346.0
1 9 7 3	4,928.6	1,280.1	1,338.2	48.1	1,290.1	2,310.2	622.2	1,688.0

Composition and Growth Rate

Composition of G.N.P. (1970 Constant Market Prices)

	G.N.P.	Agri., Forestry & Fishery	Mining & Manufacturing			Social Overhead Capital & Other Services		
			Total	Mining	Manu-facturing	Total	Social Overhead Capital	Other Services
1 9 6 0	100	41.3	12.1	1.3	10.8	46.6	6.0	40.6
1 9 6 1	100	44.1	12.0	1.4	10.6	43.9	6.0	37.9
1 9 6 2	100	40.3	13.2	1.6	11.6	46.5	6.7	39.8
1 9 6 3	100	40.0	14.1	1.5	12.6	45.9	7.2	38.7
1 9 6 4	100	42.6	13.9	1.5	12.4	43.5	7.5	36.0
1 9 6 5	100	39.4	15.5	1.6	13.9	45.1	8.5	36.6
1 9 6 6	100	38.8	16.0	1.5	14.5	45.2	9.1	36.1
1 9 6 7	100	34.3	18.0	1.5	16.5	47.7	10.0	37.7
1 9 6 8	100	31.1	20.0	1.3	18.7	48.9	11.7	37.2
1 9 6 9	100	30.5	20.8	1.1	19.7	48.7	13.0	35.7
1 9 7 0	100	28.0	22.8	1.2	21.6	49.2	13.3	35.9
1 9 7 1	100	26.5	24.4	1.1	23.3	49.1	13.0	36.1
1 9 7 2	100	25.2	26.2	1.0	25.2	48.6	12.9	35.7
1 9 7 3	100	22.8	29.4	1.0	28.4	47.8	13.7	34.1

# of G. N. P.

(In billion won)

At 1970 Constant Market Prices

G.N.P.	Agri., Forestry & Fishery	Mining & Manufacturing			Social Overhead Capital & Other Services		
		Total	Mining	Manufacturing	Total	Social Overhead Capital	Other Services
1, 129. 7	466. 5	136. 8	14. 8	122. 0	526. 3	68. 0	458. 3
1, 184. 4	522. 2	141. 7	15. 9	125. 7	520. 5	71. 6	448. 9
1, 220. 9	492. 1	161. 6	19. 3	142. 3	567. 1	82. 0	485. 0
1, 328. 3	532. 0	187. 0	20. 1	166. 9	609. 1	95. 3	513. 8
1, 441. 9	614. 5	200. 0	22. 2	177. 8	627. 3	107. 8	519. 4
1, 529. 7	602. 6	237. 4	24. 1	213. 3	689. 5	129. 6	559. 9
1, 719. 1	667. 9	274. 6	24. 7	249. 8	776. 6	156. 1	620. 5
1, 853. 0	634. 7	334. 0	27. 2	306. 7	884. 2	186. 0	698. 2
2, 087. 1	650. 0	416. 7	27. 0	389. 6	1, 020. 3	243. 6	776. 6
2, 400. 4	731. 4	499. 5	26. 5	473. 0	1, 169. 4	313. 3	856. 0
2, 589. 2	724. 5	590. 7	30. 7	560. 0	1, 273. 9	344. 8	929. 0
2, 826. 8	748. 4	690. 4	31. 2	659. 2	1, 387. 9	367. 8	1, 020. 1
3, 023. 6	760. 9	794. 0	31. 2	762. 7	1, 468. 7	389. 6	1, 079. 0
3, 522. 7	802. 9	1, 035. 6	36. 8	998. 7	1, 684. 1	483. 2	1, 200. 9

# of G.N.P. by Industrial Origin

(In per cent)

Growth Rate of G.N.P. (1970 Constant Market Prices)

G.N.P.	Agri., Forestry & Fishery	Mining & Manufacturing			Social Overhead Capital & Other Services		
		Total	Mining	Manufacturing	Total	Social Overhead Capital	Other Services
1. 9	−1. 3	10. 4	32. 4	8. 2	2. 8	6. 0	2. 4
4. 8	11. 9	3. 6	7. 8	3. 1	−1. 1	5. 3	−2. 1
3. 1	−5. 8	14. 1	21. 3	13. 2	8. 9	14. 6	8. 0
8. 8	8. 1	15. 7	3. 9	17. 3	7. 4	16. 2	5. 9
8. 6	15. 5	6. 9	10. 4	6. 5	3. 0	13. 2	1. 1
6. 1	−1. 9	18. 7	8. 6	20. 0	9. 9	20. 2	7. 8
12. 4	10. 8	15. 6	2. 7	17. 1	12. 6	20. 4	10. 8
7. 8	−5. 0	21. 6	10. 1	22. 8	13. 8	19. 2	12. 5
12. 6	2. 4	24. 8	−0. 8	27. 0	15. 4	31. 0	11. 2
15. 0	12. 5	19. 9	−1. 7	21. 4	14. 6	28. 6	10. 2
7. 9	−0. 9	18. 2	15. 7	18. 4	8. 9	10. 1	8. 5
9. 2	3. 3	16. 9	1. 6	17. 7	8. 9	6. 7	9. 8
7. 0	1. 7	15. 0	0. 0	15. 7	5. 8	5. 9	5. 8
16. 5	5. 5	30. 4	18. 1	30. 9	14. 7	24. 0	11. 3

Expenditure

			At Current Market Prices							
			Expenditure			Exports of Goods & Services	(Less) Imports of Goods & Services	Statistical Discrepancy	Expenditure on G.D.P.	Net Factor Income from Abroad	Expenditure on G.N.P.
			Con-sumption	Invest-ment	Total						
1 9 6 0			242. 8	26. 8	269. 6	8. 2	31. 0	−2. 3	244. 5	1. 8	246. 3
1 9 6 1			285. 5	38. 8	324. 3	15. 8	43. 8	−1. 9	294. 3	2. 8	297. 1
1 9 6 2			343. 4	45. 5	388. 9	18. 0	59. 1	−2. 0	345. 7	3. 2	348. 9
1 9 6 3			458. 1	90. 3	548. 3	23. 8	79. 5	−7. 4	485. 2	3. 3	488. 5
1 9 6 4			648. 3	102. 2	750. 5	42. 1	96. 4	−1. 2	694. 9	5. 3	700. 2
1 9 6 5			744. 8	120. 0	866. 8	68. 6	127. 8	−9. 9	797. 7	7. 7	805. 3
1 9 6 6			910. 1	224. 5	1, 134. 5	106. 8	207. 8	−14. 4	1, 019. 1	13. 4	1, 032. 4
1 9 6 7			1, 118. 1	281. 0	1, 399. 1	144. 6	279. 4	−16. 3	1, 248. 0	21. 9	1, 269. 9
1 9 6 8			1, 379. 7	427. 9	1, 807. 6	209. 3	416. 8	−25. 2	1, 574. 9	23. 2	1, 598. 0
1 9 6 9			1, 716. 3	620. 7	2, 337. 0	287. 8	541. 3	−26. 5	2, 056. 5	25. 0	2, 081. 5
1 9 7 0			2, 166. 1	704. 7	2, 870. 7	381. 2	642. 4	−32. 2	2, 577. 4	11. 9	2, 589. 3
1 9 7 1			2, 693. 3	805. 4	3, 498. 6	514. 2	865. 9	6. 9	3, 153. 8	−2. 3	3, 151. 6
1 9 7 2			3, 282. 7	805. 5	4, 088. 2	813. 8	1, 013. 5	−13. 1	3, 875. 3	−15. 3	3, 860. 0
1 9 7 3			3, 838. 9	1, 292. 3	5, 131. 2	1, 577. 7	1, 739. 6	−3. 6	4, 965. 7	−37. 0	4, 928. 7

Gross Domestic Capital Formation

			Saving Ratio				Total	Fixed Capital Formation	Increase in Stocks
			Total	Domestic Saving	Foreign Saving				
1 9 6 0			10. 9	1. 4	8. 6		10. 9	10. 8	0. 1
1 9 6 1			13. 1	3. 9	8. 6		13. 1	11. 6	1. 5
1 9 6 2			13. 0	1. 6	10. 8		13. 0	13. 9	−0. 9
1 9 6 3			18. 5	6. 3	10. 7		18. 5	13. 9	4. 6
1 9 6 4			14. 6	7. 3	7. 1		14. 6	11. 6	3. 0
1 9 6 5			15. 1	7. 5	6. 4		15. 1	14. 8	0. 3
1 9 6 6			21. 7	11. 8	8. 5		21. 7	20. 2	1. 5
1 9 6 7			22. 1	11. 9	8. 9		22. 1	21. 5	0. 6
1 9 6 8			26. 8	13. 6	11. 6		26. 8	25. 8	1. 0
1 9 6 9			29. 8	17. 5	11. 0		29. 8	26. 6	3. 2
1 9 7 0			27. 2	16. 3	9. 7		27. 2	25. 1	2. 1
1 9 7 1			25. 6	14. 5	11. 3		25. 6	23. 2	2. 4
1 9 7 2			20. 9	15. 0	5. 6		20. 9	20. 2	0. 7
1 9 7 3			26. 2	22. 1	4. 0		26. 2	23. 7	2. 5

Note: Industrial origin and subject origin in investment ratios are breakdowns of fixed capital formation.

on G.N.P.

At 1970 Constant Market Prices								
Expenditure			Exports of Goods & Services	Imports of Goods & Services	Statistical Discrepancy	Expenditure on G.D.P.	Net Factor Income from Abroad	Expenditure on G.N.P.
Consumption	Investment	Total						
1, 107. 1	96. 6	1, 203. 7	27. 4	117. 5	7. 5	1, 121. 1	8. 6	1, 129. 7
1, 114. 0	121. 4	1, 235. 4	38. 2	106. 6	10. 7	1, 177. 7	6. 8	1, 184. 5
1, 184. 8	119. 9	1, 304. 7	43. 0	141. 2	7. 0	1, 213. 4	7. 6	1, 221. 0
1, 229. 8	225. 1	1, 454. 9	46. 2	179. 2	−1. 4	1, 320. 4	7. 9	1, 328. 3
1, 296. 3	188. 2	1, 484. 5	57. 1	133. 3	26. 1	1, 434. 4	7. 6	1, 442. 0
1, 382. 7	197. 3	1, 579. 9	80. 3	149. 6	10. 1	1, 520. 8	8. 9	1, 529. 7
1, 482. 7	317. 5	1, 800. 2	122. 3	237. 9	19. 4	1, 703. 9	15. 3	1, 719. 2
1, 614. 9	368. 3	1, 983. 3	166. 0	320. 7	−0. 7	1, 827. 8	25. 2	1, 853. 0
1, 786. 2	509. 1	2, 295. 2	235. 0	468. 0	−1. 1	2, 061. 1	26. 0	2, 087. 1
1, 969. 8	714. 1	2, 683. 9	310. 1	583. 8	−36. 6	2, 373. 5	27. 0	2, 400. 5
2, 166. 1	704. 7	2, 870. 7	381. 2	642. 4	−32. 2	2, 577. 4	11. 9	2, 589. 3
2, 392. 0	748. 8	3, 140. 8	459. 4	773. 6	2. 2	2, 828. 8	−2. 0	2, 826. 8
2, 551. 6	667. 9	3, 219. 5	643. 3	801. 2	−25. 9	3, 035. 7	−12. 1	3, 023. 6
2, 752. 4	921. 7	3, 674. 1	1, 034. 3	1, 087. 0	−71. 9	3, 549. 4	−26. 7	3, 522. 7

and Saving-Investment Ratio

Investment Ratio						
Industrial Origin				Subject Origin		
Agri., Forestry & Fishery	Mining & Manufacturing	Social Overhead Capital	Other Services	Private & Public Enterprises	Gov't Enterprises	General Gov't
1. 4	2. 3	2. 6	4. 5	7. 4	1. 4	2. 0
1. 6	2. 4	3. 8	3. 8	7. 9	1. 3	2. 4
1. 2	3. 0	5. 2	4. 5	9. 5	1. 6	2. 8
1. 4	3. 3	5. 4	3. 8	10. 1	1. 8	2. 0
1. 4	2. 9	3. 5	3. 8	9. 0	1. 4	1. 2
1. 7	4. 1	4. 1	4. 9	11. 6	1. 4	1. 8
2. 4	6. 6	6. 3	4. 9	15. 7	2. 1	2. 4
1. 8	5. 8	8. 1	5. 8	16. 7	2. 0	2. 8
1. 9	6. 4	10. 2	7. 3	19. 4	1. 9	4. 5
1. 7	5. 6	11. 7	7. 6	18. 7	1. 7	6. 2
2. 0	5. 1	9. 6	8. 4	18. 8	1. 2	5. 1
1. 9	4. 7	8. 5	8. 1	17. 0	1. 4	4. 8
2. 2	4. 2	7. 5	6. 3	14. 7	1. 5	4. 0
2. 1	7. 0	7. 6	7. 1	19. 2	1. 1	3. 4

347

General Government Budget and Central

F Y	Revenues						Counterpart Fund
	Total	Taxes	Monopoly Profits	Misc. Non-tax Revs.	Trust Funds & Interest	Others	
1 9 6 0	48,456	24,964	2,300	2,437	—	1,992	16,763
1 9 6 1	61,354	23,198	2,645	5,034	—	6,419	24,058
1 9 6 2	93,214	28,242	4,234	6,834	1,091	24,082	28,726
1 9 6 3	75,923	31,078	4,832	6,803	1,327	5,571	26,312
1 9 6 4	79,387	37,421	4,503	5,938	1,818	1,660	28,020
1 9 6 5	105,481	54,634	3,598	7,426	2,276	1,457	36,090
1 9 6 6	153,777	87,646	7,500	11,016	9,200	—	38,415
1 9 6 7	199,018	129,241	10,000	12,467	9,271	—	38,039
1 9 6 8	275,717	194,288	16,400	18,678	12,933	—	33,418
1 9 6 9	376,041	262,823	24,250	20,265	44,802	—	23,901
1 9 7 0	445,856	334,723	30,100	21,739	35,596	—	23,698
1 9 7 1	551,452	407,683	45,373	26,391	51,056	—	20,949
1 9 7 2	706,882	433,446	42,900	23,658	100,180	95,000	11,699
1 9 7 3	691,101	521,492	57,000	27,372	82,368	—	2,868

Note: 1) On executed basis.

Central and Local

F Y	Total Finance	For Central Gov't Finance			Local Gov't Finance	Gross Finance Burden (%)	Central Gov't Burden (%)	Local Gov't Burden (%)	Tax Burden (%)
		Total	General Finance	Special Accounts					
1 9 6 1	99.65	79.75	57.15	22.60	19.90	36.9	29.6	7.4	9.5
1 9 6 2	155.72	119.90	88.39	31.51	35.82	44.7	34.4	10.3	10.8
1 9 6 3	153.36	110.99	72.84	38.15	42.37	31.4	22.7	8.7	8.9
1 9 6 4	167.67	120.67	75.18	45.49	47.00	23.9	17.3	6.7	7.3
1 9 6 5	214.82	154.15	93.53	60.61	60.67	26.7	19.1	7.5	8.6
1 9 6 6	330.27	230.98	140.94	90.04	99.29	32.0	22.4	9.6	10.8
1 9 6 7	423.67	291.25	180.93	110.32	132.42	33.4	22.9	10.4	12.1
1 9 6 8	590.61	402.88	262.06	140.82	187.73	36.9	25.2	11.7	14.4
1 9 6 9	845.50	578.04	370.53	207.51	267.46	40.6	27.8	12.8	15.1
1 9 7 0	918.60	597.67	441.33	156.34	320.93	35.4	23.1	12.4	15.4
1 9 7 1	1,126.91	731.98	546.28	187.50	394.15	35.8	23.2	12.6	15.6
1 9 7 2	1,411.42	963.11	710.14	261.97	448.31	36.6	25.0	11.6	13.5
1 9 7 3	1,504.44	958.14	651.59	306.50	546.30	31.1	19.8	11.3	13.4

Note: 1) On executed basis.

Government Loans and Investments[1]

(In million won)

	Expenditure				Compostion Ratio by Industry of Central Gov't Loans & Investments			
Total	General Expen.	National Defense	Loans & Investments	Others	Agri., Forestry & Fishery	Mining & Manufacturing	Social Overhead Capital	Other Services
41,995	16,695	14,707	10,383	210	..	..	..	..
57,153	23,314	16,599	16,965	275	..	..	..	..
88,393	43,868	20,474	23,897	154	29.1	21.6	30.3	19.0
72,839	31,844	20,479	20,333	183	23.0	19.8	42.0	15.2
75,180	33,312	24,926	16,682	260	20.8	20.7	45.3	17.3
93,534	41,815	29,874	21,445	400	28.5	24.1	34.4	13.1
140,942	59,169	40,542	40,684	547	27.7	18.6	36.5	17.1
180,932	84,721	49,553	46,108	550	25.4	17.3	37.2	20.2
262,064	116,404	64,708	80,302	650	27.5	10.3	42.5	19.7
370,532	153,843	84,382	131,656	651	27.9	11.5	38.7	21.9
441,329	189,798	102,335	148,566	630	24.4	12.2	36.9	26.5
546,278	233,600	134,738	177,350	590	24.6	15.2	33.5	26.8
701,143	286,543	173,909	240,191	500	20.0	32.5	28.0	19.5
651,586	291,367	183,468	176,750	—	32.9	8.9	36.8	21.5

Government Finance[1]

(In billion won)

Finance of Cities and Provinces (Total)										
Seoul	Busan	Gyeong-gi	Gang-weon	Chung-buk	Chung-nam	Jeon-bug	Jeon-nam	Gyeong-bug	Gyeong-nam	Jeju
3.27	—	1.33	1.08	0.81	1.28	1.26	1.61	1.99	2.13	0.20
4.74	1.33	3.44	2.37	2.00	3.28	3.21	4.55	5.53	4.72	0.58
5.72	1.87	4.47	2.72	2.36	4.11	3.83	5.26	6.28	4.98	0.72
6.69	2.10	4.97	3.16	2.68	4.73	3.90	5.94	6.98	5.16	0.65
8.41	3.09	6.42	4.30	3.45	5.79	4.86	7.66	9.03	6.81	0.80
14.18	6.85	9.72	7.03	5.22	8.90	7.68	12.93	14.60	10.64	1.50
17.88	8.02	12.64	9.03	6.94	11.55	10.73	17.54	20.82	14.83	2.38
29.53	15.71	17.79	11.23	8.44	14.23	13.90	27.95	26.84	19.60	2.45
42.98	19.92	25.66	15.61	12.43	20.03	20.32	36.56	38.08	31.89	3.95
54.62	17.41	33.39	22.09	17.52	28.23	20.01	40.35	46.79	35.81	4.65
69.35	21.32	43.12	28.47	20.94	35.23	31.60	48.69	55.75	41.56	6.17
74.29	24.89	56.87	34.24	27.28	39.69	36.69	60.40	70.69	50.21	8.09
97.57	30.77	61.88	35.88	28.23	43.80	40.13	61.45	82.04	56.37	8.26

Money, Deposits

End of Year	Money			Money by Sector			
	Total	Currency in Circulation	Deposit Money	Public Sector	Gov't Agencies	Private Sector	Foreign Sector
1 9 6 0	22,738	14,250	8,488	6,262	—	10,167	6,408
1 9 6 1	35,768	16,668	19,100	2,133	200	27,590	18,819
1 9 6 2	39,359	17,560	21,799	7,774	500	28,064	11,787
1 9 6 3	41,914	18,280	23,634	8,341	2,642	31,593	4,295
1 9 6 4	48,903	24,940	23,963	3,983	2,100	27,480	11,784
1 9 6 5	65,618	31,634	33,984	2,612	12,300	32,378	18,583
1 9 6 6	85,083	42,901	42,182	−6,807	18,500	24,534	51,789
1 9 6 7	122,998	57,609	65,389	−8,633	20,100	46,052	80,448
1 9 6 8	177,858	81,938	95,920	−29,922	27,900	117,996	81,350
1 9 6 9	252,007	111,317	140,690	−54,266	32,000	202,291	107,941
1 9 7 0	307,601	133,685	173,916	−82,752	30,000	277,269	110,247
1 9 7 1	357,974	162,071	195,903	−98,655	32,000	407,300	37,757
1 9 7 2	519,393	217,739	301,654	−17,793	34,000	420,213	102,480
1 9 7 3	730,297	311,399	418,898	−2,380	43,000	449,173	299,560

Note: 1) *Excludes the Bank of Korea and Korea Development Bank.*

Interest Rates on Deposits of Deposit Money Banks[1]

(Per cent per annum)

Effective From	Time Deposits [2]				Passbook Deposits	Notice Deposits	Extra Deposits	Install-ment Savings Deposits	New House-hold Deposits	House-hold Deposits
	Three Months	Six Months	1 year or over	2 years or over						
1960. 1. 1	6.0	8.0	10.0	—	1.8	3.65	1.1	4.0[3]	—	—
1961. 7.10	9.0	12.0	15.0	—	1.8	3.65	1.1	4.0[3]	—	—
1962. 2. 1	9.0	12.0	15.0	—	1.8	3.65	1.1	10.0	—	—
1964. 3.16	9.0	12.0	15.0	—	1.8	3.65	1.0	10.0	—	—
1965. 9.30	18.0	24.0	26.4	30.0[4]	1.8	5.00	1.0	30.0	—	—
1968. 4. 1	15.6	20.4	26.4	27.6	1.8	5.00	1.0	28.0	12.0	—
10. 1	14.4	19.2	25.2	—	1.8	5.00	1.0	25.0	12.0	—
1969. 6. 1	12.0	16.8	22.8	—	1.8	5.00	1.0	23.0	9.6	—
1971. 6.28	10.2	14.4	20.4	21.3	1.8	5.00	1.0	21.0	8.7	—
1972. 1.17	8.4	11.4	16.8	17.4	1.8	5.00	1.0	17.0	6.6	—
8. 3	6.0	8.4	12.0	12.6	1.8	3.65	1.0	12.0	4.8	—
1973. 5. 1	6.0	8.4	12.0	12.6	1.8	3.65	1.0	12.0	4.8	2.562
1974. 1.24	12.0	13.2	15.0	—	1.8	3.65	1.0	13.2	4.8	2.562

Note: 1) *Maximum rates decided by Monetary Board.*
2) *Actual rates agreed upon by the Korean Banker's Association.*
3) *Rate for maturity of less than 1 year, 5% for 1 year and over, and 6% for 2 years and over.*
4) *Applies to time deposits for 18 months and over.*

and Loans

	Deposits and Loans					
	Deposits			Loans		
Other Sector	Total	Demand	Time & Savings	Total	Commercial Banks	Special [1] Banks
−101	14,091	11,653	2,438	11,470	11,470	—
−12,973	24,730	19,311	5,419	31,951	12,777	19,174
−8,767	39,103	26,940	12,163	43,199	20,907	22,292
−4.958	39,031	26.185	12,846	49,079	22,834	26,245
3,555	43,051	28,555	14,496	53,052	23,141	29,911
−254	78,520	47,947	30,573	72,064	37,459	34,605
−2,933	120,948	50,863	70,085	102,688	57,868	44,820
−14,970	205,880	76,979	128,901	177,998	105,578	72,420
−19,462	373,073	117,535	255,538	331,216	209,971	121,245
−35,959	619,173	167,646	451,527	562,975	359,284	203,691
−27,163	789,671	213,358	576,313	722,446	441,788	280,658
−20,428	977,563	268,876	708,687	919,522	568,413	351,109
−19,507	1,323,879	412,365	911,514	1,198,016	742,487	455,529
−59,056	1,753,625	539,407	1,214,218	1,587,508	987,542	599,966

Interest Rates on Loans and Discounts of Deposit Money Banks[1]

Effective From	Discounts on Bills	Loans for Export Trade	Loans for Suppliers of US Offshore Procurement	Loans on Other Bills				Over-drafts	Loans Overdue	Call Loans	Loans on Installment Savings
				Up to 1 year	1~3 years	3~5 years	5~8 years				
1959. 7. 15	13.87	13.87	—	17.52	—	—	—	18.25	20.00	13.87	17.50
1962. 4. 1	13.87	6.00	—	16.43	—	—	—	18.25	20.00	13.87	16.43
12. 1	13.87	6.00	6.00	15.70	—	—	—	18.25	20.00	13.87	15.70
1964. 3. 16	14.00	6.00	6.00	16.00	—	—	—	18.50	20.00	12.00	15.70
1965. 9. 30	24.00	6.00	6.00	26.00	—	—	—	26.00	36.50	22.00	26.00
1967. 6. 29	24.00	6.00	6.00	26.00	—	—	—	28.00	36.50	22.00	26.00
1968.10. 1	26.00	6.00	6.00	25.20	—	—	—	28.00	36.50	22.00	25.20
1969. 6. 1	24.60	6.00	6.00	24.00	—	—	—	26.00	36.50	21.00	24.00
1970. 4. 1	24.00	6.00	6.00	24.00	—	—	—	26.00	36.50	21.00	24.00
1971. 6. 28	22.00	6.00	6.00	22.00	22.50	23.00	—	24.00	36.50	19.00	22.00
1972. 1. 17	19.00	6.00	6.00	19.00	19.50	20.00	—	22.00	31.20	19.00	19.00
8. 3	15.50	6.00	6.00	15.50	16.00	16.50	—	17.50	25.00	15.00	15.50
10. 2	15.50	6.00	6.00	15.50	16.00	16.00	16.50	17.50	25.00	15.00	15.50
1973. 5. 14	15.50	7.00	7.00	15.50	15.50	15.50	15.50	17.50	25.00	15.00	15.50
1974. 1. 24	15.50	9.00	9.00	15.50	15.50	15.50	15.50	17.50	25.00	15.00	15.50

Note: 1) *Maximum rates decided by Monetary Board.*

Summary of Exports

	Exports and Imports [1]							
	Exports				Imports			
	Total	Ordinary	Bonded Process	Others	Total	Korean Foreign Exchange	Property & Claims	Official Aid
1 9 6 0	32,827	31,832	—	995	343,527	97,168	—	231,947
1 9 6 1	40,878	38,646	—	2,232	316,142	103,138	—	196,818
1 9 6 2	54,813	52,834	—	1,009	421,782	178,989	—	218,539
1 9 6 3	86,802	76,682	4,855	5,265	560,273	232,709	—	232,635
1 9 6 4	119,058	111,035	5,355	2,668	404,351	184,503	—	142,634
1 9 6 5	175,082	153,429	16,329	5,324	463,442	248,351	—	135,536
1 9 6 6	250,334	215,848	28,750	5,736	716,441	397,835	4,079	143,629
1 9 6 7	320,229	259,557	49,788	10,884	996,246	640,729	32,786	119,176
1 9 6 8	455,401	356,320	86,965	12,115	1,462,873	921,844	42,599	125,682
1 9 6 9	622,516	478,930	130,667	12,919	1,823,611	1,052,330	34,726	120,507
1 9 7 0	835,185	659,850	152,273	23,062	1,983,973	1,229,945	26,320	161,171
1 9 7 1	1,067,607	839,162	208,802	19,643	2,394,320	1,595,435	20,166	105,569
1 9 7 2	1,624,088	1,308,867	285,328	29,893	2,522,002	1,657,476	44,730	21,725
1 9 7 3	3,225,025	2,459,112	703,098	62,815	4,240,277	3,295,581	23,328	—

Note: 1) *Exports are valued at f.o.b. and imports at c.i.f.. Both exports and imports include trade without drafts and exclude sales of goods to military forces in Vietnam. The figures are based on the trade statistics of the Office of Customs Administration.*

Exports and Imports

	Exports [1]									
	Total	U.S.A.	Japan	Germany	U.K.	France	Taiwan	Hong Kong	Canada	Others
1 9 6 0	32.8	3.6	20.2	0.6	1.9	0	0.4	2.7	0	3.4
1 9 6 1	40.9	6.8	19.4	1.0	1.4	0	0.5	7.4	0	4.4
1 9 6 2	54.8	12.0	23.5	0.2	1.6	1.0	1.4	4.7	0.1	10.3
1 9 6 3	86.8	24.3	24.8	1.3	1.6	0.5	0.7	9.1	0.3	24.2
1 9 6 4	119.1	35.1	38.2	1.1	6.5	0.8	1.9	11.6	0.4	23.5
1 9 6 5	175.1	61.7	44.0	3.2	3.6	0.5	1.9	10.8	2.5	46.9
1 9 6 6	258.3	95.8	66.3	7.0	5.1	1.0	2.1	9.5	5.8	65.7
1 9 6 7	320.2	137.4	84.7	5.2	7.9	2.1	3.1	15.2	7.9	56.7
1 9 6 8	455.4	237.0	99.7	9.6	7.0	2.6	5.8	15.7	14.2	63.8
1 9 6 9	622.5	315.7	133.3	16.4	10.6	1.8	13.3	24.4	15.1	91.9
1 9 7 0	835.2	395.2	234.3	27.3	13.0	1.6	7.2	27.6	19.6	109.4
1 9 7 1	1,067.6	531.8	262.0	31.4	14.1	2.6	12.0	41.4	28.9	143.4
1 9 7 2	1,624.1	759.0	407.1	51.2	28.7	8.2	16.1	72.9	58.9	222.0
1 9 7 3	3,225.0	1,021.2	1,241.5	120.3	75.0	23.1	40.9	117.7	124.9	460.4

Note: 1) *Valued at f.o.b. and based on the trade statistics of the Office of Customs Administration.*

and Imports

(In thousand dollars)

Loans	Others	Excess of Imports	Total	Agricultural Products	Marine Products	Mining Products	Manufactured
—	14,412	310,700	32,385	7,078	5,755	13,681	5,871
—	16,186	275,264	42,901	8,151	7,293	18,018	9,439
—	19,718	336,969	56,702	13,041	12,474	15,877	15,310
52,125	42,804	473,471	84,368	11,222	13,090	16,446	43,610
34,609	42,605	285,293	120,851	12,562	24,050	21,917	62,322
31,482	48,073	288,360	180,450	15,695	24,738	27,645	112,372
108,419	62,479	466,107	255,751	24,336	37,536	34,195	159,684
167,332	36,223	676,017	358,592	16,971	52,834	37,612	251,175
299,636	73,112	1,007,473	500,408	21,607	50,856	41,005	386,940
475,675	140,373	1,201,095	702,811	29,748	66,052	51,955	555,055
400,166	166,371	1,148,788	1,003,808	30,056	82,324	52,059	839,369
541,400	131,750	1,326,713	1,352,037	37,992	103,983	47,207	1,162,855
628,647	169,424	897,914	1,806,963	52,994	137,467	32,234	1,584,268
628,425	292,943	997,917	3,256,912	101,237	233,508	49,417	2,872,750

2) *Includes both simple remittances, exports of bonded processing, sales of goods to military forces in Vietnam and exports without drafts. The figures are based on the settlements of transactions in the Ministry of Commerce & Industry.*

by Major Countries

(In million dollars)

Imports 2)

Total	U.S.A.	Japan	Germany	U.K.	France	Taiwan	Hong Kong	Canada	Others
343.5	133.8	70.4	41.0	9.1	2.5	5.5	1.4	5.4	74.4
316.1	143.4	69.2	24.9	5.2	1.6	6.2	0.3	2.3	63.0
421.8	220.3	109.2	19.2	6.3	1.2	7.3	0.3	2.0	56.0
560.3	284.1	159.3	22.7	5.2	0.9	15.0	6.0	3.5	63.6
404.4	202.1	110.1	23.9	3.2	0.1	5.2	5.9	2.5	51.4
463.4	182.3	166.6	16.1	1.2	11.7	10.5	7.5	1.6	65.9
716.4	253.7	293.8	20.3	2.2	10.9	10.8	7.7	2.7	114.3
996.2	305.2	443.1	31.0	5.3	16.7	27.2	12.0	8.4	147.3
1,462.9	449.0	624.0	73.6	15.6	13.7	15.9	13.9	12.2	245.0
1,823.6	530.2	753.2	79.0	32.0	36.4	23.2	20.0	22.3	327.3
1,984.0	584.8	809.3	67.2	32.8	52.2	34.0	19.7	23.2	360.8
2,394.3	678.3	953.8	73.7	56.2	71.8	39.1	19.7	39.0	462.7
2,522.0	647.2	1,031.1	66.9	73.9	47.8	47.9	35.9	36.0	535.3
4,240.3	1,201.9	1,726.9	132.0	68.9	46.9	55.4	29.4	82.5	896.4

2) *Valued at c.i.f. and based on the trade statistics of the Office of Customs Administration.*

	Total	Public Loans				Subtotal
		Subtotal	Agri., Forestry & Fishery	Mining & Manufacturing	Social Overhead Capital & Other Services	
1 9 5 9~6 6	350,441	140,847	—	60,931	79,916	184,109
1 9 6 7	237,215	105,619	—	44,020	61,599	124,001
1 9 6 8	357,755	70,220	380	30,100	39,740	268,366
1 9 6 9	560,266	138,934	522	24,612	113,800	408,671
1 9 7 0	548,146	115,325	2,137	32,186	81,002	366,708
1 9 7 1	691,422	303,395	23,618	38,676	241,101	345,193
1 9 7 2	729,644	324.436	17,404	84,700	222,332	326,415
1 9 7 3	856,210	368,463	18,680	122,494	227,289	344,426
Total	4,331,099	1,567,239	62,741	437,719	1,066,779	2,367,889

Foreign Exchange Receipts

	Total Holdings		Current		
			Receipts		
	Amount	Index	Total	Visible	Invisible
1 9 6 0	155.2	112.2	111.8	32.4	79.4
1 9 6 1	205.2	148.4	166.2	42.9	123.3
1 9 6 2	166.8	120.6	179.0	56.7	!22.3
1 9 6 3	129.6	93.7	177.2	85.4	91.8
1 9 6 4	128.9	93.2	212.2	115.1	97.1
1 9 6 5	138.3	100.0	298.0	172.2	125.8
1 9 6 6	235.8	170.5	486.8	248.4	238.5
1 9 6 7	347.2	251.0	695.4	320.2	375.4
1 9 6 8	387.7	280.3	889.4	464.9	424.2
1 9 6 9	549.5	397.3	1,102.0	604.9	497.1
1 9 7 0	583.5	421.9	1,306.7	816.0	490.7
1 9 7 1	534.5	386.5	1,523.4	1,036.8	486.6
1 9 7 2	693.8	501.7	2,159.2	1,580.0	579.2
1 9 7 3	1,034.2	747.8	4,033.8	3,097.5	936.3

Investments and Loans (Arrivals)

| Commercial Loans | | | | Equity Investments | | |
Agri., Forestry & Fishery	Mining & Manufacturing	Social Overhead Capital & Other Services	Subtotal	Agri., Forestry & Fishery	Mining & Manufacturing	Social Overhead Capital & Other Services
44,345	133,675	6,089	25,485	126	25,359	—
10,934	80,218	32,849	7,595	13	6,992	590
3,192	163,840	101,334	19,169	753	13,375	5,041
13,604	169,712	225,355	12,661	33	11,839	789
9,367	147,937	209,404	66,113	291	57,428	8,394
3,291	188,611	153,291	42,834	165	28,963	13,706
11,994	214,799	99,622	78,793	139	70,569	8,085
11,263	140,361	192,802	143,321	2,548	135,082	5,691
107,990	1,239,153	1,020,746	395,971	4,068	349,607	42,296

and Payments

| Transactions | | | Net Receipts or Payments | Capital Transactions Net Receipts or Payments | Errors and Omissions | Incr. or Decr. in Foreign Exchange Holdings |
| Payments | | | | | | |
Total	Visible	Invisible				
102.2	84.9	17.3	9.6	—	—	9.7
116.1	100.6	15.5	50.1	—	—	50.5
225.7	195.8	29.9	-46.7			-38.4
247.8	211.3	36.5	-70.6			-37.2
202.4	164.7	37.7	9.8	50.5	-47.2	-0.7
282.4	244.0	38.4	15.6			9.4
367.7	324.5	43.2	119.1			97.5
690.9	605.1	85.8	4.5	98.2	8.8	111.4
1,015.6	897.2	118.4	-126.2	193.0	-7.7	59.1
1,126.4	967.0	159.4	-24.4	144.2	23.3	143.1
1,375.4	1,154.6	220.8	-68.7	90.4	12.3	34.0
1,674.5	1,380.0	294.5	-151.1	93.5	8.6	-49.0
1,859.5	1,510.9	348.6	299.7	-130.7	-9.7	159.3
3,591.1	3,107.9	483.2	442.8	-111.5	9.1	340.3

Cultivated Area, Number of Farm

	Cultivated Area and Number of Farm Households							
	Cultivated Area (thousand Jeongbo[1])			Number of Farm Households (thousand)	Farm Population (thousand)	Cultivated Area per Farm Household (Danbo[2])		
	Total	Paddy	Dry Fields			Total	Paddy	Dry Fields
1 9 6 0	2,042	1,216	826	2,350	14,559	8.7	5.2	3.5
1 9 6 1	2,049	1,221	828	2,327	14,509	8.8	5.3	3.6
1 9 6 2	2,080	1,233	847	2,469	15,097	8.4	5.0	3.4
1 9 6 3	2,097	1,238	859	2,416	15,266	8.7	5.1	3.6
1 9 6 4	2,189	1,272	917	2,450	15,553	8.9	5.2	3.7
1 9 6 5	2,275	1,297	978	2,507	15,812	9.1	5.2	3.9
1 9 6 6	2,312	1,298	1,014	2,540	15,781	9.1	5.1	4.0
1 9 6 7	2,331	1,301	1,030	2,587	16,078	9.0	5.0	4.0
1 9 6 8	2,338	1,300	1,038	2,579	15,908	9.1	5.0	4.0
1 9 6 9	2,331	1,294	1,037	2,546	15,589	9.2	5.1	4.1
1 9 7 0	2,136	1,205	931	2,483	14,422	8.6	4.8	3.7
1 9 7 1	2,290	1,275	1,015	2,482	14,712	9.2	5.1	4.1
1 9 7 2	2,261	1,270	991	2,452	14,677	9.2	5.2	4.0
1 9 7 3	2,222	1,253	970	2,450	14,645	9.1	5.1	4.0

Note: 1) 1 Jeongbo＝9,917.4m^2
2) 1 Danbo＝991.74m^2

Fishing Boat Status

	Number of Fishing Households (thousand)	Fishing Population (thousand)	Fishing Boat Status					
			Total		Non-Motor Boats		Motor Boats	
			Number	Tonnage	Number	Tonnage	Number	Tonnage
1 9 6 0	189.2	808.9	34,438	107,017	30,089	49,038	4,349	57,979
1 9 6 1	191.9	816.8	42,300	144,869	37,285	79,412	5,015	65,457
1 9 6 2	194.6	1,093.7	45,504	161,709	39,419	81,604	6,085	80,105
1 9 6 3	202.1	1,224.5	47,217	160,042	41,110	79,706	6,107	80,335
1 9 6 4	202.9	1,211.0	48,716	167,423	42,253	80,908	6,463	86,514
1 9 6 5	215.1	1,276.8	51,052	203,164	43,480	83,648	7,572	119,515
1 9 6 6	236.5	1,441.7	53,294	245,962	44,410	85,474	8,884	160,487
1 9 6 7	241.5	1,477.0	57,255	262,079	46,266	82,961	10,989	179,117
1 9 6 8	219.6	1,346.4	62,002	292,962	50,558	86,641	11,444	206,321
1 9 6 9	223.0	1,325.4	66,115	342,280	53,263	91,215	12,852	251,065
1 9 7 0	194.6	1,165.2	68,355	358,365	54,270	90,184	14,085	268,182
1 9 7 1	—	—	68,269	392,649	53,612	85,393	14,657	307,256
1 9 7 2	182.4	1,061.6	67,679	451,767	52,938	84,923	14,741	366,844
1 9 7 3	171.0	979.2	68,597	511,112	52,125	78,994	16,472	432,118

Households and Food Grain Production

Food Grain Production (thousand MT)						Production per 10 Ares	
Total	Rice	Barley & Wheat	Pulses	Miscel- laneous Cereals	Potatoes	Rice (kg)	Barley & Wheat (kg)
5,271	3,047	1,668	150	81	326	272	175
5,933	3,463	1,801	190	96	383	307	187
5,423	3,015	1,688	182	99	439	265	168
5,742	3,758	1,181	182	108	514	325	111
7,066	3,954	1,859	191	126	936	331	167
7,005	3,501	2,136	203	120	1,045	285	178
7,568	3,919	2,375	195	107	972	318	209
6,836	3,603	2,253	235	114	631	292	197
6,857	3,195	2,453	288	162	759	278	213
7,737	4,090	2,459	273	137	778	335	221
7,476	3,939	2,352	277	124	783	327	219
7,275	3,998	2,197	263	110	707	336	223
7,208	3,957	2,222	261	94	674	332	227
7,163	4,212	1,953	283	104	611	356	219

and Marine Production

Marine Production (thousand MT)								
By Kind					By Industry			
Total	Fish	Shellfish	Sea Plants	Others	Pelagic Fishing	Offshore Fishing	Cultivation	Others
357.2	..	..	..	..	0.9	..	..	..
447.6	..	..	..	..	0.4	..	..	..
470.2	298.9	32.6	51.7	86.9	0.7	449.0	18.7	1.8
532.2	252.7	82.6	57.5	139.4	2.6	442.6	85.3	1.7
599.8	323.3	99.2	61.7	115.6	2.6	521.5	72.9	2.8
636.5	393.5	79.7	61.0	102.3	8.6	553.4	73.7	0.9
702.3	428.9	101.4	69.7	102.3	26.9	583.2	91.1	1.1
750.3	481.4	95.6	87.8	85.5	40.5	611.6	97.2	1.1
852.3	511.2	99.9	119.6	121.6	50.1	688.1	113.1	1.0
862.8	596.7	95.8	80.7	89.6	82.8	692.4	86.4	1.3
935.5	596.0	110.7	116.7	112.1	89.6	724.7	119.2	1.9
1,073.7	726.8	147.8	117.2	81.9	159.3	764.9	147.4	2.2
1,343.6	947.7	160.6	128.8	106.5	224.1	957.4	160.4	1.6
1,686.5	1,121.7	211.6	224.2	129.0	360.6	1,063.2	260.5	2.2

Electric Power Generating

		Electric Power Generating Capacity (thousand kw)			Maximum Power (thousand kw)	Average Power (thousand kw)
		Total	Hydro	Thermal		
1 9 6 0		374. 3	143. 5	230. 8	228. 0	193
1 9 6 1		367. 3	143. 5	223. 8	305. 7	202
1 9 6 2		434. 0	143. 5	290. 5	343. 0	226
1 9 6 3		465. 5	143. 5	322. 0	392. 6	255
1 9 6 4		597. 5	143. 5	454. 0	492. 3	307
1 9 6 5		769. 5	215. 5	554. 0	602. 2	371
1 9 6 6		769. 5	215. 5	554. 0	696. 5	444
1 9 6 7		917. 2	300. 5	616. 8	778. 5	561
1 9 6 8		1, 274. 2	327. 5	946. 8	1, 079. 8	686
1 9 6 9		1, 630. 8	328. 7	1, 302. 1	1, 340. 0	879
1 9 7 0		2, 288. 2	328. 7	1, 959. 5	1, 555. 0	1, 047
1 9 7 1		2, 628. 0	341. 3	2, 286. 7	1, 776. 5	1, 203
1 9 7 2		3, 870. 8	341. 1	3, 529. 7	2, 097. 3	1, 348
1 9 7 3		4, 270. 6	621. 1	3, 649. 5	2, 556. 5	1, 692

Principal Mineral

		Anthracite (thousand MT)	Iron Ore (thousand MT)	Tungsten Concentrate (ST)	Refined Gold (kg)	Refined Silver (kg)	Kaolin (thousand MT)
1 9 6 0		5, 350	392	4, 915	2, 047	10, 253	51. 2
1 9 6 1		5, 884	489	6, 303	2, 616	14, 321	51. 2
1 9 6 2		7, 444	471	5, 798	3, 134	12, 843	38. 2
1 9 6 3		8, 858	501	4, 737	2, 802	13, 810	52. 3
1 9 6 4		9, 622	685	4, 656	2, 357	12, 580	90. 5
1 9 6 5		10, 248	735	3, 837	1, 954	13, 499	72. 2
1 9 6 6		11, 613	789	3, 704	1, 891	15, 530	112. 2
1 9 6 7		12, 436	698	3, 648	1, 970	18, 287	102. 7
1 9 6 8		10, 242	830	3, 769	1, 940	19, 814	120. 6
1 9 6 9		10, 273	709	3, 550	1, 578	28, 182	135. 6
1 9 7 0		12, 394	571	3, 728	1, 597	46, 483	194. 6
1 9 7 1		12, 785	504	3, 708	896	48, 005	191. 2
1 9 7 2		12, 403	492	3, 659	531	55, 043	184. 5
1 9 7 3		13, 571	595	3, 915	506	46, 340	377. 3

Capacity and Power Generated

(In million kwh)

Total Power Generated	Hydro	Thermal				Island	Power Purchased
			Steam Power	Barge	Diesel		
1,699	580	1,117	1,117	—	—	—	—
1,773	652	1,118	1,118	—	—	—	—
1,978	702	1,273	1,016	182	75	3	0
2,236	727	1,478	1,199	205	74	3	28
2,700	749	1,946	1,735	140	71	5	0
3,250	710	2,534	2,407	88	39	5	—
3,886	985	2,895	2,731	114	50	6	0
4,913	953	3,949	3,438	180	331	9	2
6,026	929	5,059	4,082	204	773	12	26
7,700	1,427	6,256	5,506	96	654	17	—
9,167	1,219	7,885	7,372	155	357	23	41
10,540	1,319	7,707	7,520	19	168	29	1,485
11,839	1,367	8,484	8,421	—	64	36	1,953
14,826	1,221	11,106	11,059	—	47	49	2,450

Production

Talc (MT)	Limestone (thousand MT)	Copper Ore (thousand MT)	Lead Ore (thousand MT)	Zinc Ore (MT)	Salt (thousand MT)	Amorphous Graphite (thousand MT)	Fluorite (thousand MT)
15,979	637	5.9	1.8	84	399	92	18.9
21,674	1,265	5.3	1.8	900	122	88	27.9
28,368	1,259	10.7	2.8	839	388	184	33.0
32,392	1,363	12.3	3.8	2,258	230	338	39.8
43,900	2,220	12.1	6.7	5,080	386	262	56.4
35,732	3,090	22.2	8.8	14,232	669	254	39.2
53,609	2,926	21.1	13.9	23,386	393	129	32.0
56,280	3,916	15.6	17.6	27,299	612	61	57.0
71,643	5,653	19.0	31.3	38,679	562	128	46.6
84,346	7,415	22.2	33.0	41,163	289	73	39.2
83,949	9,104	27.3	32.0	47,960	405	59	47.8
70,114	10,617	29.6	33.1	56,322	360	71	57.9
72,352	10,146	34.7	29.4	71,850	452	41	29.0
113,092	12,903	38.7	25.7	96,301	742	43	29.8

	Food		Fibers and Textiles				
	Refined Sugar (000 MT)	Canned Food (MT)	Cotton Yarn (MT)	Worsted Yarn (MT)	Cotton Fabrics (000 m²)	Rayon Fabrics (000 m²)	Nylon Fabrics (000 m²)
1 9 6 0	63.9	5,811	49,142	2,135	126,121	52,232	3,922
1 9 6 1	64.3	7,551	44,191	2,565	111,191	46,180	3,474
1 9 6 2	53.6	5,443	52,504	2.122	125,889	50,838	16,871
1 9 6 3	39.8	3,708	62,679	1,892	147,661	36,679	5,023
1 9 6 4	17.1	4,932	64,881	1,152	172,711	40,147	4,749
1 9 6 5	45.3	6,388	65,027	1,211	222,879	51,860	18,301
1 9 6 6	71.4	6,526	68,417	1,449	228,796	58,452	38,911
1 9 6 7	110.4	3,243	75,245	2,297	250,239	64,621	41,864
1 9 6 8	140.0	4,247	51,843	3,371	120,862	35,251	71,001
1 9 6 9	185.5	3,574	64,680	3,225	201,924	41,724	96,480
1 9 7 0	211.2	1,904	90,846	1,902	192,634	48,011	115,411
1 9 7 1	237.1	3,606	94,951	2,009	233,782	35,049	151,107
1 9 7 2	205.2	5,242	91,256	2,753	201,189	34,839	204,372
1 9 7 3	303.5	5,716	103,014	2,800	264,400	45,267	332,084

Production of Principal

	Petroleum Products				Glass, Clay & Stone Products		Basic Metals
	Fuel Oil (000 kl)	Gasoline (000 kl)	Bunker-C (000 kl)	Diesel Oil (000 kl)	Plate Glass (000 CS)	Cement (000 MT)	Steel (000 MT)
1 9 6 0	—	—	—	—	192.7	430.9	115.6
1 9 6 1	—	—	—	—	309.7	522.8	86.9
1 9 6 2	—	—	—	—	259.2	789.7	141.6
1 9 6 3	—	—	—	—	537.0	778.3	207.4
1 9 6 4	420.5	92.6	12.2	182.9	512.9	1,242.1	229.5
1 9 6 5	548.5	224.5	188.7	489.0	517.2	1,614.2	266.4
1 9 6 6	400.3	323.0	429.3	603.3	571.6	1,884.4	334.2
1 9 6 7	348.9	428.5	810.2	649.1	558.0	2,441.0	469.7
1 9 6 8	398.0	614.7	2,130.2	1,151.9	698.9	3,572.4	741.6
1 9 6 9	329.5	764.5	3,617.9	1,472.8	835.1	4,828.2	1,010.3
1 9 7 0	596.0	894.1	5,307.7	1,785.5	1,361.6	5,781.9	1,276.2
1 9 7 1	585.3	1,033.8	6,575.7	2,200.9	1,872.5	6,872.3	1,460.9
1 9 7 2	578.2	942.8	7,091.1	2,329.4	1,744.5	6,486.3	1,858.0
1 9 7 3	710.0	1,034.2	8,308.1	2,853.8	2,061.6	8,174.7	2,828.8

Manufactures (Ⅰ)

	Paper		Rubber Products			Wood	Chemical Products	
Newsprint (MT)	Vellum Paper (MT)	Kraft Paper (MT)	Motor Vehicles Tires (000)	V Belts (000 plies)	Boots (000 pairs)	Plywood (million SF)	Paint (kl)	Urea Fertilizer (000 MT)
26, 870	8, 877	2, 403	175	9, 344	56, 198	187	..	13. 3
32, 686	13, 034	5, 072	160	9, 716	53, 553	166	..	64. 7
37, 646	16, 924	9, 687	179	15, 310	63, 798	284	..	81. 3
41, 753	16, 592	15, 922	238	20, 619	68, 912	335	..	97. 8
42, 955	17, 929	18, 671	251	27, 452	78, 789	501	..	141. 1
45, 397	28, 391	36, 079	368	33, 984	90, 218	729	1, 418	163. 0
54, 626	31, 949	37, 267	443	41, 953	79, 102	1, 198	3. 812	172. 6
58, 223	35, 285	31, 367	486	55, 120	69, 437	1, 490	4, 236	318. 0
64, 832	52, 126	47, 252	669	156, 555	72, 612	2, 384	3, 942	568. 3
84, 195	66, 218	48, 731	877	181, 864	74, 252	2, 784	6, 405	664. 4
105, 709	57, 377	60, 101	923	213, 728	68, 062	2, 872	7, 676	707. 5
108, 345	69, 904	69, 840	1, 046	238, 224	82, 012	3, 471	7, 079	669. 2
113, 651	73, 195	75, 261	1, 088	278, 286	84, 401	3, 703	7, 351	690. 8
124, 561	100, 732	90, 422	1, 577	340, 316	113, 770	5, 022	8, 240	698. 1

Manufactures (Ⅱ)

& Metal Products		Machinery		Electrical Machinery and Tools			Transport Equipment	
Electrolytic Copper (MT)	Galvanized Iron Sheets (MT)	Engines (each)	Sewing Machines (each)	Electric Motors (each)	Radios (000 sets)	Dry Batteries (000)	Ships (GT)	Passenger Cars (each)
1, 010	5, 149	2, 167	22, 888	1, 224	40. 3	3, 876	4, 200	—
1, 321	4, 250	3, 345	51, 494	1, 741	162. 0	6, 244	4, 600	—
2, 210	6, 922	8, 817	123, 345	2, 350	152. 5	9, 966	4, 636	1, 710
2, 379	45, 696	7, 302	91, 744	11, 451	158. 3	14, 986	8, 869	1, 063
2, 810	19, 588	8, 351	86, 489	21, 256	202. 9	28, 285	11, 625	216
2, 506	37, 173	9, 411	82, 123	130, 040	333. 5	14, 346	13, 788	106
3, 593	29, 430	7, 867	74, 730	249, 576	805. 9	23, 380	17, 683	3, 117
3, 438	11, 618	6, 823	111, 483	214, 251	460. 7	22, 485	19, 944	4, 983
4, 257	19, 089	9, 739	112, 375	220, 038	1, 360. 8	21, 759	31, 148	11, 629
5, 655	32, 476	9, 305	114, 225	389, 829	1, 185. 8	34, 202	37, 804	19, 494
5, 118	36, 174	8, 228	117, 837	325, 989	1, 087. 9	46, 398	39, 100	14, 487
5, 671	41, 110	8, 028	128, 940	259, 494	1, 027. 8	63, 881	43, 310	12, 428
11, 060	62, 311	4, 809	111, 651	241, 397	1, 858. 1	64, 375	50, 480	9, 952
18, 044	51, 104	4, 005	228, 567	416, 055	3, 271. 9	90, 646	163, 474	12, 751

Transportation

| | Railways | | | | | Automobiles and | | | |
| | Locomotives (each) | | Coaches (each) | Freight Cars (each) | Length of Railways in Opera-tion (km) | Automobiles | | | |
	Steam	Diesel				Total	Passenger Cars	Trucks	Buses
1 9 6 0	457	95	1, 308	9, 541	4, 584	31, 339	12, 776	13, 426	4, 195
1 9 6 1	356	95	1, 303	9, 670	4, 630	29, 234	9, 809	12, 808	4, 266
1 9 6 2	280	95	1, 445	9, 770	4, 696	30, 814	8, 733	13, 093	6, 747
1 9 6 3	280	125	1, 609	10, 479	4, 730	34, 228	9, 569	13, 929	8, 132
1 9 6 4	272	125	1, 260	10, 764	4, 780	37, 815	11, 409	14, 951	8, 617
1 9 6 5	272	125	1, 390	10, 587	4, 897	41, 511	13, 001	16, 015	9, 316
1 9 6 6	261	173	1, 418	11, 454	5, 049	50, 160	17, 502	19, 432	10, 888
1 9 6 7	203	252	1, 363	12, 617	5, 132	60, 697	23, 235	22, 955	11, 499
1 9 6 8	115	252	1, 531	13, 239	5, 319	80, 951	33, 112	31, 582	12, 786
1 9 6 9	115	282	1, 662	13, 994	5, 437	108, 669	50, 299	40, 134	14, 237
1 9 7 0	109	277	1, 681	14, 407	5, 500	129, 371	60, 677	48, 901	15, 831
1 9 7 1	95	337	1, 621	15, 189	5, 500	144, 337	67, 582	53, 405	17, 411
1 9 7 2	95	336	1, 597	16, 808	5, 507	150, 035	70, 244	55, 116	17, 550
1 9 7 3	93	336	1, 577	16, 269	5, 541	170, 714	78, 334	64, 584	18, 871

Communications

| | Post Offices | Telephone Subscribers | Domestic Telephone Revenue | Overseas Telephone Calls | | Telegrams | |
| | | | | | | Domestic | |
	Each	Circuits	Million Won	Sent	Received	Sent	Received
1 9 6 0	724	86, 604	1, 250. 5	35, 544	24, 448	3, 466	3, 739
1 9 6 1	804	97, 016	1, 426. 5	21, 695	31, 524	3, 680	3, 858
1 9 6 2	1, 004	127, 686	1, 556. 8	27, 401	29, 404	3, 738	4, 192
1 9 6 3	1, 147	157, 327	2, 293. 6	28, 034	38, 942	4, 436	5, 201
1 9 6 4	1, 323	193, 075	3, 473. 4	33, 031	48, 266	5, 537	6, 301
1 9 6 5	1, 475	220, 635	4, 551. 0	36, 395	48, 736	7, 408	8, 131
1 9 6 6	1, 728	277, 756	9, 872. 4	45, 127	52, 312	7, 347	7, 616
1 9 6 7	1, 769	339, 280	12, 570. 4	59, 899	67, 038	8, 269	9, 200
1 9 6 8	1, 808	384, 514	16, 505. 2	126, 822	121, 997	9, 422	10, 643
1 9 6 9	1, 822	442, 452	20, 814. 2	202, 494	217, 283	10, 102	11, 310
1 9 7 0	1, 842	481, 207	22, 944. 6	294, 370	368, 277	11, 364	12, 676
1 9 7 1	1, 868	563, 129	28, 241. 1	406, 874	547, 729	12, 138	13, 311
1 9 7 2	1, 884	654, 339	37, 589. 4	680, 274	651, 804	13, 004	13, 934
1 9 7 3	1, 901	773, 894	46, 503. 3	1, 083, 104	1, 081, 434	13, 877	14, 593

Highways		Public Roads (km)			Ship				Airplanes (each)
(each)					Steel Ships		Wooden Ships		
Small Size	Special Use	Total	Paved	Unpaved	Number	000 GT	Number	000 GT	
588	354	27,169	967	26,202	281	153.7	10,894	189.8	7
1,863	488	27,170	1,123	26,046	353	166.8	11,860	202.3	9
1,846	395	28,145	1,259	26,886	364	166.1	12,315	207.0	14
2,029	569	28,145	1,394	26,751	259	134.1	9,561	159.9	24
2,160	678	28,145	1,558	26,587	298	151.9	10,395	164.8	31
2,385	794	28,145	1,627	26,517	430	193.7	11,396	176.7	34
1,322	1,016	34,476	1,934	32,542	584	257.2	11,978	183.0	37
1,722	1,286	34,799	2,092	32,708	844	518.1	12,631	190.2	46
2,188	1,283	34,949	2,200	32,750	1,078	713.7	14,675	204.9	53
2,531	1,468	37,169	2,970	34,199	1,297	906.8	15,601	215.4	63
2,865	1,097	40,244	3,864	36,381	1,511	999.8	15,264	206.6	75
4,068	1,871	40,635	5,789	34,846	1,476	1,087.3	15,472	206.8	76
4,398	2,727	42,868	6,769	36,099	2,053	1,263.9	14,743	200.5	78
5,407	3,518	43,581	7,820	35,761	2,255	1,259.2	14,635	195.6	82

(In thousands)

Handled		Ordinary Mail Handled	Registered Letter Mail & Parcel Post Handled		International Letter Mail Handled	
International						
Sent	Received		Registered Letter Mail	Parcels	Dispatched	Arrived
224	203	156,881	9,416	828	3,117	4,246
232	240	147,094	8,966	985	2,875	4,598
284	309	174,337	9,443	1,327	3,504	5,150
266	285	211,906	11,784	1,614	5,022	11,165
266	288	276,080	13,403	1,831	7,596	12,786
289	328	367,623	15,381	2,453	9,407	15,315
358	417	396,953	14,793	2,315	13,755	18,905
438	515	440,438	17,586	2,681	15,385	24,750
506	575	480,741	21,467	2,869	16,465	31,502
547	619	522,382	27,268	3,181	18,317	32,539
599	693	540,269	26,021	3,769	14,827	33,083
653	720	551,575	27,780	4,018	14,603	34,888
577	666	564,286	30,106	4,517	15,816	37,542
597	715	569,369	33,050	4,867	16,989	40,309

Economically Active Population

	Population[1]			Population Aged 14 & Over	Economically Active Population			Economically Active Non-economically Active
	Total	Male	Female		Total	Male	Female	
1 9 6 3	26,987	13,570	13,417	15,085	8,343	5,462	2,881	6,742
1 9 6 4	27,678	13,923	13,755	15,502	8,449	5,571	2,878	7,053
1 9 6 5	28,327	14,255	14,072	15,937	8,859	5,808	3,051	7,078
1 9 6 6[3]	29,160	14,684	14,476	16,367	9,071	5,965	3,106	7,296
1 9 6 7	29,541	14,837	14,704	16,764	9,295	6,058	3,237	7,469
1 9 6 8	30,171	15,145	15,026	17,166	9,647	6,203	3,444	7,519
1 9 6 9	30,738	15,429	15,309	17,639	9,888	6,413	3,475	7,751
1 9 7 0[3]	31,435	15,779	15,656	18,253	10,199	6,516	3,683	8,054
1 9 7 1	31,828	15,985	15,843	18,984	10,542	6,723	3,819	8,442
1 9 7 2	32,360	16,260	16,100	19,724	11,058	7,064	3,994	8,666
1 9 7 3	32,905	16,534	16,371	20,438	11,600	7,286	4,314	8,838

Note: 1) *Figures are estimated on the basis of the results of the 1960, 1966 and 1971 population censuses. Midyear population.*

Household Earnings

	Number of Persons per Household		Number of Employed per Household	
	Urban	Rural	Urban	Rural
1 9 6 3	5.56	6.39	1.19	3.19
1 9 6 4	5.56	6.44	1.25	3.27
1 9 6 5	5.56	6.29	1.25	3.15
1 9 6 6	5.47	6.22	1.25	3.12
1 9 6 7	5.46	6.12	1.29	3.12
1 9 6 8	5.44	6.02	1.30	3.00
1 9 6 9	5.42	5.99	1.31	2.96
1 9 7 0	5.34	5.92	1.33	2.91
1 9 7 1	5.28	5.83	1.34	2.92
1 9 7 2	5.27	5.71	1.31	2.98
1 9 7 3	5.25	5.72	1.36	2.93

and Employed Persons

Population and Employed Persons[2]

Employed			Unemployed			Employment by Industry		
Total	Male	Female	Total	Male	Female	Agri., Forestry & Fishery	Mining & Manufacturing	Social Overhead Capital & Other Services
7,662	4,988	2,674	681	474	207	4,837	667	2,158
7,799	5,082	2,717	650	489	161	4,825	690	2,284
8,206	5,322	2,884	653	486	167	4,810	849	2,547
8,423	5,482	2,941	648	483	165	4,876	913	2,634
8,717	5,655	3,062	578	403	175	4,811	1,115	2,791
9,155	5,855	3,300	492	348	144	4,801	1,282	3,072
9,414	6,088	3,326	474	325	149	4,825	1,346	3,243
9,745	6,167	3,578	454	349	105	4,916	1,395	3,434
10,066	6,371	3,695	476	352	124	4,876	1,428	3,762
10,559	6,665	3,894	499	399	100	5,346	1,499	3,714
11,139	6,923	4,216	461	363	98	5,569	1,821	3,749

2) *Based on sample survey.*

3) *Census population and excludes foreigners.*

in Urban and Rural Areas

Earnings (won)			Average Income per Member of Household (won)		
Urban (A)	Rural (B)	B/A (%)	Urban (A)	Rural (B)	B/A (%)
6,680	7,765	116.2	1,201	1,215	101.2
8,100	10,474	129.3	1,457	1,626	111.6
9,380	9,350	99.7	1,687	1,486	88.1
13,460	10,848	80.6	2,461	1,744	70.9
20,720	12,456	60.1	3,795	2,035	53.6
23,830	14,913	62.6	4,381	2,477	56.5
27,800	18,156	65.3	5,129	3,031	59.1
31,770	21,317	67.1	5,949	3,601	60.5
37,660	29,699	78.9	7,133	5,094	71.4
43,120	35,783	83.0	8,182	6,267	76.6
45,850	40,059	87.4	8,733	7,003	80.2

Wholesale Price Index and

	All Commodities	Foods	All Commodities Excluding Foods	Raw Materials	Capital Goods	Consumer Goods
			Wholesale Price Index			
Weight	1,000.0	313.0	687.0	395.9	52.6	551.5
1 9 6 0	31.0	24.4	35.2	34.1	38.5	29.1
1 9 6 1	35.1	28.9	39.0	39.0	39.2	32.9
1 9 6 2	38.4	32.6	41.9	42.9	41.1	35.8
1 9 6 3	46.3	44.8	46.3	47.6	47.1	45.7
1 9 6 4	62.3	61.4	61.5	63.4	60.1	62.1
1 9 6 5	68.5	60.4	73.0	75.9	68.3	64.6
1 9 6 6	74.6	65.3	79.8	81.9	74.4	70.6
1 9 6 7	79.4	70.9	84.1	84.0	78.6	77.0
1 9 6 8	85.8	79.7	89.3	88.0	88.3	84.6
1 9 6 9	91.6	89.3	93.0	91.2	89.1	92.0
1 9 7 0	100.0	100.0	100.0	100.0	100.0	100.0
1 9 7 1	108.6	115.0	105.7	106.3	105.8	110.5
1 9 7 2	123.8	137.5	117.5	120.7	118.1	126.5
1 9 7 3	132.4	143.5	127.3	135.6	123.6	130.9

Index Numbers of Prices

	All Farm Products	Farm Products Excluding Vegetables	Grains	Fruits & Vegetables	Livestock, Cocoons & Poultry Products
			Prices Received		
Weight	1,000.0	909.2	523.9	123.1	287.2
1 9 6 0	20.9	21.0	22.2	19.4	18.0
1 9 6 1	24.6	25.2	27.8	17.2	20.0
1 9 6 2	27.1	27.8	29.4	18.4	23.4
1 9 6 3	40.1	40.4	47.3	34.1	24.5
1 9 6 4	50.2	51.4	60.4	35.3	31.0
1 9 6 5	52.2	53.1	54.7	40.8	47.4
1 9. 6 6	55.4	55.7	57.5	50.4	51.5
1 9 6 7	63.5	64.9	64.5	44.7	66.6
1 9 6 8	74.3	76.5	73.1	47.7	86.4
1 9 6 9	84.8	86.8	88.9	55.2	84.6
1 9 7 0	100.0	100.0	100.0	100.0	100.0
1 9 7 1	122.4	123.9	124.9	101.8	121.1
1 9 7 2	147.9	152.8	158.3	106.1	143.1
1 9 7 3	164.2	170.4	169.0	113.0	173.9

Seoul Consumer Price Index

	Seoul Cosumer Price Index						Engel Coefficient
All Commodities	Foods & Beverages	All Commodities Excluding Foods	Housing	Fuel & Light	Clothing	Miscel- laneous	Current
1,000.0	443.8	556.2	99.8	52.7	103.3	300.4	
28.6	25.6	32.4	36.8	33.1	32.5	30.7	55.1
30.9	27.9	34.6	36.5	39.3	34.1	33.3	57.6
32.9	30.2	36.7	39.5	42.0	34.6	35.1	55.9
39.7	40.1	40.2	45.5	42.6	39.5	38.1	58.4
51.4	54.7	48.2	52.7	48.1	55.4	44.8	64.0
58.4	59.3	57.5	59.4	58.4	67.6	54.0	59.6
65.4	63.9	66.9	70.3	68.3	76.4	63.0	55.9
72.5	68.9	76.0	83.9	80.7	85.1	69.9	54.3
80.6	76.5	84.5	89.2	90.4	89.9	80.2	52.4
88.7	85.5	91.8	94.1	94.7	95.4	89.4	52.7
100.0	100.0	100.0	100.0	100.0	100.0	100.0	53.9
112.3	117.0	108.6	106.6	107.6	107.8	109.7	54.7
125.6	132.4	120.3	117.6	121.0	118.9	121.5	55.0
129.5	136.3	124.0	122.0	128.4	131.1	121.5	52.9

Received and Paid by Farmers

(1970＝100)

	Prices Paid				Parity Ratio
Others	All Goods & Services	Farm Supplies	Household Goods	Farm Wages & Charges	
65.8	1,000.0	258.5	603.2	138.3	—
21.5	26.6	26.0	29.4	17.5	97.2
25.4	28.7	29.3	31.4	19.5	85.7
30.7	31.8	33.4	34.3	21.7	85.2
39.9	35.3	33.2	38.3	27.2	113.6
48.8	44.8	38.8	49.5	36.6	112.1
63.2	51.8	51.3	55.1	40.2	100.8
57.7	58.1	57.3	61.8	46.0	95.4
64.8	65.8	64.0	69.6	53.8	96.5
69.7	78.8	83.8	80.3	65.7	94.3
83.8	86.8	89.1	87.6	80.5	97.7
100.0	100.0	100.0	100.0	100.0	100.0
132.0	114.4	116.5	112.3	119.5	106.1
164.7	130.5	136.3	125.3	142.7	113.3
179.2	143.1	158.6	133.3	157.1	114.7